W9-BNQ-851

BECKHAM

CELEBRITIES
Series Editor: Anthony Elliott

Published
Ellis Cashmore, *Beckham*
Charles Lemert, *Muhammad Ali*
Chris Rojek, *Frank Sinatra*

Forthcoming
Dennis Altman, *Gore Vidal*
Ellis Cashmore, *Mike Tyson*
Cynthia Fuchs, *Eminem*
Richard Middleton, *John Lennon*
Daphne Read, *Oprah Winfrey*
Nick Stevenson, *David Bowie*
Jason Toynbee, *Bob Marley*

BECKHAM
Second Edition

ELLIS CASHMORE

GV
942.7
B43
A3
2004

polity

LIBRARY
NORTHERN VIRGINIA COMMUNITY COLLEGE

Copyright © Ellis Cashmore 2004

The right of Ellis Cashmore to be identified as Author of this Work has been asserted in accordance with the UK Copyright, Designs and Patents Act 1988.

First edition published 2002 by Polity Press in association with Blackwell Publishing Ltd

Reprinted 2003

Second edition published in 2004 by Polity Press Ltd

Polity Press
65 Bridge Street
Cambridge CB2 1UR, UK

Polity Press
350 Main Street
Malden, MA 02148, USA

All rights reserved. Except for the quotation of short passages for the purposes of criticism and review, no part of this publication may be reproduced, stored in a retrieval system, or transmitted, in any form or by any means, electronic, mechanical, photocopying, recording or otherwise, without the prior permission of the publisher.

ISBN: 0-7456 3366-8
ISBN: 0-7456 3367-6 (pb)

A catalogue record for this book is available from the British Library.

Typeset in 11 on 13 pt Palatino
by Kolam Information Services Pvt. Ltd., Pondicherry, India
Printed and bound in Great Britain by MPG Books Ltd, Bodmin, Cornwall

For further information on Polity, visit our website: www.polity.co.uk

CONTENTS

PREFACE   vii

INTRODUCTION   1

one   OF FROGS AND PRINCES   9

two   DISASTER OR DELIVERANCE?   25

three   INTO THE WHIRLPOOL   43

four   ARTISAN AND ARTIST   63

five   THE WORLD IS JUST ABOUT ENOUGH   83

six   VICTORIA'S MACHINE   100

seven   MANCHILD IN PURGATORY   121

eight   SEX, MASCULINITY AND THE
         TEMPTATION OF GAY MEN   139

nine   CUSTODIANS OF THE IMAGE   156

ten   MADONNA'S PACT   176

eleven   AN AD, A PRODUCT AND A BRAND   196

twelve   YOUR FIFTEEN MINUTES ARE ALMOST UP   211

Bibliography   221

Index   224

Calumnies are best answered with silence.

Ben Jonson, *Volpone*

Let fame, that all hunt after in their lives,
Live register'd upon our brazen tombs.

William Shakespeare, *Love's Labour's Lost*

I think you should never be famous just for the
sake of being famous. You should be famous for something
that's well-remembered.

Naomi Campbell

His life changed when he met his wife ... I saw his
transition to a different person.

Alex Ferguson

PREFACE

When he was 19, David Beckham moved from Manchester United to Preston North End on a short-term loan. What if he'd stayed put? There would be some likely consequences. He wouldn't have played for England's senior team as early as he did, for a start. And he might not even have played in the fateful game against Argentina. It's possible that he could have acted as a catalyst for Preston, a once-proud club that might have mounted a campaign to reclaim its former glory. Or, he could have moved to a different club and affected its fortunes.

Would sport be different? We can hardly imagine football without Pelé or Maradona. They actually changed the game, as Muhammad Ali changed boxing and Michael Jordan changed basketball. Beckham didn't have a comparable impact on soccer.

He would still be a high-class footballer: a figure known, admired and respected in the same way as, say, Michael Owen or Alan Shearer. His image would probably appear on cereal boxes and pizza commercials, but it wouldn't have been the image we grew to adore and, in some cases, even worship. People would have talked about him. People, that is, who are interested in football: not grandmothers and prepubescent girls who wouldn't know adidas from adenoids.

The world would have been different without the iconic Beckham. It would be filled with celebrities and we would still obsess over them. But, it wouldn't have a supreme, one-man, all-purpose figure on which to project every wish, fantasy, craving, ambition, even dream. All this was made possible because he returned to Old Trafford, and it was there, in 1997, that he met the woman who would effectively transform him from David Beckham, footballer, to Beckham, global icon. And what of her? Had she not met Beckham, Victoria would now be known in the same way as we know Mel B., another ex-Spice Girl, who found solo success elusive. Not entirely forgotten, but a long way away from the A-list. Her association with Beckham changed her life, but not as much as it changed his. Remember: she was a fully paid up celeb when they met. She was part of one of the biggest brands (not just bands) in the world, had sold dozens of millions of cds, held an eight-figure bank balance and was one of most recognizable women on the planet. She'd been in showbusiness practically since leaving school, had been through the entire celebrity production process and had memorized most of it.

For seven years, David and Victoria lived a fairy tale life, which mixed calamity with redemption, fate with fortune and anguish with joy. Its dramatic narrative matched its visual beauty. It captured the emotion and intellect of just about the entire planet. Then suddenly, the fairy story was exposed as exactly that: an enchanting, but fabricated, tale of mythical beings. The fourth of April was a famous date: on that day in 1968, Martin Luther King met his death. The Beckhams will remember it differently. It was on Sunday, 4 April 2004 that the *News of the World* carried a seven-page report that fully justified the newspaper's title. This was indeed news of the world. Everywhere – even the USA, which had up till now been indifferent to the Beckham phenomenon – the totally unexpected, some might say iconoclastic, story made headlines.

The image of the sensitive soul who adored, cherished and pampered his wife and who could have had any woman in the world, but was interested in only one, was no longer. The perfect godlike creature who violated every known norm associated with testosterone-pumped, homophobic, macho footballers and who acknowledged a large, devoted gay discipleship was a bit more ordinary than we thought. Far from the sanctimonious, whiter-than-white New Man many had suspected him to be, Beckham might actually be made of the same raw material as the rest of us. Maybe he would succumb to temptation just as any flesh-made man might.

In subsequent weeks, Beckham was plunged into the kind of media whirlpool in which he had once found his forte. In previous years, he had profited like no other from the attention of the media. Even his expulsion in June 1998 had been turned to his advantage. Sent off ignominiously in a crucial World Cup game, Beckham stealthily turned to his advantage the hue and cry that followed. The Red Card was actually the greatest blessing ever bestowed on a professional athlete. It sparked a career of heroic proportions. Heroic, that is, in the age of celebrity.

Beckham caught the heartbeat of a time in history. His was a simple tale told at a time when simplicity was preferred over complexity. But, the brush with reality was inevitable. As a symbol of celebrity culture, he was unbeatable. But you don't have to be a student of that culture to know that celebs have a habit of self-obsolescing. Or, rather, we render them obsolescent; not because they actually do anything, but because we grow tired, bored or just plain exhausted.

Beckham-fatigue was diagnosed long before 2004. Yet, every time pundits predicted its onset, a new surge of enthusiasm would undermine them: a locker-room incident, a farewell kickabout at Old Trafford, an epic transfer saga – and, of course, the Easter 2004 scandal. For a while the Beckham story looked like turning from an innocent fable into a squalid soap opera. The ink had barely dried on the *NoW*'s pages before doom-watchers were asking: is this the end of Beckham? The answer wasn't long in arriving. Irresistibly, every newspaper, magazine, radio and television station was drawn to the latest Beckham disclosure. For weeks, it displaced the Iraq conflict, Palestine, the European constitution and other trivialities from the front pages. As ever, a Beckham story obscured other world events. If he was in danger of losing his appeal, why were we all so entranced by the possibility that his spoon was long enough to sup with the devil, so to speak?

And then they appeared and it looked just like any one of their countless photoshoots. He wore a black jacket, blue jeans and several crucifixes hung on chains. She wore a black bodice, asymmetrical skirt and impossibly high stilettos. They preened, pouted and pirouetted for cameras outside London's Albert Hall. Tactile as ever, they touched, hugged and clutched each other, smiling continuously while the click-whirrs of the cameras provided supporting evidence that they were still the most sought-after couple in the world. But their world had changed.

Now they were no longer in a place over which they seemed to have sovereignty and where all the major calls were theirs to make. They were adrift in a different world, one in which all their money, glitz and opulence still counted, but not as much. The Albert Hall scene was a defiant gesture, the equivalent of one of those swivel-on-it fingers footballers sometimes show to booing crowds.

Body language readers would no doubt have interpreted the cloying, the frolicking, and the general raillery as proof that family life with the Beckhams was as blissful as ever. If David's new cropped hairdo was a sort of penance, then he was absolution personified. Reports of trouble in paradise had been exaggerated. Here were the Beckhams, as radiantly, rapturously, rhapsodically happy as they ever were.

We'll never know what really happened between DB and VB over the three weeks between the first revelations and their public exhibition of affection in west London. What we do know for sure is the way the media apportioned blame. Wronged women are usually candidates for sympathy. Not this time: even writers who described themselves as feminists found themselves consoling the golden one and censuring his Mrs for concentrating too hard on trying to revive her professional recording career. Why hadn't she just given up chasing success independently of her husband and gone with him to Madrid, taking the two boys with her? Victoria was never popular. Celebrated, yes. Most photographed, talked-about, and fêted woman in Europe and beyond, yes. Popular? No. But think about it: who had the know-how, the experience, the skill, the training and the sagacity to make exactly the right decisions about Beckham's career? And every decision was spot-on.

Who was habituated to the demands of celebrity life? Who had the judgement, the practice and the wisdom to advise when catastrophe threatened? None of this underestimates the talent of Beckham on the football field. Not his looks, his manner, or his sheer likeability. Yet, these composite parts don't make up a global celebrity. Something or someone was needed to make the conversion. Victoria responded valiantly to the *NoW*-brokered scandal, but, in a sense, it was like someone had stolen her notes and was acting on them. The story ran in the best-selling Sunday paper and was followed, after a modest break, by an exclusively contracted interview on Sky One tv. Both media outlets are part of the Rupert Murdoch empire, which was essential to the rise of Beckham – as we will see in the chapters that follow. Terrestrial tv appearances followed and, amazingly, the Beckhams seemed to be outmanoeuvred. This was a different Beckham story: one in which neither David nor Victoria was actually visible. Maybe it was another case of the "Cinderella syndrome": pa to a celeb secretly envies his wealth and fame and decides to get some of her own. Or, payback time for a discarded companion.

The motive was less interesting that the effects.

It must have felt like being sucked into that same old whirlpool that had always delivered Beckham safely to dry land, except this time, it was too much like drowning, as images deliriously changing shape and proportion flashed before him. As the bewilderment – I mean ours as well as his – disappeared, he emerged, his celebrity status intact, though with some interesting modifications. Decorous male he had always been, but never devilish. Perhaps the new variation in image would build towards an even greater celebrity payoff.

Of course, if Beckham had stayed at Preston, none of the events of Easter 2004 would have happened and we wouldn't be nearly so interested in him. But that's in a parallel universe; in this one, we've been absorbed in Beckham's life. This book is about that life and our interest in it.

INTRODUCTION

"I'm flattered and honoured. Only the other day, I had a 90-year-old woman writing to me for a shirt", answered Beckham. My question was: "With the possible exception of Michael Jordan, no athlete in history has commanded the interest of the global media in the way you have. Yet, no one has asked how you react to this?" And then, I asked: "Do you understand it?" – to which Beckham's answer was a straightforward "No."

Around the time of the first edition of this book, I tried to visualize Beckham's response to the elevation of his life to the vertiginous heights of celebritydom. I thought of Peter Sellers's character in the 1979 Hal Ashby film *Being There*. A simple gardener who speaks in sayings and proverbs ("after every spring, there is a summer"), his supposed wisdom is soaked up by the US President, who takes him into his confidence and introduces him as a sage to his distinguished colleagues. The gardener can't comprehend why he's invested with this gnomic status, but just keeps blurting out his adages and lets his audiences read into them whatever they want. All he really wanted to do was tend his garden.

All Beckham wanted to do was to play football. If he ever made it to the Manchester United first team, it would have been a much-appreciated bonus. When that came true, the rest was literally, as they say, beyond his wildest dreams. He could never have possibly imagined he would become the most celebrated figure in sport, a global icon and the raw material of a zillion fantasies. It would have been outside the frame of his, or, for that matter, anyone's, comprehension. When he found himself in that position, it was no easier to understand it.

Still, the *Being There* analogy is inadequate. The gardener might not have figured out what he was doing in the White House but he didn't have to contend with the utterly unfamiliar experience of being adored, if not worshipped, of having people throw themselves prostrate at his feet. Nor of witnessing the growth of a minor industry with the purpose of generating money from his image. No, the experience of Being Beckham is closer to being in *The Matrix*. Readers may recall that the premise of the Wachowski brothers' series is that the world we experience around us is a virtual reality plugged into our brains by robots that use human bodies as a source of energy. Once unplugged, we see that the earth is a forbidding, arid wasteland. What's better? we're induced to ask, a fake utopia or a real dystopia?

Beckham must feel like someone crept up and plugged him in. As if by magic, the ordinary world became paradisiacal. Then, it got better: he became the most celestial of beings. People began to honour, then venerate, then adore him and he didn't know why. Occasionally, he doubtless asks himself: is all this really happening? And probably answers: who knows? who cares? If he's in the Matrix, it's an eminently agreeable one – and one in which he has no Agent Smith or octopoid robots to make life uncomfortable.

After all, Beckham's Matrix is populated by fans who fawn over him, managers and agents who set up multimillion euro deals for him, fellow celebs who vie with him for the media's focus and a family that might have been designed by the author of a *How to have a 2+2 family and live in bliss* manual. He enjoys the kind of status that used to be the special reserve of only the most humongous rock or movie stars. His wife continues to be the numero uno celeb in Europe, occupying more media photographs than any other woman on earth – and she hasn't made a hit cd or movie in years.

Beckham's incomprehension or perhaps reluctance to try to make sense of it all is, in a way, justified. I mean, who would want to stop the Ferrari while driving along the Mediterranean coast and get under the bonnet just to figure out how the internal combustion engine works? All the same, his ascent does throw up some interesting questions and ones that deserve a little more consideration than those that have been popularly offered. Beckham, as most sensible football watchers know, is not the best player in the world and wouldn't figure in any serious analyst's dream team. Photogenic as he is, he's asked to model not because of his poise, presence or other qualities that are supposedly possessed by professional models, but because he's the most instantly recognizable human being on the planet. And, in the looks department, he may be well endowed, but does he have the symmetry of Keanu Reeves, the bone structure of Johnny Depp, or the teeth of Tom Cruise?

Broken down into his component parts, Beckham doesn't really seem so special. Nor do two alka seltzer tablets and a glass of tap water when they're looked at separately. Put them all together and there's a collective effervescence. The things that make the seltzer and water fizz are, of course, the air bubbles. In Beckham's case, the bubbles come from many sources. Without the showcase of his club, the guile of his wife and the attention of the media, Beckham is a footballer plain and simple – just like a Michael Owen or a Roberto Carlos. Yet, in a sense, the most important of all the ingredients is Us. We, his public – and I mean *all* of us – make Beckham *Beckham*.

This doesn't mean that we have been duped by the Beckham aura. We put it there. The aura didn't diffuse from him. All he did was look good and play decent football. We did the rest. For years he hardly spoke at all and yet still somehow contrived to communicate with us. The sarong, the nail varnish, the hairdos, the tattoos, the plucked eyebrows, the public appearances with the kids and, obviously, the deeds, good and bad, on the pitch. We picked up the messages and spun them into a coherent narrative that was, at once, dramatic, exhilarating and moralistic. It had everything: growth and decay, defilement and castigation, redemption and deliverance, abundance and extravagance. And we made it possible; all he did was give us some raw material.

Admittedly, the timing was exquisite. The extravagant *faux royale* wedding of Posh and Becks in 1999 came in the aftermath of the death of Princess Diana. While it's crass and perhaps insulting to the memory of Diana to suggest that the celebrity couple slid into the emotional vacuum created by Diana's death, we have something else to consider. There is a sense in which the royals have been victims of a historic collision of time and place. At a time when we demand to know more and more about the people we make famous, the royal family just happens to be famous by virtue of its position. As we've got to know more and more about the royals, we've discovered that they're just as fallible, untrustworthy and inadequate as other human beings. Vengeful servants have provided evidence. In recent years, scandals, secrets and rumours, many of them involving sex and corruption, have beset the royal family. We may not have completely lost faith in the institution of the monarchy, but we have probably had some of our idealistic notions about the royal family shaken loose.

Maybe we've begun to suspect that the Windsors are so uncomfortably like ourselves – except with more wealth and power – that we can't really glorify them as we used to. In any case, they're a little too starchy for the times: they don't emote enough, dress coolly, or use language the way we do. Consorting with the Spice Girls was never a credible undertaking for Prince Charles, even if he is the same age as Bruce Springsteen.

The Beckham fairy tale – which, like all fairy tales, embodies ideas about ourselves – grew out of this fertile soil, a context in which people had lost trust in established, traditional forms of authority, in which they no longer looked to monarchic, military, religious or political leaders for guidance and in which they found gratification in immersing themselves in the lives of glamorous and flamboyant celebs This book is about the construction of the fairy tale.

———

You know you've made it to the very top once people know you by just one name. Just think about Oprah, Kylie, Bowie, Madonna. They all exist at a level somewhere above the usual layer of celebs. Beckham has now arrived there.

There's never been an athlete quite like Beckham. Or, more accurately, there have been any number of athletes like Beckham, but never a celebrity and never a brand. Other athletes have pushed gently at the thin membrane that separates sport and show business, of course. Michael Jordan, in particular, broke into pure entertainment, even making an animated feature, *Space Jam*, in which he co-starred with Bugs Bunny. Vinnie Jones adapted the hard image he cultivated in football for the big screen. They were both happy to let their public and private personae coexist. The public can see their movies, buy their books, consume them as celebrities. Beckham faces a different situation: he shows no interest in diversifying. All he wants to do is play football. At least, that's what he says. Yet he keeps turning up in all sorts of places: in ads for mobile phones, in film titles, in internet rumours, and, of course, in countless media stories. His global audience knows it's being served up a public image. It doesn't seem to mind.

A few years ago, Beckham was evasive, talking sparingly in public and sheltering from the media's hailstorm. Now, he's neither as elusive as he was, nor forthcoming. He no longer resists the media, appearing to maintain a distance between his private and public selves and prompting the question whether he has a private self: is there actually anything else apart from the Beckham served up on our tv screens and in print? It's possible that he's become adept at projecting a particular image of himself as a slightly unworldly character lacking in guile. Once asked by a gently teasing *Cosmopolitan* writer if he had bad hair days like everybody else, Beckham answered deadpan, as if he were explaining the mechanics of a free kick.

It's equally possible that this is a man who has become a kind of willing accomplice in a global design. At some point, he must have realized that he was no longer seen as just a footballer, nor even a star footballer, perhaps not even just a star footballer of international renown. Round about the turn of the millennium, he must have thought to himself: "I've become a phenomenon." His choice must have been either to try to resist and reassert his humanity, playing football and refusing to countenance any other kind of pursuit, or just go with it. He went with it, agreeing to the photoshoots, the commercials, the strategic interviews, the rare, but crucial appearances and any other performance that contributed to the image.

No one forced him into it. After all, when the cheques kept featuring more zeroes, it would have been hard to shout: "Stop! I just want to be an ordinary footballer again." Instead, he did what he was told to do. Who wouldn't? Even his most confident advisers must have secretly harboured doubts about Beckham's longevity. Of all the lessons we draw from the age of celebrity, the main one is that consumers are fickle. They'll love you one year and have forgotten you the next. Surprisingly, the love affair with Beckham had legs. Every time there seemed to be a lapse in interest, a new story would leap back into the headlines and a reminder would be served: Beckham is still news.

Clearly, Beckham's relationship with the media has become a central part in his professional and private life. A sports celebrity lives in the public glare. The second it stops, the career is over. Beckham may be a footballer – and a good one – but his celebrity status is one conferred on him by the insatiable (and what seem carnivorous) consumers and media that feed them. They, rather than his football, have shot him into his astral position. At this stage, he and his advisers must know that; which is why he cooperates with the media so much. Once the media senses an abatement of enthusiasm, or perhaps precipitates one, Beckham will be returned to earth.

Beckham captivates a global audience that includes young females who have no obvious interest in sport, gay men for whom Beckham has acquired almost fetishist properties (his hairstyle, accessories and clothes are assigned status as gay symbols), working-class kids who proclaim their nationalism through their champion and countless other groups who have become enamoured by him. Whether we like it or not, we're all part of this fandom. We may not be consciously aware of it; we may openly despise the inordinate amount of coverage given to Beckham. But, we watch tv, read newspapers, listen to the radio, surf the net. We just can't help but be aware of him. We can't escape images of him, stories about him. He's become part of the contemporary cultural landscape.

Should we be surprised that someone whose talent extends only as far as the touchlines of a football pitch has been recreated as an icon of our times? Not really: Beckham is actually perfect for our times. He may be superficial, but who wants depth? He may give us only image, but who wants reality? He may even come across as a bit phoney, but who wants authenticity?

I raised much the same questions in the first edition of this book and my answers are the same, except this time I have more evidence from around the world. Beckham's superficiality, image and inauthenticity have found favour almost everywhere in the world. Only the USA seems to have rebuffed him (though, curiously, Beckham got mentioned on Missy Elliott's 2003 album *This is Not a Test*). And yet, apart from adding to his formidable assembly of acolytes, Beckham has been busy in many other areas. His life and times have been full of incidents and episodes that have made a second edition of *Beckham* inevitable.

Apart from revising the text in the light of developments since 2003, I have adjusted the emphasis of the first edition, especially in relation to the roles of Victoria, his wife, and adidas, the global corporation that has Beckham under contract. Events after the middle of 2003 revealed that the influence of both these parties was even more pronounced than I had suggested in the first edition of *Beckham*. Although I stressed the vital part Posh played in the transition of David Beckham, footballer, to Beckham, celebrity, I still understated the way in which she moulded her husband. I am now persuaded that she masterminded the Beckham project. There are no sinister connotations intended. Victoria was the most astute and self-aware member of a band that few pretended had an abundance of talent. Her experience with the Spice Girls taught her that talent comes a distant second to marketing craft in popular culture. At some critical point in their relationship, she noticed that interest in Beckham was of a different scale and intensity than interest in other footballers. People who didn't know offside from off-licence were paying attention. He seemed to engender emotions typically associated with rock performers. Whether she consciously proposed to apply the same kinds of celeb-making principles and operations that had worked so certainly for the Spice Girls to a footballer, we'll never know. In chapter six, I raise the possibility.

When adidas, the sportswear manufacturer, signed Beckham to an endorsement contract, it could not have imagined what a *coup* that was. A talented player in a fashionable team, Beckham was not yet a fully fledged celebrity. Yet, he developed beyond adidas's most improvident expectations: he became the world's premier celebrity athlete. For years, it must have been tormenting for adidas to have had him on the books, yet have to sit back and watch him play every week in the red shirt of Manchester United, a shirt that bore the "swoosh" logo of adidas's market rivals, Nike. adidas is rarely mentioned in Beckham's rise, if at all. The corporation remains silent, presumably content to utilize his fabulous image to shift its merchandise off the shelves. I paid insufficient attention to adidas in the first edition. In this edition, I examine the kind of money a sports manufacturer might expect to earn from an endorser like Beckham, and suggest why adidas may, in future, be an even bigger influence than Victoria.

Second editions are rarely published so soon after the first, but, in this case, it's amply justified. The past couple of years have seen Beckham at the centre of (yet another) spell of media delirium, this one lasting several months and culminating in Beckham's trading his Manchester United shirt for the adidas-emblazoned shirt of Real Madrid. He failed to conquer the USA, but annexed another huge market in Japan. They were a revealing couple of years. Exactly what they revealed about Beckham and the phenomenon he has propagated will become clear.

Had he surfaced twenty, or ten, or even five years before, would he still have commanded the adulation of the planet? If he'd played for any other club, would he have attracted the attention of the world's media? Supposing he hadn't married who he did, when he did, would he have become a global celebrity? The short answers to these questions are no, no and no. The longer versions are in the pages that follow.

one

OF FROGS AND PRINCES

There was once a frog whose best friend worked as a kitchen maid. The maid dreamt of going to a ball and dancing with a handsome prince. Sometimes after dark, dressed in rags, she would dance in the parlour, never expecting that her dream would ever come true. One night a fairy godmother appeared, waved a magic wand and transformed the maid into a Lady, complete with exquisite ball gown. But, who would accompany her to the ball? Once more, the fairy godmother motioned her wand and the frog became a prince. Not the prince of the kitchen maid's dreams: far more handsome and dressed in clothes so fine that they put even hers to shame. And, when they arrived at the ball, he danced so divinely that the others withdrew from the floor in awe and simply looked on in admiration – and in envy.

He basked in the admiration so much that he forgot to get home by midnight to break the spell and so ended up trapped in a human body. But what a body! Adorned with resplendent satins, perforated with elegant jewellery, his supple, creamy flesh was enchanting. The maid fell in love with him; so too did countless others. In fact, they not only loved him, they adored, idolized and worshipped him. They devoted large parts of their life to him, copied his clothes, his hair, the rings in his ears, the patterns on his body. How they wished they could be like him, or a part of him, or even be him.

So enchanted by the image of the handsome prince were they that they forgot completely that he was once only a humble frog. It really didn't matter, anyway. Folks came from far and wide to stare at the prince, bestowing on him great praise and gifts.

Some folks sneered; most gazed in wonderment. How could it be possible that one so comely, so gifted, so rich could have all these qualities in such abundance and be able to dance like no other?

One night, a tattered vagabond roamed into town. The locals told him of how the great one was once a frog who had been charmed by a fairy godmother. "You don't believe in fairy godmothers, do you?" laughed the scoundrel. When the maid, by now a fair princess, heard of the vagabond, she was furious. She banished him from town. As he left, the wanderer turned back and looked at the castle of the illustrious couple. "There's no fairy godmother, my friends", he shouted to the townsfolk. "If you want to know the truth behind the prince's secret, ask the princess."

Fairy stories, folk tales and myths are fantasies. David Beckham's life, his experience, his very being is a fantasy of sorts. A working-class boy with generous athletic skills who, after a modest start to his sports career, became the most celebrated athlete of his time, perhaps ever, Beckham seems to live in a fantastical landscape, in a world that resembles our own, but one in which the rules are different. In the Beckham landscape, our hero scores vital goals that compare with any dragon-slaying feat achieved by St George. He marries a pop star, an event that could have been stolen from *Sleeping Beauty*. His hairstyles, clothes and body ornamentation are emulated with the kind of obedience commanded by the Pied Piper.

The evidence is, quite literally, all around, from huge bill-boards bearing his image, to the fact that every newspaper and radio station carries at least one story about him. He appears on television, on chat shows, on commercials and, of course, playing football, whether for his club or country. Beckham is near-ubiquitous. News that he has acquired a new tattoo or body pierce is instantly relayed around the world, reported, interpreted and discussed. A new haircut sparks an occasion for deep thought: what does it mean? is it appropriate? should we follow the example? He holds hands with his wife: the *Guardian* runs a story on the significance of hand-holding. And even a minor injury makes front-page news and sends journalists scurrying to medical dictionaries: "metatarsus, *n.*, part of foot between ankle and toes; set of bones in this".

Every move is closely monitored and minutely dissected by the media. Every gesture, mannerism, haircut, body pierce, tattoo becomes a subject of scrutiny and analysis. His clothes are taken apart, label-by-label, invested with the kind of significance that used to be reserved for rock or movie stars. There have been enough television programmes dedicated to him to justify a new genre, "Becksdox", as the *Daily Telegraph*'s Jim White called it.

Beckham's life is closely monitored by a voracious media prepared to report the most seemingly minute and insignificant detail and expand it into a full-blown adventure. The presentation of a speeding ticket is changed into a life-and-death chase, with Beckham attempting to flee the predatory paparazzi who track him everywhere. A samurai-style hairdo becomes a moral and psychological discourse, with discussions centring on the propriety of the do and the motivations behind it. A sense of national catastrophe follows reports of a kidnap plot, which turns out to be bogus, anyway. His departure for Spain is an occasion for reflections on whether things will ever be the same. Every feature of his life is spun into a tale. We devour every one of them.

Fairy stories tend to embody our own experiences. Some might say that they secrete a kind of eternal human truth. A world in which frogs turn into princes, cross-dressing wolves masquerade as sick grandmothers and ducks transmute into swans engages the listener with a message of change. Things are not always what they appear: they have hidden qualities which, under certain conditions, will surface. In the process, they will change and, during the metamorphosis, something different will emerge. Beckham turned from an ordinary kid, his father a manual worker, mother a hairdresser, to first global celebrity of the century.

We'd all like to experience that kind of change. We'd like to look a little more like Beckham, take off a few pounds, put on some muscle. Maybe we'd like to be taller, or shorter, or have bigger breasts, fuller lips, narrower thighs, smaller noses or whiter teeth. Unsurprisingly, we would all like to have money like his. If we did, we'd have enough to afford the cosmetic surgery needed to effect a complete transformation.

Desire is everywhere. Princes have always had an edge over frogs, but slimness has only recently surpassed fatness as a valued property; and, while it's possible that some form of self-dissatisfaction always existed, contemporary culture dictates clear priorities. Wealth, fame and glamour are valued; poverty, obscurity and ordinariness are not. Some aspirant singers or actors toil away in pursuit of the break that will give them access to the world of wealth, fame and glamour; others try for a few years then resign themselves to a more mundane life; still others fanatisize about it. A few others actually get into the parallel world, if only for a few years. That is, the Beckham world of fame, glamour and celebrity.

―――――

When he played in Manchester, the United fans used to chant (to the tune of José Fernandez Diaz's *Guantanamera*): "One David Beckham. There's only one David Beckham." Actually, the fans were wrong. There are two Beckhams: the flesh-and-blood father with a fondness for cars, decorously pale looks and fine soccer skills; and the icon, the celebrity, the commodity, the brand, the Beckham that exists independently of time and space and resides in the imaginations of countless acolytes. For women, he's *le beau idéal*, a figure on whom fantasies are spun; for men, he's a colossus standing astride all dominions of sport, commanding their admiration, affection and devotion. He's become a global phenomenon, a towering presence, not only in football but in all of popular culture. The Beckham phenomenon is so perfectly congruent with our times, it could have been created. Actually, it was. This book is about how.

Two years ago, when the first edition of this book was published, it would have seemed ridiculous to suggest that Beckham could get any bigger: he was, after all, the world's leading sport celebrity with a fan base that spanned the globe and a package of endorsement contracts that guaranteed him about €30 million per year. No one could have imagined that his stock could go any higher. Yet, that's exactly what happened.

12

Beckham and his wife have expanded their scope, making well-documented assaults o n the US and Japanese markets and meeting with mixed success. Beckham's fraught relationship with his erstwhile manager and surrogate father Alex Ferguson has been the subject of expansive and occasionally preposterous speculation, especially after an apparent accident in February 2003 that became known as the Flying Boot incident. Many thought that this incident worked as a catalyst for Beckham's departure from Manchester to Madrid (I'll consider this later). The transfer itself was one of the commanding media stories of 2003, occupying television, radio, print media and internet sites for a full two months. In terms of coverage, it came close to eclipsing the war in Iraq. The coverage ensured that Beckham's name was known everywhere in the world. His image was the most recognizable on the planet. Ask anybody in the world outside the USA to name the three most famous men and Beckham is likely to appear as number one on every list.

By the time Beckham's autobiography *davidbeckham: My Side* was published in September 2003, Collins Willow was confident enough to publish twelve translations and a North American edition simultaneously, ordering a first print run of more than a million. In a way, it validated Beckham's status as a genuinely global figure and a brand in his own right.

Clichés that would normally seem crass feel oddly appropriate: A-list celeb, gay icon, brand. Somehow, they all fit. Beckham is not just a footballer. He is the twenty-first-century celebrity *par excellence*. Whichever way you hold him to the light, Beckham is an extraordinary being, a rare thing, a total one-off. He's everywhere in the world, in newspapers, television, the internet, on countless posters that decorate young people's bedroom walls. Some writers even reckon he and his wife have wandered into the emotional territory once occupied so serenely by Princess Diana. They've certainly commanded the attention of the paparazzi in much the same way as Diana did.

Yet, when you think about it, what does he do? Does he lead armies into battle, discover cures for diseases, perform miracles? Has he won the Nobel Peace Prize, saved the planet? Does he make pronouncements that influence opinions or issue advice that changes the way we live? No. He plays football – primarily. Auxiliary activities include wearing lots of extravagantly expensive jewellery and clothes, being a doting father, accompanying his wife to glittery premieres, appearing in ads and, well, that's about it. Yet Beckham has invested the sports pages, the tabloids, the internet websites and the television networks with more stories than they can ever wish for. He hasn't even tried to transcend football in the kind of way that rock stars like Sting or Bono have tried to reach beyond music.

So, why is he exalted to the point where you can almost imagine his being beatified, let alone honoured with an OBE? The answer is not because he is a good footballer. When the first edition of this book was published, I risked upsetting his legions of fans by having the temerity to suggest this. Now, no one is kidding himself or herself that he is in the same class as the likes of Zidane or Ronaldo. Some used his transfer from Manchester United to Real Madrid to bolster the claim that he wasn't even the most valuable player in Manchester, let alone the world. Beckham is good-looking, but there's good-looking and *good-looking*. He's photogenic, but fashion editors don't rate him as highly as scores of professional models. And when he talks, you realize that this is no George Clooney.

No, the answer is because he's a product that we all consume. We're parts of a generation of emotionally expressive, self-aware, brand-conscious, label-observant, New-Man attentive, gossip-hungry, celebrity worshippers. We, the fans, the television viewers, the writers, the audience, make Beckham *Beckham*. We've become an unpaid backing choir for his aria, and we can stop singing any time we like. The moment we do, Beckham turns back into a footballer.

This book is a departure from the usual sports biography. It's neither an extravaganza, celebrating the wonderful and unique gifts of the subject in question, nor a piercing insight into the subject's personal life. It certainly isn't a muckraking exercise, dishing the dirt on private secrets that have previously escaped the public's attention. But, it *is* about Beckham. It starts from the premise that there is more than one way to understand somebody. Looking inside them, trying to disclose their inner core, their intimate character, their true personality, is only one means of discovery. Another is to look outside them. This is my approach. Understanding Beckham in this way requires me to look both at him and also at the culture of which he has become an important part. That means us.

———

Making sense of Beckham by looking outside him to the influences that have made possible and assisted his creation takes me into unusual territory. I am not, of course, neglecting his startling talents on the field of play. Yet, the clues to understanding his status lie elsewhere: in his club, his culture and his environment, as well as himself and the people who surround him. So, this is how I proceed, mapping out the circumstances in which Beckham came into being, both as a human being and as an athlete, but also, most importantly, as a sports celebrity.

The tribulations of Beckham are pretty well documented. The hell-and-back-and-beyond drama in which he was turned from a dashing young knight to accursed soul before discovering deliverance is a tale in its own right. Chapter two describes how this experience changed not only Beckham, but, more vitally, the media's and public's perceptions of him. Together, they created a singular position for Beckham. Yes, there have been other athletes who have become world famous through either their great accomplishments or their scandalous private lives. And there have been other sport stars who have been idolized by women. And, I suppose, there have been sportsmen who have at least approached, and maybe reached, the same levels of fame as showbusiness celebrities. But, all of these? In this respect, Beckham is out on his own.

I then sketch out the "good life" that Beckham and his wife started to symbolize once Posh and Becks became an item. Of course, everyone knows they form one of the most glamorous, designer-clad couples around and sport–showbiz liaisons are always newsworthy. In chapter three, I show how the Beckhams have become living advertisements, commodities in their own right and a demonstration that there is a grand life for those daring enough to shoot for it, or even for those timid enough to fanatisize about it. In other words, Posh and Becks present a vision of the good life to which others aspire. And just when it seemed that life could get no better, it did. While the physical Beckham moved to Spain, the celebrity encircled the world.

Football lies at the core of Beckham's celebrity status, though it has become just a small part of his overall repertoire of activities. Still, the fact remains: if he hadn't been a good athlete, we'd never have heard of him. This raises a question: if he'd been a good footballer, yet had signed for, say, Tottenham Hotspur, near his birthplace, or perhaps a less fashionable club like Everton, or even Preston North End, a club to which he was loaned for a while, would he still have become a global celebrity?

Beckham's inauguration in football was through a club that was in the process of building one of the world's leading sports brands: Manchester United is not only the world's richest club; it has also surpassed Dallas Cowboys as the world's most valuable sports franchise. Almost by default, Beckham became part of a brand. He acquired the cachet associated with United. Playing for a global brand was vital for Beckham: it drew him media attention in a way that would have been impossible if he had played for a lesser club. Imagine if Matthew LeTissier, a player of uncommon technical ability, had moved from Southampton to, say, Arsenal or Leeds United in 1992. Would football history have been different? He may have challenged Gascoigne as the country's leading player and perhaps even favourite celebrity footballer. He may have helped one of those teams supplant Manchester United as the dominant club of the decade. His club might then have provided Beckham with the kind of showcase United later gave him.

My interest is in what happened rather than what might have happened (though I am tempted into this kind of speculation throughout the book). This was that Manchester United allowed Beckham, first, to exhibit his skills in front of the world and, second, to lend his name and image to a range of merchandise that would sell around the world. Both were integral to the Beckham phenomenon. In chapter four, I highlight how Manchester United changed from an ordinary and, at the start of the 1980s, lacklustre club, into the powerful brand it now is. I pay particular attention to the key role played by Martin

Edwards in this transition. Edwards is an interesting man, loved and loathed, though not in anything like equal proportions. While he's demonized, particularly by Manchester United fans, he's also responsible for many of the plans, perhaps even visions, that worked to establish ManU as the power it now is. You might be misled into thinking the mains of that power are on the field of play. They're not.

At the time of the first edition of this book, ManU, the brand, seemed invulnerable. The club boldly maintained that no player was bigger than Manchester United. And remember: this is a club that can list names like Best, Charlton and Law among its alumni. Beckham, perhaps not by design, demonstrated the falsity of that claim. The irony is that, without Manchester United and the brand it created, Beckham would have had no stage big enough to contain him. Only Manchester United could have presented him as it did – to a world audience.

There is a bigger presence in David Beckham's professional life. While you rarely see him, Rupert Murdoch is everywhere in football. His influence has been total. His television company BSkyB, or Sky as it started life, changed football the moment it pitched for the rights to show Premier League soccer "live". By the time Beckham emerged in 1992, satellite television had barely begun to wring its changes. But, by the time he established himself as a Manchester United regular, the revolution was in full swing. Football, the working-class game of yore, was not so much modified as converted wholesale into a tv-friendly competition thriving with well-paid players from all four corners and a queue of commercial sponsors, all eager to associate their brands with the now-fashionable pursuit of the affluent.

This was Beckham's world, of course: bursting with tv and sponsors' money, mixing with film, fashion and rock music as partners in showbusiness. World stars, like Jürgen Klinsmann and Ruud Gullit, were among the first overseas sojourners to base themselves in the newly glamorized English league. Soon, the whole sport was cosmopolitan.

Football's place in popular culture had been under threat throughout the 1980s. Its image as a drab and soggy sport afflicted by recurrent violence and racism had not been helped by the sequence of disasters culminating in Hillsborough. Had Beckham developed in this environment, he would never have snared the lucrative endorsements, the television documentaries and the many other deals that have brought him his riches and status. The fact is that he rose to prominence when football was more than just a game. In chapter five, I trace the changes that turned football into a showbusiness-like spectacle.

As football was turned on its head, so other cultural changes were afoot. "Girl Power", for all its vagueness, was a term on many people's lips: it chimed with the times. Victoria Adams, as she then was, personified Girl Power. As a member of the Spice Girls – Posh – she was known as much for her bubbly audacity as for her gender. When she met Beckham, her band was, as she remembers, "on fire", selling millions of cds all over the world and lending its name to enough merchandise to fill an Argos catalogue. She was well-versed in the demands of celebritydom. This, we can safely assume, included the business side.

While Beckham had shown potential and was being touted as a future star, he was by no means a celebrity athlete. News of his relationship with Posh changed all that: he soon became part of a paradoxical world of separateness and intimacy. Progressively, he was separated from other footballers, identified as a special case, deserving special treatment. He was, after all, the beau of one the world's most famous women. Intimacy was no longer his: he quickly had to get to grips with the fact that personal life for a celeb is not, strictly speaking, that personal. The media wanted to know more about him; they wanted to share his secrets. His relationship with Victoria was in the public domain from the moment it became known that they were an item.

Victoria has played a central role in Beckham's career, a role that has become even more conspicuous since the first edition of this book was published. In that edition, I wrote about her as an inspiration. Now, I realize that even this understated her part. In this edition, I investigate not only how Victoria's status transferred to him as if by osmosis, but how she may have designed a project that, when completed, must have surprised even her. Chapter six looks at the ways in which she made this happen.

Of course, Beckham wasn't the first British footballer to have been granted celebrity status. According to some writers, Stanley Matthews was a celebrity of sorts, but that was in an age when the media were much, much less invasive and interested primarily in his sporting prowess rather than his personal habits. Even George Best, who sprung out of a Beatlemaniacal sixties culture and became the first athlete to be given the same kind of attention as a pop star, wasn't subject to the elaborate scrutiny and saturation coverage afforded subsequent sport celebrities. Paul Gascoigne, on the other hand, was.

Gascoigne was the first genuine celebrity athlete to contend with a media ready to feast on any morsel: truths, half-truths, hearsay, tittle-tattle, gossip and downright lies were all staples for the media in the 1990s. Tabloid war had broken out, celeb magazines were being launched, satellite and cable television were pitching in. Gascoigne stood at what some writers call a junction, where football changed direction and headed towards becoming the product we now consume, rather than just watch.

Gascoigne was like a bottle of Budweiser: shake him up and he spurted over everyone within range. Even when not shaken, he was prone to spontaneous discharges, usually playful, but occasionally violent. Every foible – and there were many – of Gascoigne was recorded and, often, relayed around the world. And, for a while, he appeared to love the attention. In fact, one suspects, he played up to his part as the idiot savant, as Germaine Greer once described him. Eventually, Gascoigne buckled under the weight of the media and turned against them. By this time, it was probably of little consequence: they'd found new prey. Chapter seven is devoted to a study of Gascoigne and his importance. I compare Gascoigne with Beckham, though not as footballers, but as celebrities.

Many of the feats for which Gascoigne is famous concern manliness. His treatment of people, including his wife and members of the media, said something about being a man. Beckham's conduct and bearing also say something about being a man. The contrast between the two is illuminating.

Like Gascoigne before him, Beckham offered a version of what it is to be a man. Not for him the boozing, farting and no-holds-barred debauchery that characterized Gascoigne's odyssey through the 1990s. And certainly not the wife-beating that disclosed an unheeding cruelty in Gascoigne.

Beckham offered a quite different palette of masculinity: sweet-natured, caring, nurturing, doting, full of soft, human touches. It's a type of manliness that has earned him admiration from unexpected quarters. A devoted following of gay fans would be enough to guarantee most footballers a punishment course. Football fans are traditionally not known for their tolerance in this department. Yet, somehow, Beckham got away with it, even to the point of appearing on national television and endorsing his gay following. How is he able to do it? This is the subject of chapter eight.

Appearing in advertisements is not simply an added bonus for being famous. It's integral to the process of remaining famous, or becoming even more famous. There are a few celebrities who would never stoop to lend their name or image to commercial products. Not many though: even A-listers such as Madonna, Liz Taylor and Britney Spears have all done endorsements. Perhaps they were once regarded as vulgar. Now, their benefits are well recognized. Not only are they hugely remunerative; they can also help position a celeb in the public consciousness.

Football's entry into the entertainment industry has had many consequences, one of which is that its leading lights enjoy a similar kind of status to pop and movie stars. One of the first things a footballer does after securing a first team place is sign an endorsement deal, even if it's with the local timber merchants. The more the player is seen and recognized, the greater the potential rewards.

Beckham's image is everywhere: on tv, in magazines, in advertising and countless other media. His extensive presence isn't a matter of chance, but the product of a controlled enterprise. There's a virtual industry charged with the responsibility of managing a diverse portfolio of lucrative endorsement contracts, ensuring that the kind of publicity generated is exactly appropriate and extracting the right rewards for merchandise bearing Beckham's name and image. Beckham's decision to split from his agents SFX is arguably the single most important event in his celebrity life since the first edition of this book. And, I'm not neglecting the move to Madrid. In chapter nine I explore the decision to move to Simon Fuller's 19 Management and suggest the reasons behind it.

In chapter ten, I open my account even further, looking at how fans contribute directly to Beckham's status. We think we know celebrities: after all, that's why they're celebs. We think we know Beckham. Actually, we know very little. The rest, we make up. One fan claimed she heard him issuing personal commands to her. No doubt there are many, many more who experience similar visitations.

Madonna changed the rules of engagement with the media in the late 1980s/early 1990s: she offered herself to them totally, completely and wholly. She granted access and gave full disclosure. In return, she demanded media coverage, the likes of which had never been seen or heard before. Madonna's pact with the media had consequences that we are still experiencing. Fans were no longer content to read about the stars' favourite foods or colours, or to stare at pictures of them in magazines. They demanded to know them intimately.

I offer the view that Beckham is like a book, a piece of text, something we can read, interpret and know. How do fans make sense of Beckham in an age when most of the strategies, tactics and tricks used to keep celebrities in the public eye are well known? It's as if a fairy tale was postscripted with the equivalent of one of those "The making of ..." documentaries that explain how all the special fx of movies were achieved. You imagine a Brothers Grimm tale would lose its magic if it were to contain details of how the story was concocted and scribed. Many aspects of Beckham's story are fairy tale-like. How do fans come to terms with a fairy tale that includes an account of its own production?

Beckham's extraordinary status is due less to him and what he does and more to what people attribute to him and believe he does. The special "gifts" he's thought to own haven't been granted him through divine revelation, as Mozart's were thought to be. The fans who read him and read about him are the ones who credit him. His playing abilities are beyond question and his accomplishments are undeniable. Attempting to strip away his mystery doesn't involve denying that Beckham has masterly technique and fearless resolve on the football pitch. It merely means that, to understand him, we need to understand what fans make of him.

There's an answer to the big question that lies beneath this and, for that matter, any other book that tries to tap the sources of a celebrity's spell. Why are we enchanted by Them – Them being the fabulous creatures with wealth, glamour, fame and the kind of lifestyle that qualifies as the good life? We never used to be. There have always been famous people. It's just that, in recent years, there have been more of them. Lots more. And they seem to multiply. What's more, many of them haven't distinguished themselves for anything more than the capacity for being known. Beckham doesn't fall into this category: he has athletic skills and these were the original reason he came to the fore.

Exactly who wants to be rich and famous? The answer is, of course: we all do. While this may not strike readers as surprising, we are talking serious fantasy here. There is a generation out there that clings to celebrities, not in a physical way, but in the kind of way that takes a lot of perseverance, devotion and time. Many fans index their own lives to those of the celebrities they respect, honour and perhaps even idolize (that's not too strong a word). They are parts of a new type of culture, one in which celebrities, whether from sport or other branches of entertainment, wield unprecedented influence. Beckham has emerged from precisely this culture. Chapter eleven explores the reasons why today we have all been caught up in the cult of celebrity.

The final chapter examines Beckham against the background of a culture that places an exorbitant value on celebrities. There have been other celebrity footballers, including George Best and Kevin Keegan, but never one that surfaced at the moment in history when he was regarded as something much more than an athlete, even a great athlete. The evidence of our senses tells us that Beckham surely is. If he had come to the fore fifteen, no, ten years ago, he would have been recognized as a good, perhaps even great sportsman. The honours that have become common-place might still have poured in. But, he wouldn't have been the unique phenomenon he is. He wouldn't have had a fan base that encircles the globe; nor would he have attracted a border of zealots who endow him with spiritual significance. Gay men might have found him appealing, but they wouldn't have granted him iconic status. Beckham himself would probably not have had the nerve to pose in the kind of fashion shots that would earn him that kind of status. Advertisers might have offered him a few endorsements (remember Keegan's homoerotically risqué shower room commercials with Henry Cooper?), though he wouldn't have had a bulging portfolio valued in millions, as he does today. No, Beckham is a product of this time, this place.

This is actually the argument I put forward in this book and, running the risk of being repetitious, I'll restate my point: Beckham would simply not have happened in another era. He's perfect for today. He's the most adored, most copied athlete and, probably, the most persuasive, should he ever try to exercise his opinions on anything. He's very much a product of his time, his culture, yet he transcends his time and culture in a way that no other athlete has done. He's accessible but not exactly open, and he deflects the very attention that other, perhaps less talented, celebrities pursue. As athletes go, he appears among the least egocentric, the most psychologically transparent, the simplest yet the most artful. We know practically everything there is to know about one Beckham; virtually nothing about the other. He doesn't say or do much apart from play football and accompany his wife. In these respects he seems so ordinary. Perhaps that's the key: everyone knows there's a public face of Beckham; they assume the private face is much the same. What more can there be?

Even if there are hidden depths, I'm concerned less with the physical Beckham, so to speak, and more with the global celeb-rity. Beckham the celebrity embodies cultural changes that have transpired over the past two decades. These changes have affected us, rendering us all celebrity idolaters. Not content to watch athletes compete or actors act or politicians govern, we've demanded to know them. Their character, their private life, and their tastes: we demand that these be displayed for our delectation. The media collude and, as we'll see later in the book, connive in this. So do we.

We haven't spontaneously started getting interested in these things. Our changing interests reflect other kinds of change all around us. Many of them will come into view throughout the book. For example, there have been shifts in the status and operations of sport in contemporary culture, changes in perceptions and understandings of masculinity and family life, and changes in the way we formulate our plans, ambitions and our relationships to others. The engine behind all these changes is known as commodification – the seemingly irresistible process in which everything is subject to being turned into an article of trade that can be bought and sold in any marketplace in the world. Over the past few decades, we've all become consumers. We don't buy because we need things; we buy because we desire them. A whole industry has grown around trying to access our desires, shape them and convert them into spending habits.

In other words, potentially anything can be made into a commodity. This includes people. Footballers. Beckham himself is not only living evidence of this process, but also an embodiment of the culture that has advanced it. This is, after all, a culture capable of turning frogs into princes.

two

DISASTER OR DELIVERANCE?

It seems a long way from the Bernabéu. It seems to be from a different age. A minor game at Brighton and Hove Albion's now-defunct Goldstone Ground in the second round of what was then called the Rumbelow's Cup. On 23 September 1992, Manchester United, not yet the ascendant force, held the home team to a 1–1 draw. In the second half of the game, the Manchester team brought on a slightly built 17-year-old with a blanched face and highlighted hair, who made barely any impression on the game. He reappeared at intervals over the next couple of years and was then loaned out to Preston North End before returning to Manchester. For four years after his début at Brighton, he was a southerner adrift in the alien Northwest, opting to go to bed early instead of carousing, and staying behind for extra training to perfect ball skills instead of heading straight to the wine bars, playing occasionally in the first team, but failing to make his presence felt. Then, surprisingly and perhaps implausibly, he became a cross between Bobby Charlton and Brad Pitt.

David Robert Joseph Beckham was born in Leytonstone, East London on 2 May 1975. Manchester United was at its post-war nadir: after its triumphs of the mid-1960s, it had plummeted into the second division and was losing money (it's now the richest sports club in the world, valued at over £600 million). Footballers had rid themselves of the maximum wage of £20 per week in 1961, but the retain-and-transfer rule that was introduced in the 1890s was still in place, severely restricting the mobility and earnings capacity of players (it was replaced in 1978 and

25

blown away by the Bosman ruling of 1995). *The Sweeney* captivated television viewers, who were served by only the basic terrestrial networks, of course. Football came to them largely as highlight packages bereft of all the gizmos and "analyses" to which today's viewers have become accustomed. Margaret Thatcher was poised to start her unforgettable reign. The *Sun* newspaper was in its sixth year under the ownership of Rupert Murdoch and on its way to becoming Britain's biggest selling newspaper.

Changes in laws affecting football helped turn the game into a fully fledged business. Television was absolutely central both to the football business and to the cult of celebrity, which flowered from the 1980s. Thatcherism, as it became known, fostered an environment in which industry, initiative and self-help were shibboleths. In this environment, Murdoch thrived to the point where, in what at first appeared an act of suicidal pomposity, he tried to revolutionize the entire television industry. As we'll see, all these people, things and the changes they contrived became influential factors in the rise of David Beckham.

Beckham spent his youth in Chingford, Essex, which is part of Greater London. His father was a self-employed gas fitter and his mother a hairdresser. He came to public notice in 1986, when he won a national soccer skills tournament at old Trafford. His dad, Ted, had been a decent non-league player for Barking and trialled with Leyton Orient. Like many sons of aspiring athletes who never quite made it, the young Beckham became something of a beast of burden, freighting not only his own ambitions, but also those of his father. This can be a profligate cause: sport claims the ambitions and lives of countless young people, the colossal majority of whom never enjoy a single season as a professional. In Beckham's case, the encouragement of his father was the electric charge behind a professional career like no other.

Playing with a Sunday league team, Ridgeway Rovers, Beckham attracted interest from the scouts of Arsenal and Tottenham; the latter invited him to train with its youth team. At eleven, Beckham won a ball skills contest, the prize for which was a chance to train with Barcelona's youth team. Terry Ven-

Figure 1   For a while, the young Beckham was considered too small to withstand the rigours of the physically demanding Premier League. *Source*: Getty Images

ables was then coach of the Spanish team. Beckham had trials for the England Schoolboys team, but was considered too small to hold his own at international level. Unable to mix it with the heavier players, he compensated with an unerring accuracy in his passing and an exceptional power to drive a still ball towards goal.

Still, there was enough potential to arouse the interest of Manchester United scouts. After trooping off a Sunday morning game, his mother congratulated him. "It's good that you've played well today, because Manchester United were watching", she said, "and they want you to come down and have a trial." Beckham's reaction was to cry: "I just stood there and cried." It wasn't what you'd call a manly response, not in the traditional sense, anyway; and it wasn't the only time Beckham was to flout the conventions of football machismo. Much more was to come.

By the age of 14, he had signed with Manchester United and became a full professional two years later in 1991. The club, in many ways, epitomized football. The once-great Manchester United was struggling, its manager Alex Ferguson apparently out of his depth in the English league, having had success at Aberdeen and, before that, St Mirren. But he was finding England's top flight to be much more demanding. Ferguson moved to Manchester in 1986, the same year that the 11-year-old Beckham won a national football skills contest. English football was in the doldrums and, according to some analysts, destined never to find fair wind enough to navigate itself out of them.

United emerged from its fallow period and was two years away from beginning its domination of British football when Beckham signed. The shape of things to come could be discerned from United's defeat of Barcelona to win the now-discontinued European Cup Winners' Cup. Ferguson, who had, by some accounts, been close to being dismissed after his first four years with the club, was starting along a laurel-strewn path that was to lead, among other achievements, to manifold trophies and a knighthood. The club had banished the memory of a Granada television documentary, *World in Action*, shown in 1980. The programme had exposed the club's darker side, detailing payments to schoolboys, suspect business practices and the then chairman's underhand methods of procuring contracts for his meat company. The following year was the start of a new era for the club: Martin Edwards took over as chairman and effectively ushered in a new age of undreamed-of wealth and salubrity.

Beckham's rise was far from meteoric; in fact, at 19, he was loaned out to Preston North End, then a lowly, third division club. Doubts about his size and physical strength remained and the spell with PNE was intended to toughen him up. Play in lower divisions tends to be of a more physical character, demanding a certain robustness of it players. The Preston period may have been critical in Beckham's development. Fixed on a career in professional soccer since he could remember, his experiences immediately after leaving school must have seemed like a dream: playing not just for any club, but for the club he – and his father – followed and the team that, in the early 1990s, was emerging as the dominant force in England.

Preston was only a 25-mile stretch of the M6 from Manchester, but it might have been the Road to Damascus for Beckham. Somewhere along the way, he must have imagined he saw a road sign with "Lower Divisions" across it. The properties that were to become his signature must surely have come from that short, but crucial time with PNE. Blessed as a boy, gifted as an adolescent, but blighted, so it seemed, as a young man, the slightly built Beckham faced a formidable opponent. The indefatigability, tenacity and doggedness he manifested in later years weren't the products of a charmed life, but of one that, for a while, looked to be cursed. But in football, if you survive the Darwinian process, you emerge as the strongest and remain with your team. The weaker players either perish or move to other clubs. Beckham might have looked weak, but he fought his way into the ranks of the strongest.

By the time he returned to Manchester in 1995, the United team was enjoying a hegemonic period, in which it won eight Premiership titles and the European championship. It's supremacy compared with that of the Chicago Bulls of the USA's National Basketball Association, during Michael Jordan's apogee, and the New York Yankees baseball club in the late 1990s. Many of Beckham's contemporaries had established themselves as valued bit part players supporting the star of United, Eric Cantona. A tempestuous, often nihilistic maverick, Cantona played for United for five years between 1992 and 1997 before unexpectedly announcing his retirement at the age of thirty-one. A self-styled philosopher and lover of poetry, Cantona was arguably the most influential and definitely the most controversial player of his day in Britain. He presaged a significant change in the composition of British soccer, one that initially stirred parochial fears. Manchester United and a handful of other clubs formed an elite group, with money enough to tempt well-paid players from France, Germany, Italy and elsewhere in continental Europe. This was made possible by television revenues, the source of which was Rupert Murdoch's BSkyB.

Playing alongside Cantona in August 1996, Beckham scored a goal of such distinction that he made headlines nationally and featured in incalculable video replays. Fifty-seven yards out and, with the rival goalkeeper (Neil Sullivan, then of Wimbledon) off his line, Beckham struck what was either a wildly hopeful punt upfield, or an adroitly executed attempt on goal. Either way, it resulted in the ball's moving in a long, sweeping arc over everyone's heads, coming to rest in the net. Alex Ferguson introduced comparisons with Pelé's famous shot against Czechoslovakia in the 1970 World Cup championships. The raptures of the national media ensured that the name "Beckham" made its impress in the public consciousness. Widespread interest in and consumption of what many took to be a "wonder goal" guaranteed Beckham an audience. From this point, his progress would be tracked.

In many ways, Beckham's career at this stage was ordinary: working-class kid with his eyes on the big prize, but without the physical means to match his desires, gets early break, then begins to meet the big boys and gets smacked down; kid goes away, steels himself and returns ready to face the music, pulls off a sensation, is greeted by ecstatic crowd, goes on to triumph over adversity. This classic narrative has been recycled in novels and movies galore. Beckham added new twists to the plot.

At another time in history, it's entirely possible that Beckham would have been recognized as a technically proficient athlete, his looks perhaps making him into what was once called an idol – an object of adolescent approval. But only at the hinge of the twentieth and twenty-first centuries would he have become a global celebrity. Once the domain of film, television and fashion industry, showbusiness acquired a new confrère in the guise of sport. Football adapted more quickly than any other sport to the demands of showbusiness. Its players were the first to prosper: not only were they rewarded with huge salary hikes and an assortment of other commercial opportunities, but their status changed too: they all became celebrities of some order.

In 1996 – the year in which the Spice Girls were launched – Beckham represented England in international competition. While captain of the England Under-21 team, he'd shown the kind of qualities, particularly of leadership, that would eventually stand him in good stead. At 21, he assembled in the company of Alan Shearer, Bryan Robson and Paul Gascoigne, regarded by most as the best British player of the period and an athlete who was rarely out of the headlines.

Beckham had already been earmarked as a football star of tomorrow by the time he met his future wife. A scorer of memorable goals, an escort of models or model-like women, an England Under-21 captain, he seemed to have all the credentials. Even better: he was a member of not just any old club, but of one of the biggest brands in sport, the ideal showcase for a man who would wear the number 7 shirt discarded by Eric Cantona when he retired in 1997. Cantona had done much to restore the Manchester club. Apart from performing on the field, he was also a merchandiser's dream: as we'll see later, Cantona, more than any other player, promoted the growth of the ManU brand.

While Beckham wasn't in the same league as Cantona when it came to shifting merchandise in the early 1990s, he looked as if he could be groomed. Brylcreem, the maker of hair preparations, cleverly spotted his marketing potential when it offered him an endorsement deal. Brylcreem had something of a historical link with footballers, having signed Denis Compton to an endorsement contract in the 1940s. Known as the "Brylcreem Boy", Compton was perhaps the best-known athlete of his generation, playing both cricket, for Middlesex, and football, for Arsenal, as well as representing his country in both sports. A deal worth £1 million to Beckham was surprising, given the fact that the player was a rising, but not yet established, player. Yet, on reflection, it represented good value for Brylcreem: Beckham always seemed to be present at the right occasions and with the right woman (advertisers especially prefer models, of course), and, in those days, had longish, fashionably unkempt hair. Doubtless, his later abandonment of the blond locks in favour of a brutal crop would not have pleased Brylcreem.

The mandatory "boot deal" that many footballers enjoy came Beckham's way: footballers of any renown are signed to a sportswear manufacturer, which typically stipulates that the player should wear its footwear during competition and in training. The shoes bear the trademark logo or some other sort of recognizable feature of the manufacturer. Even if a player insists on playing in a rival manufacturer's shoes, an accommodation can be made, like blacking out the signature of the rival and painting on the sponsor's design. Beckham, not yet one of the elite players, was missed by Nike, which had the likes of Cantona and Ian Wright (as well as dozens of other top athletes) on its books, but was signed by its most ardent rival, adidas, which also had the services of such soccer dignitaries as Zinedine Zidane and Alessandro Del Piero.

Signing deals with brands like these can often propel individuals to fame, though Beckham's signing of his wedding vows in 1999 was unarguably more influential in his own ascent. Marrying the pop singer Victoria Adams, then at the height of her powers with the Spice Girls, sent Beckham's cultural stock spiralling upwards.

———

In March 1997, Adams attended the Manchester United–Sheffield Wednesday game at Old Trafford as a VIP guest and was introduced to Beckham. She noticed that, while the other players made a beeline for the bar in the players' lounge, Beckham spent time with his mother. Adams and Beckham had been introduced earlier, though they exchanged only cursory greetings. This time, they spent more time together. Indeed, they became an item and were soon noticed together in public. Picking up a scent, the paparazzi pursued the couple, largely because of the interest in Adams, who was then part of a group proclaiming "girl power" and already an international marketing phenomenon. Apart from records and movies, the Spice Girls brand spawned seemingly limitless merchandise, from dolls to computer games.

A regular in England's qualifying games for the World Cup, Beckham, at 22, was emerging as one the nation's foremost players. Manchester United's continuing authority in the Premiership of English football ensured that his every appearance on the field would be monitored by television cameras. The surprise retirement of Cantona didn't exactly leave United bereft of stars, but it tended to disperse the media's attention. As the player who inherited Cantona's number 7 shirt, it was not surprising that Beckham should come under close scrutiny, though perhaps not more so than his celebrated colleague Ryan Giggs. A representative of the Welsh national team, which did not qualify for the 1998 World Cup finals, Giggs commanded less media attention as the finals approached.

The unified power of the sport, entertainment and media industries impose their collective wills on the public every so often. Global sports events, such as the World Cup, the Olympic games and heavyweight title fights, are opportunities for the culture industries to engage their full artilleries in their efforts to sell newspapers, magazines and merchandise to ordinary consumers and advertising space to institutional clients. As a good-looking, well-dressed young man with a manifest talent in playing football, Beckham progressively occupied the media's attention as the finals drew near.

Beckham's relationship with Adams soon became a narrative, perhaps even a saga; a predatory media monitored each episode and image, so that, individually, Posh and Becks – as they were quickly dubbed – became quarry. While Beckham may have been initially uncomfortable with the surveillance, he soon lost his camera-shyness: one week before the World Cup finals began, he and Adams were photographed leaving a restaurant in the south of France, where they'd been staying with Elton John. A fascinating picture emerged: Beckham looking saintly and wholesome, wide-eyed and self-aware, wearing a sarong. This type of garment originated in Malaysia and Java and is a long strip of fabric worn by both sexes, tucked in at the waist or, for women, under the arms. Western traditions dictate that undivided below-waist clothes are associated with femininity. Beckham's flouting of this tradition drew derision and indignation. It wouldn't be the last time Beckham would provoke such responses, but this was the first time a heady combination of

33

motifs came together to form one image. This was, after all, a professional athlete out of his natural environment, consorting with platinum showbusiness celebs in, of all exotic places, the south of France, the very mention of which excites thoughts of riches, extravagance and abundance. And, he was wearing what most newspapers referred to as a "skirt".

Beckham's assault on the established version of masculinity prevalent in British sport, especially soccer, is a subject worthy of more detailed attention and I'll reserve this for a later chapter. Suffice it to say that his lambasting at the hands of the media was a foretaste of things to come. It also put the media on full alert: this was no ordinary football player. He was capable of providing news in ways that others couldn't imagine. Deprived of Gascoigne, who'd been the source of invaluable stories for years, but who wasn't selected for the England squad, the media turned to Beckham. This was a figure who, unlike Gascoigne and co., wasn't going to get legless in nightclubs, slag off journalists and engage in unspeakable vulgarities. Yet, he was still going to provide great copy. One can almost imagine enthusiastic editors imploring their staff to track every movement of Beckham; his competitive achievements were good news, but his off-field behaviour held even greater promise.

Here, thought journalists, is a new agenda. Forget the kebabs, the brawling, boozing and birds. Beckham was capable of shaping an entirely different subject matter revolving around sexuality, fame and celebrity. In this sense, he was perfect for the time. The suspicion that he could be a commodity athlete, a copy-generating phenomenon, arose in this period. His ability to maintain public interest was not in question: the real question was whether the media could adapt with suppleness and creativity to a character who had few of the established bankable traits of high-profile footballers, but did have other qualities worth revealing. Eventually, the media came up with an ingenious strategy: make the images available, but keep the copy so vague that consumers themselves had to construct their own interpretations, create their own meanings – decode the cipher.

The Posh and Becks affair possessed a synergy: while each was a celebrity in their own right – she much bigger than him at the time – the marriage conferred on them a distinction typically reserved for Taylor and Burton, Kelly and Prince Rainier, Douglas and Zeta Jones. These and a few other relationships were played out in public focus: the liaisons didn't come to the attention of the world fully formed, but were initiated and blossomed in the public gaze. Beckham's meeting with and subsequent marriage to Adams was chronicled minutely by the media. It's impossible to imagine any other sportsman in history having an intimate relationship opened up for public examination in the way Beckham's was, not even Joe DiMaggio's short-lived marriage to Marilyn Monroe, and certainly not Billy Wright's marriage to Joy Beverley of the Beverley Sisters (not exactly the Spice Girls of their time, but nationally famous and makers of hit records).

While the other liaisons were celebrated affairs, they happened at a time when sport was a competitive pursuit, an industry, even a business. But, it wasn't showbusiness. It maintained a critical distance from its artificial cousin: sport was real; its players were ordinary people, its culture unadulterated by the kinds of impurities awash in the more obviously false areas of entertainment. But, by the time Posh and Becks became an item, all that was changing. Some writers think they actually helped bring about the integration of football into showbiz. "Symbolically, Beckham's relationship with Victoria Adams... consummates the relationship between sport – football in particular – and the popular music and entertainment industries," wrote Raymond Boyle and Richard Haynes in their 2000 book *Power Play* (p. 103).

By the time of Posh and Becks's friendship and subsequent marriage, the division between the two spheres of football and entertainment was less distinct. This was a development that was and remains vital to Beckham's status. The relationship changed Beckham, if only because of the relentless attention he received as a result. His home was staked continuously by the British media; he was followed to training, where each trip and tumble sent photographers into a frenzy: even a Beckham ankle twist or bruise became newsworthy. Press activity that would once have been regarded as intrusive was now considered fair game for Beckham. Relaxing his once trademark policy of silence, he ventured onto television chat shows and faced tv interviewers, as if acknowledging that he had become public equity.

As a member of the Spice Girls, Victoria had grown used to living like this. In fact, she would have been well aware of how indispensable publicity was to someone like her; she knew how to turn it to her own advantage. Some of this must have rubbed off on her man. Visibly uneasy with the media at first, Beckham seemed to relax into his new role as partner of a world-famous pop singer. It was a slow process, though: he granted few interviews and modelled for photographs only on assignment. His elusiveness served only to encourage more interest. In the years after the courtship, Beckham became the globally publicized sports celebrity nonpareil. By the end of the century, no athlete in the world, not even the golfer Tiger Woods, had the minutiae of his life studied in such fine-grain detail by the world's media.

British football has had celebrities before, of course. When Beckham moved towards a position vacated by Paul Gascoigne around 1997, he almost immediately became the new darling of the media. "Darling" is not exactly the right noun: "nobody's darling" might be more apt. Welcomed as a exhilarating young player with a promising cache of talent and an illustrious show-business partner, Beckham had already alerted the media to his potential – not just as a player, but as the new occupant of Gascoigne's station. Then there was That Red Card.

"A moment of madness during the World Cup in June 1998 sealed his fate as an object of hatred and derision", writes *Posh & Becks* author Andrew Morton (p. 126). An imprudent boot aimed none too precisely at the Argentinean Diego Simeone at Saint-Etienne brought two forms of retribution, one from the referee, the other from a wider assembly of fans, media and all sorts of other indignant types. The Red Card changed everything. No longer a bright young up-and-coming star, he became the man responsible for England's defeat. A scapegoat. The papers hunted and haunted him, one tabloid setting up an effigy

Figure 2 Every minute detail of their lives is analysed in detail: they are caught holding hands and the media immediately begins debating the significance of hand-holding in public.
Source: Big Pictures

burning outside a pub. A special ad run by adidas prior to the game proved oddly prophetic. In an allusion to the 1986 "hand of God" goal scored by Diego Maradona, the strap over an image of Beckham read: "After tonight England v Argentina will be remembered for what a player did with his feet."

In his book *Manchester Unlimited*, Mihir Bose writes: "David Beckham had returned from the World Cup in France as the most reviled man in England, his sending off being held to be responsible for England's defeat." For a while, Beckham was notorious: a man hated by an entire nation. At least, it seemed that way. Concerns over his personal safety might not have been

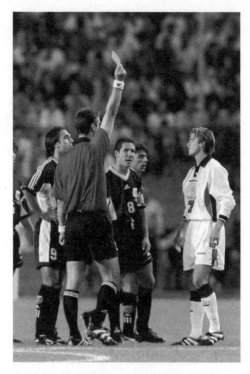

Figure 3 The Red Card incident that sent Beckham not only off the pitch but also towards a living hell, from which he emerged with god-like powers.
Source: Empics

magnified: the police turned out in force for the first few games of the 1998/9 season, one officer detailed to escort Beckham to the dressing-room at a game against West Ham where the vitriol flowed.

His calamity was disastrous from one perspective; from another, it was deliverance. Two things happened. First, like most notorious figures, Beckham acquired qualities seemingly beyond him in earlier stages of his career. The hate mail was expected, of course. But, far from being universally vilified, he gained respect from at least some layers of his already considerable fandom. No longer a one-dimensional, submissively placid, perhaps acquiescent youth who never reacted to provocation,

Beckham became a flawed character, normal in his fallibility, liable to snap when the pressure against him built up. Rendered transparent in full view of a global television audience, he disclosed a new aspect of himself, unconstrained and entirely capable of the kind of crass misdemeanours everybody engages in at some point. As the condemnation faded, Beckham was left intact, his standing enhanced, his communion with fans seemingly more authentic than ever. After all, he was capable of anger, hostility, impetuousness and other emotions, just like everybody else.

There's an enjoyment in censuring others: it probably involves reminding ourselves how we wouldn't have behaved in similar circumstances and how virtuous we are by comparison. We do it all the time, of course, tut-tutting about others' mistakes and violations, firming up our own sense of righteousness. The media exploited this fully in the months following the 1998 World Cup, ceaselessly repeating the reprimand and at the same time priming football's fandom to upbraid Beckham when the new football season got under way. Beckham, it was thought, should brace himself for a campaign of abuse such as had never been seen. As the object of this supposed calumny, Beckham was made more visible than any other player from the England squad; even those, such as Michael Owen, who had been a success, were totally eclipsed. The media continued to advise on how Beckham could expect the barrage.

This is the second thing. The media fully exploited the opportunity to exercise themselves on a new hate figure. The effigy, the dartboard (with his face as a bullseye, given out free with the *Mirror*), the admonishing editorials: with these, the media gave anyone – no, everyone – licence, without any dereliction of intelligence or reasoned morality, to despise Beckham.

As a young, good-looking footballer with a pop star companion, Beckham was famous. As the nation's *bête blanche*, he was infamous, notorious and inescapable: his image was everywhere. It was impossible not to have seen, heard of, read about, talked of or just been aware of David Beckham. His travails and rehabilitation were conducted not quietly, away from the public gaze, but right out in the open. His personal affairs were like the contents of Tracey Emin's bedroom: every stain and wrinkle in her boudoir made available for public inspection as a work of art. More than this: his entire life was turned into an adventure, each scene and each line of the script closely examined in a way that may have looked, and probably was, intrusive at the time, but which also served to position Beckham as the leading sports celebrity in Britain and, later, the world. What is it about this world of ours that makes us want to create superhumans from mortal beings? Elevate them, smash them down, hoist them up again and worship them as if deities? Why did we spend so much time, so much energy, so many brain cells attending to the affairs of another whose life had no significance for our own?

Feelings of envy and ill will begin to rise in us when a celebrity appears to be doing better than expected. We take pleasure in seeing high flyers fall Icarus-like to earth with a bump. Beckham took off at exactly the right time: a matchless coincidence of personality and history. Emerging as Gascoigne faltered, he rose, at first majestically, then somewhat conceitedly, consorting with showbusiness types and straying outside the airspace of sport. The crash landing was almost too perfect.

Everybody, not just football fans, was prompted, cajoled into loathing him. The media all but scripted an impending disaster. As the new 1998/9 season approached, they connived to predict calamity for Beckham, conveniently neglecting to write about their own role in hastening that calamity. In the manner of a self-fulfilling prophecy, the media forecast a nightmare, surreptitiously creating conditions under which that nightmare would become a reality. In the event, the reaction from the crowds wasn't nearly as intense or sustained as the media predicted. There would probably have been hardly any reaction at all if the media had downplayed it. Within six weeks, the Beckham-taunting subsided. A grudging admiration took over. The mockery didn't subside completely, of course. Adams once joked that he wore her underwear and the media took it more seriously than she'd wished. And critics would often make fun of his high-pitched voice. The admiration, I stress, was grudging.

The appreciation started to appear only after Beckham had withstood the raillery of football fans and the derision of the media and still managed to exceed the standards of play demanded by both his club and country.

"I can't understand the level of interest in every detail of our lives", Beckham once wrote, referring to the habitual coverage of him and his wife. It's tempting to paint Beckham as a "victim", a handsomely paid victim, but a victim all the same. Maybe he just wanted to play football. It wasn't his fault if he happened to play well and score spectacular goals. It wasn't his fault that he was attracted to a woman who happened to be one of the world's leading pop stars. It wasn't his fault that he got the Red Card at a crucial time. Well, actually it was, but a slightly more charitable referee may have ruled differently. But it certainly wasn't his fault if his looks, his taste in clothes, hairstyles and jewellery happened to be just like those of a generation of young people all over the world.

Tempting, but not true. Beckham, at some point, became very canny. He gave interviews selectively, strictly for publications either he, his agents or Victoria (or all) believed right for him. He modelled clothes for photoshoots, but again, they had to be right for him. He did endorsements, but not for products like denture adhesives or kitchen cleaners: only for those that, again, were right. If he threw a party, it wasn't just an ordinary bash: it was a £250,000 white-tie-and-diamonds affair with drinks served by geishas – the kind of fare eagerly consumed by the gossip mags. From around 1998, a distinct image was being cultivated. It was an image that would be consumed all over the world. What might have started off as spontaneous gradually changed to a carefully controlled exploitation of an image, a process that required a minor industry to keep it going.

Beckham once came across as an unpretentious, impulsive, unrehearsed individual who could just play football. Turning him into a celebrity was made possible by a culture ready to bow to a new young god and an industry geared to maintaining such a being. The Red Card alerted Beckham to the caprice of the media. Worshipful one moment, damning the next, they had, perhaps unwittingly, made him into an icon, something that can be either loved or hated, depending on the circumstances. How did he answer back? With silence. Hounded out of the country after the sending-off, he returned a different man – in the eyes of the nation. In the run-up to the 1998 World Cup, he was the good-looking guy with nice taste in clothes and a pop star partner. All the publicity prior to the game enhanced his credentials as a bone fide celebrity. Becoming a hate figure may have changed public perceptions of him, but only temporarily. And he emerged an even bigger sport celebrity than before. All this without hardly saying a word.

As we'll see later in the book, his manager at Manchester United, Alex Ferguson, worried that the showbusiness element of his life might eclipse his sport. Dropping him from the squad, ordering him to report for training soon after his wedding and reminding him of a footballer's priorities with regard to women-folk were, from one angle, no more than a manager's routine duties. From another, they may have been part of an attempt to bring the player back to earth at a time when many might have believed he could fly. Christmas 2001: Beckham was sitting on the bench, criticized from some quarters for failing to reproduce his England form for his club, the suspicion being that his motivation was greater when performing on a world stage.

Soon after, it didn't really matter what motivated Beckham: simply everything he did was interesting to the media. Playing well, or badly; at football grounds or in shops; with his team mates or his wife. It didn't matter. He was a celebrity. And celebrities are as famous for being as for doing.

——— three ———

INTO THE WHIRLPOOL

Life with the Spice Girls must at times have been something like walking the gauntlet. With so much media attention, the idea of having private moments was not usually a practical one. But even Victoria Adams must have been taken aback when she left hospital with her newborn son. The media not only waited for her, Beckham and Brooklyn to emerge, but they deliberately set up roadblocks to slow down their progress and enable them to take a few photos. The assistance of the police was needed to escort Victoria and co. home and the whole manoeuvre was staged, in Beckham's words, as a military operation. Anything resembling privacy had become a thing of the past.

After 1998, Beckham seemed to lurch from one episode to the next, hauling with him a dragoon of cameramen and writers, all awaiting a new development. The new baby gave them sustenance, and Beckham's new tattoo incorporating the name of his son, gave them even more. Beckham and Adams acquired that designation "newsworthy": everything, every little thing, they did was potentially a story. Within ten months of meeting, the couple announced their engagement at a press conference that resembled a royal occasion.

Even more regal was their wedding at Luttrellstown Castle, Ireland, in July 1999, four months after Adams had given birth to Brooklyn. By then, Beckham had become one of the premier players in England, and possibly Europe, and Adams a pure celebrity – meaning that, while her actual deeds or accomplishments were minimal, her renown had grown exponentially. While her erstwhile colleagues pursued solo careers (with mixed success), she simply became more celebrated. Adams epitomized Daniel Boorstin's oft-quoted definition from his book *The Image*: "The celebrity is a person who is known for his [or her] well-knownness" (p. 67).

Such was their status – and perhaps appetite for publicity – that Beckham and Adams were able to contract exclusive rights to their wedding photographs to the British gossip magazine *OK!*, which claimed a record circulation for the two issues featuring the shots. The magazine typically sells between 5,000 and 6,000 copies; it sold two million of the first issue featuring the wedding shots and five million copies in total for the next three issues. The magazine paid £1 million for the right to publish the photographs.

Few countries in the world didn't carry news of the wedding. The fascinated media wouldn't relent: after the wedding, Beckham caught the interest not only of sports writers, but practically every other kind of journalist. Interest centred less on his football, more on his domestic behaviour. But, of course, one reinforced the other. Once established as a legitimate target by the popular media, his athletic performances automatically drew closer attention.

While both Beckham and Adams had shown a certain craft in exploiting media attention, neither had, until the wedding, employed machinery, manipulation and commercial packaging to intrigue consumers. Adams, of course, being a member of an assembled pop group, was fully practised in the processes and it was she, presumably, who was able to bring her expertise to bear on the media arrangements for the wedding. Whether she aspired to a kind of ostentatious royal occasion, or actually entertained visions of occupying the role vacated by the death of Diana, we can't know. What's certain is that, like Madonna, she liked to control events, orchestrate them in a calculating, finessing, work-the-system kind of way that yielded precisely the results she wanted (as we will see in chapter six).

By contracting public representations of the event to a magazine known to specialize in photo-journalistic coverage of the marriages, divorces, births, operations and deaths of celebrities, Adams could exercise her dominion. While critics from other media understandably questioned her motives (avarice?) and wisdom in selecting the journal, Adams, or Victoria Beckham, as she became after the wedding, must have been flushed with her success in directing coverage to perfection. Effectively, this was a form of copy approval: a condition demanded by celebrities who deign to give interviews, but insist on reading and, in most cases, editing the text prior to publication.

The Posh and Becks wedding became a lever: it bestowed an element of control on the otherwise uncontrollable environment inhabited and run by the world's media. It also showed how Adams, and maybe Beckham himself, deeply mistrusted journalists. The million was surely neither here nor there to a couple whose joint income that year alone probably exceeded £10 million. The real purpose of the *OK!* deal was public relations, ensuring that images and words reached the public consciousness via print and electronic broadcast in a particular kind of way. After the mauling he took in the immediate aftermath of the Argentina game, Beckham was, we can safely assume, amenable to his wife's intervention. As Morton recognized: "Like any other commercial concern, fame is a business and Victoria is a skilful entrepreneur" (p. 23).

Beckham's marriage turned him from football star into an all-purpose celeb. The permeating influence of the market, most evident in television, impinges on everyone, everywhere. The media work with and off one another in a process that Garry Whannel calls "vortextuality". Some events that may have no significance beyond the media's interest in them are reported and analysed simply because all the other newspapers, magazines, tv networks and internet sites are carrying coverage of them. It's as if they're all sucked into a fast-swirling and irresistible whirlpool. In his essay "Punishment, redemption and celebration in the popular press", Whannel argues that the death of Princess Diana was a case in point: it was so all-pervasive that it effectively removed many otherwise newsworthy items from the agenda and dominated all media globally.

"If not on the same scale, the wedding of Beckham and Posh was also an example of the vortex at work", writes Whannel. "Television presenters alluded to it, politicians made asides about it, radio phone-ins discussed it, and comedians make jokes about it" (p. 143). The event was a key moment in their passage to an exalted status. The synergy produced in the fusion of two performers, each drawn from different spheres of entertainment, created new and perhaps undreamed-of possibilities in marketing, merchandising and promotions in sports, pop, fashion and, eventually, patriotism – Beckham was later appointed captain of the England national soccer team and so became a national emblem.

The vortex continued to envelop and propel Beckham. Spotted at a launch party for a Jade Jagger jewellery collection, he was instantly drawn into the whirlpool. Manchester United was travelling to Austria the following day for a Uefa Champions' League tie against Sturm Graz. Athletes are not, of course, expected to be fraternizing with fashion and showbiz types so close to a big game. Beckham was fined by United for the oversight. Perhaps more important were Beckham's regalia at the launch: he wore a silk bandanna, not unlike the thousands of others that young people all over the world were wearing around that time. But when Beckham wore one, it became big news. Even the minutiae of Beckham's appearance were under constant review by 1999.

A retaliatory gesture at Leeds United fans who barracked him during a game at Old Trafford resulted in a meeting with an official of the Football Association (FA), presumably intended to remind Beckham of the responsibilities attendant on being the leading member of football's elite. A similar gesture, with much the same import, landed him in trouble during an England game against Portugal. Caught vividly on camera, the gesture made newspapers all over the country. Interestingly, the stinging criticism that typically accompanied a Beckham faux pas such as this was averted when the then England manager, Kevin Keegan, offered mitigation. He was, suggested Keegan, the target of vapid abuse directed at his wife and child. "There is a limit to what anybody can take", announced Keegan, who is quoted by Fergus Kelly in his *David Beckham: Portrait of a Superstar*: "It got way beyond that. I think David handles himself fantastically well" (p. 103). Of course, the endorsement would have held more authority had Keegan himself not been prone to emoting in public and if he hadn't walked out so despondently from the England job soon after.

Interestingly, Beckham appreciated Keegan's support and, in a way, reciprocated after Keegan's resignation, calling him to offer condolences. "He had been in a similar position to me, dealing with the pressures of celebrity", reflected Beckham, perhaps overstating Keegan's plight. Keegan was, for sure, the eminent celebrity of his time; but the media surveillance of his life was neither so exhaustive nor as explicit as that accorded Beckham. Keegan's life was mapped out, while Beckham's was painted as if by pointillism – in tiny spots of various colours, which are blended by the observer's eye.

Keegan's departure from England's national team led to the very temporary (one game) appointment of Peter Taylor, who gave Beckham the captaincy, a responsibility he seemed to relish. Already under the microscope, his quirks were invested with moral qualities. A new mohican haircut was an occasion for the media to probe whether this was a fit and proper thing for an England captain be doing.

While his wife dabbled in modelling, tv presenting, talk show appearances, the occasional cd release and a spat with one of the ex-Spice Girls, Beckham combined his athletic career with all manner of pursuit typically associated with rock or movie stars. His public appearances wearing couture items and a photoshoot in military fatigue-inspired clothes helped earn him a new following. The term "gay icon" was added to his appellations.

Bizarrely and for the first time, a soccer star attracted a gay following. Conventionally, soccer players exhibit often belligerently macho behaviour. Drunken binges, wife-beating and serial model dating are normal fare for players. Beckham, by contrast, showed no penchant for the kinds of excess preferred by his colleagues or any attachment to the kinds of value associated with professional soccer. Many players might have reasserted their heterosexuality or rebutted gay patronage for fear of retribution from soccer's virulently homophobic retinue. Not so Beckham: he acknowledged his gay following on British national television and confirmed that he wasn't embarrassed by it.

Without saying or even doing much, Beckham became a truly transgressive character amid a megamasculine, homophobic culture which, according to many critics, still perpetuates sexist stereotyping, reinforces patriarchy and functions as an agent of women's oppression. The quiet dignity with which Beckham ceded place to his more loquacious wife, the doting commitment to fatherhood and the lack of interest in hellraising are so extraordinarily atypical that Beckham invited the possibility that he was too good to be true. Yet, in a different way, Beckham had shown that he was quite capable of behaving badly and this too contributed to his status. Taunts about him, his wife and baby eventually faded or were eclipsed by the adulation afforded him by a wider fandom uninterested in his athletic exploits, but fascinated by his image: a stylish coxcomb with a taste for the extravagant designer wear.

The Beckhamwatch was vigilant: front pages and websites around the world kept a keen eye on every whimsy; and, in periods of quietude, they started to fabricate them. The Beckham rumour industry had a kind of independent status. This troubled the all-controlling Beckhams who had, by 2000, assembled a promotional enterprise of their own to ensure authority over and direction of all things Beckham. Victoria's fury when, in 2001, she suspected a store of selling unlicensed Beckham gear landed her in hot water: it was found that the proprietors had done nothing wrong and Victoria was ordered to pay £55,000 damages to settle a slander action.

It was a relatively minor incident, but one that reflected the zeal with which she oversaw the development of what had become her own commercial fiefdom. More evidence of this appeared in 2002 when she challenged the legal right of Peterborough United Football Club to trademark its nickname "Posh", a name by which the club had been known by fans since 1934 when the club was created. Ever-protective, Victoria's lawyers argued: "The name Posh is inexorably associated with Victoria Beckham in the public's mind" and, if the football club sold merchandise bearing its nickname, consumers might erroneously believe Victoria had endorsed the products. An easy mistake to make.

Imagine the frenzy when an internet rumour initiated by a celeb-attentive website pulsed it way around the worldwide-web. Like the rumour about Prince Charles in 2003, it flashed around the world in less time than it takes to boil a kettle. Only swift action prevented the media from disclosing contents of the rumour – which were, in the event, unfounded. It served notice that people were prepared to take seriously any item of chat, hearsay or gossip or full-on lies that passed along the electronic grapevine. As long as it involved the name Beckham.

The Beckham story that dominated 2002 was actually true: a foot injury threatened to rule him out of the World Cup finals in Japan and South Korea. The media coverage of the injury and its implications for the England team's chances were comparable with that typically afforded a General Election campaign. It dominated lead stories in television and radio not only in Britain, but in virtually every soccer-playing nation for several days, which then became weeks. Daily checks on "will he or won't he be healthy enough to play?" subsided only days before England's first game when it became clear that he would, after all, play. England's undistinguished campaign involved wins over Sweden and Argentina, but defeat by Brazil. Beckham's performances paralleled that of his team, though, by this stage, his on-field behaviour was incidental.

Then, something ordinary happened and it became extraordinary. On 15 February 2003, Arsenal beat Manchester United at Old Trafford in the fifth round of the FA Cup. It was a disjointed display from United and one that guaranteed that Ferguson would not be at his most mellow when he joined his players for a post-match debriefing. Earlier, during the halftime break, Ferguson had expressed his unease with the way Beckham was playing. Beckham himself disagreed with the tactical changes Ferguson prescribed for the second half. After the game, Ferguson's first words as he entered the changing room in volcanic mood were: "David. What about the second goal? What were you doing?" Beckham refused to take the blame, to which Ferguson blasted back: "The problem with you is you don't let anyone talk to you. You don't listen." At least that's how the incident is recorded in Beckham's own book.

Beckham's father, Ted, told the Manchester United fans website redrants.co.uk, that Ferguson "came in [to the changing room] and was fuming. He was effing and blinding and, unfortunately, he saw a boot and just kicked it." Nearly all of the kicks that become enshrined in football's history have been on the field of play. This one took place behind closed doors and though it wasn't captured on video or film, it became the stuff of myth. The Flying Boot, as it became known, may or may not have been the catalyst for a sequence of events that led ultimately to Beckham's departure from Manchester. But, it was retrospectively depicted as precisely that.

Only Ferguson will ever know whether he actually kicked the football boot that had been discarded by one of the players towards the object of his anger, or just lashed out in rage. Wherever he meant it to go, it ended up colliding with Beckham's forehead, leaving a gash over his left eye. "I don't know if I've ever lost control like that in my life before", reflected Beckham on his reaction: "I went for the gaffer."

Ferguson, on his own account apologized immediately: "Sorry, David, that wasn't meant to happen." But, it seems, Beckham was not inclined to accept the apology. He hastened his way to the treatment room and had two stitches. While Ferguson dismissed it publicly as a freak incident, Beckham himself remained privately angry, as his father testified.

Beckhamwatchers went into paroxysms the next morning when Beckham turned up for training with his hair swept back and fastened in place with an Alice band, revealing the cut like a battle scar. As celebrity wounds go, it was up there with the right foot Michael Jackson fractured while playing on his Neverland ranch and the rotator cuff Arnold Schwarzenegger tore on the set of *Terminator 3: Rise of the Machines*. Actually, it was probably nearer Evander Holyfield's ear. The soothsayers were called in to divine the true meaning of the injury. Did it signify a break between a player and his manager whom he had once regarded as a surrogate parent? Was it the culmination of a bubbling conflict over Beckham's overcommitted showbusiness diary? Had Ferguson's well-known discord with Victoria become so intolerable that he was using Beckham as a scapegoat? Had there been a clash between two distinct types of men from two different generations? Or, was it just an accident?

If Beckham had chosen to wear his hair loose so as to conceal the laceration and the players were told not to mention it, the whole business could have escaped even the most prying media eye. Countless changing-room incidents never reach the light of day. Even a Beckham episode could have been hushed up without too much effort. But once Beckham pulled back his hair to allow a full inspection of the injury, it was immediately endowed with global significance.

The *Sun* led with the story "BECKS: I AM LIVID" and fired three bullet points beneath: "• Fergie nearly left him blind; • Bleeding star spat at gaffer; • Posh wanted to hit Sir Alex." And, just to make clear that there was trouble in the Beckham paradise, the paper included on the same front page a story headlined: "Mel C sinks Spice reunion."

Beckham himself reckoned that he pulled his hair back to stop it falling against the eye and insisted that the extensive attention paid to it by the media made it hard for him to patch up matters with Ferguson. "It seems like millions of people are looking over your shoulder, waiting to see what's going to happen, speculating about what might before it does", he wrote in his 2003 biography (p. 337). One wonders how he could have countenanced any other possible outcome. Speculation followed Beckham like ducklings follow their mother. Even fabricated events drew consideration. So, when he actually provided tangible proof, the conjecture veered out of control.

At least that was the impression. It's conceivable that he and his wife, who was adept in manipulating the media to her own ends, could have designed the reaction. The Alice band wasn't just a fashion accessory: it might have been a calculated way of bringing Beckham's displeasure to the attention of the world. If so, it worked like a charm. The reason they wanted such widespread public speculation over Beckham isn't clear. Maybe they had both grown tired of Manchester and wanted to move to more exotic climes. Maybe there were commercial interests bigger than those of Manchester United, urging Beckham to move. Maybe transfer negotiations were already under way and it worked better for Beckham if he was seen to be pushed rather than jumping. Maybe it was convenient to obscure the fact that there were larger forces at work by personalizing the dispute between two individuals. If so, the aim was achieved: the Flying Boot incident provided the starting point for a new subplot in the Beckham story.

Beckham's status as an automatic first team regular was destabilized by Ferguson when he began to bench him for key games, including a Champions' League game against Real Madrid. Beckham came off the bench in that game to score two goals in the last thirty minutes. Although United lost the tie, Beckham had played commendably and the meeting between the two teams ignited even more speculation about his move. Public denials from United's chief executive officer Peter Kenyon and his opposite number in Madrid seemed disingenuous, especially when Manchester presented Beckham with a new contract. This happened in May 2003. Less than a year before, Beckham had agreed to a new contract that had taken eighteen months to negotiate. It included a hard-fought clause regarding image rights (which will be discussed in chapter nine). The newly presented contract provided for an improvement in Beckham's salary, but was hardly necessary.

About twenty minutes after leaving the pitch following the last game of the 2002/3 season at Old Trafford, Beckham reemerged with his son Brooklyn. The handful of stragglers in the crowd still making their exits stopped and watched as father and son engaged in a kickabout, gradually covering all areas of the field and finishing with a salute to all four sides. Was he saying goodbye to Old Trafford, returning briefly with his son as a father might take a child for a final drive in a beloved car before he exchanges it for a new model?

Beckham was never a great talker. Yet, he was quite a communicator. His gestures, signals, expressions, even his body language were potent means of conveying thoughts and emotions. Not that Beckham is any different from anyone else in this respect: we all make visible our experiences. But, when Beckham traipsed languidly from the field, as he did on that Saturday, his posture, facial cast, even eye movements were telling people something. Perhaps they were a coded epilogue to the narrative that had occupied the world for the previous few months.

The mark of genuine 22-carat global celebrities is that they can accelerate a media frenzy *in absentia*, so to speak. While Beckham and his wife were taking a vacation in California, heaving into view only to attend the MTV awards concert, suppositions, hypotheses and guesswork spiralled upwards. Amid all the conjecture about whether Beckham's Manchester days were numbered, Ferguson, then 61, remained silent. In fact, the most categorical comment came from Barcelona's then president-elect Joan Laporta, who announced on 13 June that he had reached an agreement with Manchester United and would be offering contractual terms to Beckham himself. Set against Real Madrid's "never, never ..." response to the question of whether the club wanted Beckham, the Barça statement seemed plausible, at least on the surface.

Those familiar with the terms of the Bosman ruling of 1995 would have realized that a player under contract to a club can't simply be transferred without his consent. He has a contract that is legally enforceable and can insist that the club honours that contract. Both Laporta and the directors of Manchester United would have been aware of that fact. So, when Beckham released a statement prepared by his agents expressing his disappointment, surprise at being used as "a political pawn", it seemed somewhat ritualistic. Still, the signal was clear: he had become – incredible as it sounded – superfluous to United's needs.

Day-to-day rumour-milling had the effect of preparing the world for an event that would have been ungraspable a few months before. By the time it was announced that Beckham would definitely move to Madrid after all, the only unexpected aspects of it were the modest size of the fee involved and the way in which it was structured: €7.5 million of the total fee would be paid on completion of the contracts, with a further €17.5 million over the following four years, in equal instalments. Another €10 million was contingent on Real Madrid's performances in the European Champions' League. The maximum possible was €35 million, or about £23 million. United had paid more than that for the signature of Rio Ferdinand, the central defender. Real itself had paid a reputed €75 million for Zinedine Zidane, €60 million for Luis Figo and €45 million for Ronaldo. Yet, as United's Kenyon confirmed: "We [United] believe this is a good deal for the club."

Perhaps he meant that it unburdened them of the €7 million per year they paid Beckham in salary, or that it relieved Ferguson of his most exasperating player, or that, with the sinking value of football's transfer market, the money could be better used to buy several younger players. Or, perhaps, the club believed that Beckham's value as a player had been exaggerated by his celebrity status. Not that celebrity status is without its value, of course. With the likes of Zidane, Figo, Ronaldo and Raul on its roster, Real already had a surplus of talent. Beckham may not have had the technical proficiency of these players, but he had something they lacked: global renown. At the time of his transfer, he was the supreme celebrity athlete. Real was buying a commodity as much as a player.

In sport, there are puppets and puppet masters. The former are usually in evidence, while the latter operate behind the scenes. In the months leading to Beckham's transfer in June 2003, the media focused on the player, his wife, the clubs and their executives. They wondered if Real had really wanted Beckham as a player or just as an instrument in a marketing onslaught. After all, in playing terms the club consistently outshone Manchester United and had the trophies to prove it. But, it must have looked on with envy at its rival across the North Atlantic, which remained the world's best-known, best-supported and hence most valuable brand in sport. Perhaps Real thought Beckham could change that.

There is another scenario. In 1998 Beckham had signed an endorsement contract with adidas, the sportswear makers. It was worth between €5 and 6 million, spread over six years. Now, 1998 was the year of Beckham's Red Card; in other words, the very start of his trajectory. But adidas couldn't possibly have known that it had captured the future. Indeed, at the start of 2003, it must have been tormented. Having the world's leading sport celebrity under contract was the good news. The bad was that something like 90 per cent of the images that circulated around the globe featured him wearing the United shirt – emblazoned with the logo of adidas's deadliest rival, Nike.

How adidas must have longed for Beckham to appear week in week out wearing an adidas shirt. Then it could set about exploiting the Beckham image to the hilt. Maybe it's pure coincidence that the club to which Beckham moved had an agreement with adidas and that, after the transfer, there was a proliferation of images of Beckham in adidas gear, plus a new range of Beckham-themed adidas leisure wear, complete with its own logo.

The puppet masters in sports are not the clubs, or the leagues and certainly not the players. A corporation the size of adidas could buy every club in La Liga without its accountants raising a finger in protest. In the same year that Beckham moved to Madrid, adidas had its nose put out of joint when LeBron James, a teenage basketball player who had never thrown a ball through a hoop as a professional, opted to sign an endorsement contract with Nike valued at $90 million, or about €103 million – about three times Beckham's total possible transfer fee. Perhaps adidas entertained thoughts about getting its own back, but, with Beckham continually witnessed in Nike, it was helpless. An adidas-clad Beckham, however, was a new kind of magic with which to fight Nike. I'll return to this possibility later; for now, I just raise it as a way of understanding a transfer deal that never really added up.

––––––

I stated at the outset that there were two Beckhams, but, in the mind of the consumer, there is but one: an infinitely mutable being who can accommodate any number of apparent contradictions – straight and gay; disobedient and respectful; ostentatious and bashful; transcendent and earthy. Yet, this double helix-type quality is but one source of his appeal: he has "climbed the foothills of fame", claimed Morton, and has now reached the rarefied atmosphere in which his life has "become a metaphor for life in modern Britain". We should add: and in the world.

Perhaps he's not just one metaphor, but a series of overstated and inconsistent metaphors. His life bears a likeness, a resemblance not so much to the life of others, but to the life others aspire to, wish for, or just dream about. Beckham and wife are young and affluent, with glamour, money and cultural authority. They are apparently devoted to each other, yet have the devotions of countless others, straight and gay. The media's depiction of them projects what Christopher Lasch, in his *The True and Only Heaven,* called "a vision of the good life", which is narrowly conceived as consisting of excitement, luxury, novelty, romance and endless stimulation, but which also "mocks decent people" with the prospect of wealth and glamour (p. 524). How then can we understand the power of a status that both attracts and mocks, that is genuine yet counterfeit, sought-after and unattainable?

We can all see Beckham in a fast-flowing escapist narrative of love, intrigue, chat, art and hedonism served up by an alliance of tabloids and celeb-watching tv shows. Yet he's also in a different narrative, this one involving the emergence of a special kind of culture that reveres and pays homage to celebrities.

One of the most apparent features of culture today is the irresistible fixation we have for celebrities. Not only do we have lots more celebs around us, but we all want to be, and actually try to become, like them. This is a relatively recent development, as I will show. But, without a clear conception of the *how* and the *why* of celebrity, we can't approach the Beckham phenomenon. Even then, we have to factor in the recognition that contemporary culture has a special place for sports celebrities, athletes who, for reasons that will soon be uncovered, have risen in our esteem to the point where they vie with rock and movie stars.

This is a special time in history, when athletes can rub shoulders with celebs from what's traditionally regarded as the entertainment industry. Sport, in particular football, is now very much part of that industry. Without understanding how this state of affairs has come about, we won't be able to divine the special place Beckham currently occupies. In other words, the answer to my question lies less in Beckham the man, more in the extensive changes that have affected contemporary popular culture, a culture that has created Beckham the phenomenon.

The sport celebrity is a relatively new and unique animal whose natural habitat is as much the *Star* and *People* as it is the football field, and who is often seen prowling the savannahs of movie premières and nightclub launches. Until recently, only rock and movie stars could command the kind of status that guaranteed invitations to gala openings, launches or benefit concerts. Now, it's almost mandatory that such events include sports celebs. This suggests a change not only in the structure of sport, but also in the overall configuration of the entertainment industry of which sport is now a part, as well as in the culture that commissions the voracious consumption of people as well as goods. And our appetite for people has never been so great.

While many think of George Best, Muhammad Ali and, even deeper in history, Babe Ruth as sport icons, these were all operating before the advent of the multimedia. These historical characters were certainly universally famous and may well be icons of sport; but they were not celebrities in the contemporary sense of the word. "The defining characteristic of celebrity is that it is essentially a media production ... celebrities are well known (through the media) for nothing in particular, whereas the truly famous are in some way deserving of individual recognition", writes David Giles in his *Illusions of Immortality: A Psychology of Fame and Celebrity* (pp. 3–4). There may be a case for arguing that some athletes deserve individual recognition, but today's celebrity athletes are different. They seem to be altogether bigger, glitzier, more glamorous than ever.

Something has happened over the past ten or fifteen years. More and more of us have become fascinated by what the old tv series narrated by Robin Leach called "Lifestyles of the rich and famous". We've long had an interest in how the other one-ten-thousandth live, though now there's something approaching a preoccupation, coupled with a growth in the numbers of people who can legitimately claim to be among that tiny fraction we call celebrities. They may not hang on to that status for long; in fact, almost by definition the status is short-lived. But, the proliferation of celebrity chefs, politicians, criminals, lawyers and so on has made celebrity something of an equal opportunities sector. An alphabetically ordered hierarchy has evolved that either honours or condemns someone to A, B or C-list status, or worse.

Today's culture is one in which celebrities are more prized than ever. The ones who manage to get into the fabulous world of movie premières, late-night chat shows and supermarket openings milk it for all it's worth, while the rest stand back in awe, behind the rope barriers at the premières, in their living-rooms watching tv, among the throng of shoppers at the super-market. They remain on the outside, not just looking in, but often being willing to do anything to get in. As the title of Gus Van Sant's 1995 movie about a nobody who is determined to become a tv presenter at all costs, being a celebrity is (literally, in the film) *To Die For*.

Beckham is a part of this culture. It's a culture that possesses what might in other eras be seen as a pathological fixation with celebrity. In fact, it was depicted as just this in another film, made by Martin Scorsese thirteen years before Van Sant's. In *The King of Comedy*, Rupert Pupkin obsesses over getting his own tv show, creating his own mock studio, complete with cut-out guests, at his apartment. Not only does he follow the stars: he uses them as his own, imagining he's with them, that he has what they have, that he can do what they do. It's a triumph of fantasy. At least, until he decides to buttonhole a real tv pre-senter, and then fraudulently gains entrance to his home. What was unambiguously pathological in 1982 does not seem so ex-treme nowadays. We suspect that there's any number of Rupert Pupkins out there. Beckham has certainly had one or two of his own, though the most famous case involved former tennis player Steffi Graf, one of whose fans kept a shrine in her honour and, at one stage, ran on court to stab her opponent Monica Seles.

We've all become a little more like Pupkin than we're com-fortable admitting. How else do we explain the almost scarifying success of magazines such as *Heat, Closer* and *People*? These have taken their stories to a new level. Not content to report on the celebs, they have become part of the stories themselves, often – openly – commissioning stories that they can then report. Beckham's wedding was contracted exclusively to *OK!* which played an integral role in the planning and organization of the event as well as carrying pictures. Three years before, Paul Gascoigne commissioned his wedding photographs to a magazine. Some measure of the value of celebrity footballers to the media might be gleaned from the respective fees: Gascoigne and his wife Sheryl received £150,000 from *Hello!* while Posh and Becks got a million. This didn't mean that Gascoigne was a less valued footballer, but, in the short period between the two weddings, the celebrity fixation had grown more intense. And, of course, Gascoigne's bride was not a global celeb in her own right.

Even before his wedding, Beckham could claim some of the celeb hallmarks, including being the recipient of death threats, having a monument built around his image and inciting a generation of young people to style their hair like his. Having a home with the almost mandatory electronic gates at its entrance, a home that is the subject of its own website and called, in an allusion to royalty, "Beckingham Palace", suggests that he was prepared to meet his side of the bargain. Fans like it when celebrities live up to their expectations. Perhaps most audacious of all was his medical examination when he moved to Madrid. The club sold the rights to the "live" performance to a Japanese television company.

We've always admired, revered, cherished and even worshipped great figures. When news of great deeds travels, then great figures emerge: their greatness has been a product of a particular form of relationship. Winning battles, conquering new lands and dominating territories may, at times in history, be grand deeds. Yet the figure responsible for the deeds won't be acknowledged as great unless there is a wide and receptive population to hear of, talk about and recognize him or her as great. In other words, the audience confers greatness on a person, not a deed. Today, the relationship still stands, albeit with an interesting modification. The audience is still vital in bestowing status on people, but somehow, in the mix of history, the actual deeds that were once the sparks have been disregarded. Now, to use the insipid but accurate phrase, people are "famous for being famous".

The media is filled with stories about celebrities who, on reflection, have no particular gift, talent or achievement to their name, but who are simply *there* – in the public imagination. We know of them; often we know a great deal about them. We're even curious about them and eagerly consume bits of tittle-tattle, gossip and sundry other trifles for no other reason than that we know them or know about them. The reasons we know them in the first place become irrelevant.

Yet, Beckham is a doer and, like great leaders of old, he goads, inspires, influences and offers himself as an example to others. Clearly, he's come to terms with the fact that he does all these and still arouses more curiosity than any other celebrity. This is a man who revels in the status he has been granted. Other athletes, like Gascoigne, have wallowed in the attention then become exhausted by the persistent badgering. Beckham has shown no signs of this. He plays at the highest level, building a protective canopy to shield him from the kind of intrusions that eventually plagued Gascoigne, yet slaking the media's thirst with controlled releases of information.

Other athletes have crumbled under the weight of either expectation or media overload. Football especially has a roll of honour featuring once-great players who, as they say, "couldn't handle the pressure", from Best to Gascoigne via Frank McAvennie. Once suspected of instability, Beckham seemed to acquire a sureness of presence in the eyes of many. Somehow, he appeared to have discovered new depths in his self, showing his fans and detractors alike that it's not necessary to be unhappy or tormented to be creative, that maturity comes with responsibility more than age.

Beckham's occasionally heroic deeds on the football field brought him to the attention of the sports media. In a six-year period, from 1998 to 2004, the media's wrath turned to adulation. Crucial goals, a penchant for graft and a commandeering presence as England captain convinced sport fans that Beckham's skill was of pharmaceutical purity. Yet, while his status as a footballer grew, something else was happening. He became a global celebrity whose fame eventually extended far, far beyond soccer's media and fandom and whose allure appeared to be without limits. Perhaps just a minority of his

Figure 4 Beckham picked up his first Red Card in a Real Madrid shirt in January 2004 during his team's 3–0 win over Valencia at the Bernabéu. He was cautioned for dissent before clipping an opponent's heels, after which he received his marching orders. Even an event like this was publicized all over Europe and beyond.
Source: Empics

acolytes were sport enthusiasts. And by the time the suspicion that he wasn't among the world's best players emerged, nobody cared. He was simply *there*. He was Beckham.

Nobody else commanded such an ecstatically reverent patronage. Tiger Woods was appreciated rather than revered, valued more than adored, followed not mimicked, liked rather than worshipped. Jonny Wilkinson was admired, not loved, honoured but not adulated. Why does Beckham engender these kinds of emotion in his fans?

There's an easy answer and a hard one. The easy one centres on Beckham himself. He's good-looking to be sure. But there are other handsome young men in sports who go largely unnoticed. His technical skills are undoubtedly ample, though not on a par with those of a dozen or so other world-class footballers. His marriage to one of the Spice Girls gave him public exposure few other athletes had enjoyed. Then again, a few years before another prominent soccer star, Jamie Redknapp, had married another pop star, Louise, without being launched into the media stratosphere.

The harder answer starts from the assumption that it's not something that Beckham is or has done that separates him from all others: it's how we consume him. The reasons for his remarkable status are less to do with him, more to do with the media that carries the images and narratives, and the audience that receives, translates and interprets them – Us. This relationship has been forged in a culture that values image, illusion and perhaps fantasy.

—— four ——

ARTISAN AND ARTIST

There is an adage in football, "no player is bigger than his club". In February 2002, Beckham left a meeting at Old Trafford to find a swarm of reporters awaiting the outcome of his talks over a new contract. He assured them that progress had been made, adding that the clause in the proposed contract about image rights needed "perking". Setting aside for the moment what he meant by "perking" (he probably meant "tweaking"), the reporters were left to ponder whether Beckham was challenging the adage. Just over a year later, Beckham had started to demonstrate that it was false. He was bigger than Manchester United. Yet, there was an irony as Beckham flexed his muscles: had he played for any other club, he might today be seen as another good player, an England captain and perhaps a serial endorser of household products. Nothing more.

The adage had been under pressure since the days of George Best, though only in the 1990s was it put to the test. The advent of celebrity footballers meant that some individuals could claim justifiably to be portable brands. Whatever club they play for, wherever, they retain their status. Obviously, moving to a club like Real Madrid, AC Milan or Bayern Munich brings rewards in terms of brand enhancement for the player. Conversely, it could also be argued that the crème de la crème adds value to any club, whether it's globally famous or not.

Prior to the long-winded negotiations, specifically over image rights, Beckham's relations with his club were unproblematic. His agents negotiated his various contracts, including that with his club, and things seemed harmonious. Alex Ferguson might not have exactly welcomed the appearance of Victoria in Beckham's life, but the club appreciated his and her commercial value.

Image rights have been vital to celebrities: they include legal ownership, or perhaps hypothetical ownership of such things as a name, like "Gazza", a distinct signature, like the one that appears on Paul Smith labels, and most importantly a person's likeness or image. In Britain, the law doesn't recognize such rights, at least not in a technical sense. Each case has to be evaluated on its own merits. The copyright in any picture, unless specifically assigned, is presumed to belong to the person who took it, or the organization for which he or she works, and not to the subject in the picture. Celebrities have fought cases using a variety of means, such as trademark violations, libel and invasion of privacy, in efforts to create some sort of defence against what they regard as intrusion. Footballers are as helpless as anyone else when newspaper and magazine photographers or television cameramen shoot them in action, though there has been talk of an attempt to copyright key goals.

Players' agents are well aware that the Premier League opened an Aladdin's cave and they sought a way of capturing some of its contents for their clients. Older contracts would seek to incorporate image rights in the basic salary arrangement of a player, effectively including them in his labours: signing for a club meant not only playing and training, but also engaging in promotional events and allowing your name and image to feature in club-authorized articles. But, as players began to acquire celebrity status, some began to question whether their value was fully reflected in this type of arrangement.

Beckham was already familiar with the troublesome nature of image rights. In 2001, he and his wife successfully obtained an injunction preventing a national newspaper from publishing unauthorized photographs taken outside their house. They invoked the Human Rights Act to assert their right to a private life. The newspaper responded by agreeing to pull the photographs, but asked for an assurance in return: that the Beckhams should not allow pictures of the interior of their house to be published elsewhere. In other words, why ask for the right to privacy if you're going to allow other publications, which are prepared to pay a fee and agree to copy approval, to feature equally private shots? The court granted only the Beckhams' request and imposed the injunction without requiring them to cease authorizing photographs of themselves. This presumably made an impression on Beckham when he entered negotiations over his contract.

Victoria also had experience with image rights, though in her case with less satisfactory results. In 1997, with the Spice Girls going strong, the band tried to stop the publication of an unauthorized sticker book. They failed, the ruling being that, just because the words "not authorized" were not on the book's jacket cover, the consumer would not necessarily believe that the book was endorsed by members of the band. Twenty years earlier, ABBA failed to get an injunction to prevent the sale of unauthorized merchandise, the court decision being that buyers wouldn't take it to have been officially approved by the band. In both cases, the inference was the same: the consumer isn't easily duped into thinking something is authorized.

By contrast, courts in the USA are well geared up to celebrity requirements and typically grant much more protection. In California, for example, the Diana Memorial Fund effectively stopped the production and distribution of Princess Diana memorabilia, the market for which was considerable. Michael Douglas and Catherine Zeta Jones, like the Beckhams, sold the rights to their wedding to *OK!* Unauthorized shots were taken by the magazine's arch rival *Hello!* and Douglas and Zeta Jones argued that this was an invasion of their privacy.

There's an important difference between Diana, Zeta Jones and other figures, on the one hand, and footballers, on the other: the latter play for clubs, which are themselves brands. This takes us back to the question: is the value of the player's image enhanced by his membership of a known brand, or is the value of the club's brand enhanced by the ownership of a celebrity player? Probably both, though Manchester United favours the former, according to Rob Draper, writing for *soccernet* in 2002: "The United board's view is that in the modern game only Diego Maradona and Ronaldo, before his injury problems, have driven sales of shirts purely by their name, rather than that of the club they played for. They do not feel Beckham fits into that category".

That might have been the official line, but, when he was CEO of United, Peter Kenyon acknowledged that the club's own players too were drivers: "Top players drive sellouts at the stadium, sponsorship, television audiences and showcases Old Trafford to a huge audience" (*Guardian*, 30 March 2002). He might not have had Beckham in mind, though.

———

Wise heads rarely take retirements in sport too seriously. So when Eric Cantona declared he was finished with football, the response was more "for how long?" than "we'll all miss him". After all, Michael Jordan retired twice, annulling both departures by returning to competitive action. Children of lesser gods, such as Chris Eubank and Chris Waddle retired, then unretired to re-enter the fray. George Best, of course, was a serial retiree; but Alex Ferguson can claim the distinction of announcing his managerial retirement only to make a comeback before the retirement actually started. All the same, there must have been some concern among Manchester United's merchandising division in 1997 when Cantona told the club he would retire at the end of the season, still only 30 years' old (improbably, he stayed retired).

Cantona had electrified merchandising operations. He joined the club at precisely the time it was gearing up and powered a merchandising stratagem that would establish ManU as one of the leading sports brands in the world. His name and dark, conceited countenance adorned millions of articles sold around the world. And yet: "There wasn't any drastic dip in circulation or product selling with Cantona away." So said Edward Freedman, who headed up United's marketing. Ironically, Cantona's "departure was good publicity and it was all over the world and everyone was talking about Manchester United", Freedman is quoted as saying by Mihir Bose in his book *Manchester Unlimited* (p. 199).

When, in April 1995, Beckham started his first Premiership game, his club was already the indomitable force of British football. It was mutating from Manchester United the team to Manchester United the brand. In the process, it was charming fans away from the modesty of local clubs and towards the grandeur of United. Twenty-seven per cent of 7–19 year-olds describing themselves as football fans across England supported Manchester United in 1996, according to research by BMRB. Distributing the club's inhouse magazine, promoting replica kits and distributing merchandise nationally were elements of a marketing strategy designed to position the club as the market, as well as league leader. Beckham débuted for a club in the throes of becoming a label.

He was in distinguished company. As well as the thrillingly unpredictable Cantona, Ryan Giggs was acknowledged as one of the best players in the country. By 1996, Beckham had won medals for the Premiership and FA Cup (the double) and been selected to play for England. Not yet a national figure, he attracted minor media interest, if only by virtue of his boyish looks and his choice of partners. Julie Killelea, the daughter of a wealthy builder and later to marry player Phil Neville, escorted Beckham to various functions, as did Leoni Marzell. Both women were models. The footballer/model item is always a temptation to newspaper photographers, of course. The media were discovering that consumers liked to see, read and hear about footballers and attractive women. They were neither subtle nor elusive, rarely offering resistance to invasive reporters and photographers. After all, publicity was like hard cash. One of the indispensable ingredients in Beckham's celebrity was a relationship with one of the best-known women in the world. But, in the mid-1990s, his status was less to do with the glamour and renown of women, more to do with the glamour and renown of his club. If he had débuted for his club, say, four years before, his destiny may have been quite different.

No individual is responsible for turning Manchester United into a legitimate brand, but Martin Edwards realized, perhaps more clearly than most, that to prosper or even just survive in the late twentieth century, football clubs needed to generate cash outside their sport. To do this, they had to reach beyond traditional consumers. This meant creating emotional as well as

Figure 5 When Martin Edwards and Alex Ferguson called a press conference to announce the unexpected resignation of Eric Cantona, they must have wondered about the effects of the departure of the man who had propelled marketing operations at ManU. Edwards realized that to prosper, or even just survive, football clubs needed to market themselves as brands.
Source: Empics

instrumental bonds, making the name Manchester United resound everywhere, so that the impress of United could be used for selling almost anything. The success of the brand, Edwards suspected, could be achieved independently of competitive success. For instance, Ferrari's Formula One team's failure to win a driver's championship for over two decades from 1979 did little to damage its brand value.

The exemplar, however, is Dallas Cowboys. A force in the mid-1990s, though a spent one by the early 2000s, the club's dextrously managed relationship with consumers maintained its position as the most valuable brand in the world, beating even United into second place. Research published in 2001 by FutureBrand, a consultancy owned by Interpublic, a global advertising group, valued the Dallas franchise, which positions itself as the representative of Texas, using a lone star emblem (even though there are several other ball clubs in the state), at $274 million, or £193 million. The Manchester United brand was worth £179 million, which was still more than the brands of Real Madrid or McLaren Mercedes at the time.

No one can be sure precisely when Edwards came to this crucial realization, though his actions from 1991 suggest that a lightbulb over his head might have lit up during one particular meeting.

Time: November 1990. *Place*: London Weekend Television Centre, Southbank. *Occasion*: dinner. *Host*: Greg Dyke. *Invitees*: Representatives of Arsenal, Everton, Liverpool, Manchester United and Tottenham Hotspur. Dyke, later director-general of the BBC, was, at the time, boss of London Weekend Television. At the head of his agenda was a simple, but consuming, prescription: Stop Rupert Murdoch.

Mindful that Murdoch's newly merged Sky/BSB would probably be casting an admiring glance at the television rights for football, Dyke wanted to pitch an idea at the chairs of the five biggest clubs as a way of wooing them away from the dishonourable attentions of Murdoch. Martin Edwards's heart must have leapt at what he heard: Dyke proposed a new league comprising the elite plus a select number of other clubs, which would remain financially distinct from the Football League clubs.

Since the Football League's inception in 1888, the principle of sharing revenues as a way of maintaining competitiveness had been taken for granted. Television money, which became increasingly important from the 1970s, was divided between the ninety-two league clubs, the first division teams taking the lion's share, but the lower league teams receiving a proportion. Edwards, the chair of Manchester United, could never see the fairness of this arrangement. In fact, he thought the lower ranked clubs were like bloodsuckers. "They're bleeding the game dry", he once said, adding his favoured solution: "They should be put to sleep."

While Dyke's plan didn't allow for such a terminal resolution, it did introduce the basis for a completely new type of economy in which the money received by the big clubs would be ring-fenced, with the rest of the league left to fend for itself amid the vagaries of the market. As David Conn writes in *The Football Business*: "The dinner was the start of what would become the Premier League" (p. 147).

Martin Edwards took over as chair of Manchester United in 1981 when his father Louis died. A devout United fan from Salford, Louis had worked as a butcher under the tutelage of his father. Louis Edwards & Sons (he had a brother, Douglas) expanded in the aftermath of the Second World War, developing a wholesale operation and a chain of retail outlets. Douglas moved into politics, while Louis diversified into football. During the 1950s, Louis petitioned to join the Manchester United board of directors. Known locally for his business interests, he rubbed shoulders with manager Matt Busby and his famed Busby Babes, who delighted crowds and drew the sympathy of the nation after the Munich air disaster of 1958. Louis Edwards was appointed a director on 7 February 1958, the day after the plane crash in which twenty-three people died. Running a business left him with only limited time to involve himself in club affairs and, as only a minority shareholder (he owned 17 out of a total of 4,132 shares of club stock) his interest in the club was hardly significant. Yet he wanted it to be and, when Louis Edwards & Sons floated on the stock exchange, he pursued this ambition. Released from the more time-consuming responsibilities of the meat business, Edwards set about boosting his holding.

During the early 1960s, Edwards embarked on his mission to acquire a majority shareholding and thus control of Manchester United. His crusade was tenacious and his methods, at times, dubious: "bullying and underhand dealings", as Conn calls them, were revealed, though only twenty years later. In their 1989 book, *Manchester United: The Betrayal of a Legend*, Michael Crick and David Smith recount how Edwards secured a copy of the club's share register and used a Tory councillor to solicit shareholders, offering to buy their stock. Sellers were presented with "thank-you" presents: cuts of meat. At £15 per share, Edwards offered over the market value. When fellow sharehold-ers grew edgy at the scale of his holding, Edwards used his brother and brother-in-law to buy shares in their name that were later transferred to him. By 1964, Edwards's monstrously successful endeavour was complete. For a total amount of probably less than £40,000 he had bought 2,223 shares, amounting to 54 per cent of the total. A year on and, in a development that must have resembled an instance of Manifest Destiny, the club's chair, Harold Hardman, died. Edwards was the outstanding choice to succeed him.

Edwards presided over United during one of the club's finest hours: it won two league titles and, in 1968, the European Cup. Featuring players like George Best, Bobby Charlton and Denis Law, United seemed to have emerged from the remnants of Munich and restored itself to the position of Britain's, indeed Europe's, leading club. The period also saw the beginning of the modification of Old Trafford from a functional monument to the industrial Northwest to the current theatre of dreams. These were the days before football had become a product and the players commodities. Edwards witnessed the emergence of football's first legitimate celebrity in Best, though it's far from certain that he approved of the inordinate attention his player received from the media. Best's well-documented benders would have been a source of extreme discomfort for Edwards. But, there were worse travails in store.

An unexpected relegation to the second division and the retirement of Sir Matt Busby compounded a scandal that surrounded Edwards's business operations. A contract to supply meat for school dinners haunted him: a tv documentary detailed how gifts to local authority buyers preceded the deal and that the meat supplied was of poor quality. Edwards's company was fined. Economies of scale enabled the bigger supermarkets to offer cuts of meat at keen prices and shopping patterns generally changed, making it hard for retailers to compete. Consumption of meat was also affected by the rising health consciousness of the 1970s: jogging, gym workouts and health food diets became popular. Meat wasn't part of any popular health food diet, of course: in fact, red meat was shown to contribute to heart disease.

Sales slumped, and Edwards's business foundered. Crick and Smith argue that, as the meat business started to hurt, the

Edwards family, which by then owned 74 per cent of United's stock, began to detect the money-making potential of the club. While Louis Edwards could not have realized it at the time, his venture to gain effective control of Manchester United proved to be his deliverance. Like many chairs of the time, Edwards was involved with his club not exactly for philanthropic reasons but nor was he in it for the purpose of making money. Indeed, FA rules prohibited profit being taken out of clubs. People like Bob Lord and Bert Millichip were rich benefactors with an evident passion for their clubs; their purpose was not to make an ancillary business out of football, but to act as custodians of their clubs.

Nor was Edwards motivated by baser aims: his instincts were to contribute to and share in the glory of the club he loved. But times changed and, while the club was thriving financially, his business was not. A controversial plan was hatched whereby the club was to have a share issue, entitling shareholders to buy 208 shares at £1 each for every share held. This would increase the flow of cash to the club without threatening Edwards's power. Opposed by, among others, Busby (then a director) and secretary Les Olive as well as supporters, the plan was rolled out nevertheless. Enter son Martin.

Martin Edwards had been nominated as a director of Manchester United in 1970, when he was only 24. At the time, it was a controversial move: Martin wasn't a soccer fan, opting to spend his Saturdays playing rugby. He was given preference over Matt Busby's son Sandy, who sought a place on the board. If there were any doubts that Martin wasn't driven by the same motives as his father, they were confirmed years later when he offered to sell the club several times.

The continuing decline in the meat business, of which Martin was a director, prompted drastic actions. In 1977, Martin took out an overdraft and used the money to buy United shares, which bolstered his family's holding to 74 per cent. With a rights issue planned, the family was accumulating shares in the confident expectation that their value would soon appreciate. According to Conn, Martin's total overdraft was £600,000 and this represents "the sum total of his 'investment' in United, ever" (p. 40). This may sound a humble investment by today's standards, but in the 1970s and early 1980s, this was, as Bose suggests, "slightly more than the going rates for clubs". He provides comparisons: in 1982, Doug Ellis bought control of Aston Villa for £600,000 and, the following year, David Dein paid £300,000 for a share of Arsenal (we might also add that, in 1982, Ken Bates bought Chelsea for the princely sum of £1, though the club was effectively bankrupt). At this time, television revenue was distributed equitably between all league clubs. Clubs such as Rotherham or Torquay United could expect about £25,000 per year.

With backroom manoeuvres affecting power arrangements at United, other changes were set to change the business of football. Since the 1890s, English soccer had operated under the retain-and-transfer system. This meant that clubs held both contracts with players and their registration. Even when a contract had expired, a player wasn't free to move to another club until the first club decided to release him. In effect, this placed players in the position of indentured labour. The system was challenged in 1912 by an Aston Villa player, who lost his case. Not until 1978 was the system abolished. In 1995, the Bosman ruling created the concept of free agency: at the end of their contract, players were at liberty to move to any employer they wished. While the 1978 removal of the retain-and-transfer system did not introduce wholesale changes, it made club directors realize that they were competing for the players in a labour market rather than a controlled environment. Over the following years, players' salaries increased sharply as clubs began to calculate their value. Transfer fees also rose: within two years, Trevor Francis became the first player to move from one club to another for £1 million. In 1979, United paid Chelsea £700,000 for Ray Wilkins's services.

After the share issue at Manchester, there were dividend payments, the main beneficiaries being the Edwards family, of course. Louis died in 1981, leaving Martin to become chair of the club. Two crucial changes in rules introduced around the same time as Martin's assumption of the chair greatly enhanced his status at the club. One raised the maximum amount of dividend that could be paid to shareholders. United took full advantage of this, paying its shareholders as much as was legally permitted. The other was even more crucial: clubs were allowed to employ a full-time salaried director. This was recognition that football had progressed beyond the days when directors could run a club in their spare time. Football was coming to terms with the fact that, like other sports, it was also a business and needed to be organized as such.

Martin Edwards immediately installed himself as a paid member of United's staff, awarding himself a starting salary of £30,000, increasing to £100,000 by 1990 and £600,000 by 1998. His control was near complete. He brought to the club a dispassionate commercial mentality that had been absent during his father's reign, or perhaps was simply not necessary prior to the 1990s. We should remind ourselves that the Manchester United of that period wasn't the United of the 1990s or of today. Liverpool was the dominant club, winning eleven league titles and two European Cups in eighteen years. United was a strictly distant contender. Nor was the club profitable. As Bose puts it: "It had never done better than break even" (p. 157). This was a time when the United fans, who made up average gates of 25,000, were mostly from Manchester rather than all four corners, and before the expansion of ManU from a football club to a global brand. Edwards played no small part in bringing about this expansion. But, before his grand project took shape, he suffered mortification when he "sold" the club to Michael Knighton in 1989 for £10 million. The sale fell through, as did another attempted sale fifteen years later. But, when Rupert Murdoch pitched his bid, the club was valued at £625 million. What had changed?

———

It's interesting, but no more than a coincidence, that Manchester United's fortunes changed at the same time as Beckham signed to the club as a youth trainee. That was in 1991, on 8 July, actually his sixteenth birthday. But it was the stock market rather than Beckham that precipitated United's rise. Flotation on the stock exchange was Edwards's response to the misbegotten Knighton affair. In fact, the affair may well have acted as a catalyst for the extensive changes that followed. When the millions failed to materialize one way, he found another. Edwards personally made £6 million from the flotation, while keeping 3.4 million shares, leaving him with 28 per cent of the total. His salaried position was unaffected. Institutional investors fought shy of the club, presumably unaware of the potential. In fact, few people would have regarded football as a growth industry in 1991. The club was valued at just £47 million. The share issue was not an unqualified success, being undersubscribed, a small percentage of the stock remaining with the underwriters.

Technically, Manchester United plc wasn't just the football club following the flotation; it also included two other divisions: catering and merchandising (itself subdivided into merchandising (domestic) and merchandising (international)). Later, a fourth division concentrated on associated concerns, such as MUTV and hotels. Eventually, the merchandising division would generate around 40 per cent of the plc's income, or about £25 million per year in the early 2000s. The club's hugely successful and, in many ways, visionary marketing operation was vital both to the ManU brand and, by implication, to Beckham.

_____

The fateful meeting with Dyke and the owners of the four other biggest football clubs in England happened within a year of United's flotation. Edwards was, by then, into his stride, bringing to United a new finance director and a head of merchandising, each dedicated to exploiting what Edwards detected was a newly emerging market made possible by television. Edwards's desire to split from the lower league clubs was one of the worst kept secrets in football. The market possibilities he envisaged just could not be realized if the needy clubs continued to leech off their prosperous cousins. As a public corporation, United had new responsibilities: not to fans, but to shareholders. Edwards took these responsibilities seriously, exploring every way of maximizing profits. In this sense, he was perfect for the times: untrammelled by the restrictions of other clubs which remained rooted in the traditions, values and even morality of a bygone age, he had no compunction about bringing all his powers to bear in turning a penny. If this meant casting adrift the majority of football clubs in the country, then the deed had to be done. So it was – but not in the way anticipated by those at the LWT dinner in 1990.

The "Stop Murdoch" assignment failed. BSkyB blew away all other bidders with an astonishing £304 million, which bought them exclusive rights to "live" games from the first division, which was to be rechristened the Premier League (and, later, the Premiership). The money wasn't to be distributed throughout the league, but divided up among the clubs in the top division. The FA had hitherto repulsed all suggestions of an autonomous elite, insisting it would sound the death knell of the league structure. But it too had been sounding out the market, hiring consultants to prognosticate on the possibilities of a breakaway. It was persuaded not just by them or the chairs of the clubs, or even the television companies, though they all added weight to the argument. The context was also important: this was a time when the social historian James Walvin wrote in his book *Football and the Decline of Britain*: "The game in recent years has plunged deeper and deeper into a crisis, partly of its own making, partly thrust upon it by external forces over which football has little or no control" (p. vi). Football, Walvin speculated paralleled the British economy, both being in "sharp and seemingly uncontrollable decline" (p. 127).

Gates had fallen; English teams had been suspended from European competition following the disaster at the Heysel Stadium in Brussels in 1985. The fire at Bradford City's main stand in the same year had exposed the dilapidated, unsafe state of many of the country's grounds. Most savage of all, the Hillsborough disaster, which claimed ninety-six lives, had blighted the whole sport. Soccer's more persistent problems continued: it struggled with hooliganism, racism and an association between fans and hard right political movements (which was not unrelated to the continuing racism).

A glance around shopping centres revealed an aspect of the malaise: young people were more likely to be found wearing warm-up jackets or baseball caps bearing Washington Redskins or Raiders than clothes displaying their loyalty to a local soccer club. Channel 4's slick and inventive package of National Football League games sparked immense interest in American football and, perhaps, prompted other television companies to reflect on their styles of sports presentation, which had remained substantially unchanged for twenty years.

More than any other chair, Edwards represented the new rich, a class of marketers with none of the nostalgia that older practitioners in football felt. Football, for this group, was a background to a more lucrative trade in accessories. Television, merchandise, hospitality and sponsorship: these became watchwords. The antipathy many factions of ManU fans have for Edwards is at least in part attributable to his being among the first to realize that football's priority customers were *not* fans, but television companies and sponsors. Fans had to be catered for, but, by the 1990s, Manchester United was selling out every home game: demand always exceeded supply. The next challenge was to sell them and anyone else merchandise – everything from duvet covers to whisky.

Other owners had understood this as clearly as Edwards. Irving Scholar, of Tottenham, was especially keen on merchandising and, in 1986, appointed Edward Freedman to fire up marketing operations. By 1992, Tottenham was turning over more in merchandise than any club, including Manchester United.

Impressed by his accomplishments, Edwards enticed Freedman from North London to Manchester and so started what Bose calls "the Freedman marketing revolution". There followed a rapid retail expansion, production and wholesale facilities, overseas operations and a new publication, the first official club magazine and, now, the best-selling football monthly in the world. Licensing was cut back as the club cranked up manufacture of its owns goods, sourcing materials from all over the world. A monthly video magazine was introduced. These kinds of innovation were instrumental in building Manchester United into the most valuable sports brand in the world bar none.

One of Edwards's most crucial acts during the early 1990s was in brokering the transfer of Eric Cantona from Leeds United for only £1.2 million. The value the player added to the club brand, as well as its competitive achievements, is inestimable. "I marketed Cantona to the hilt", reflected Freedman, in Bose's book. "He was on T-shirts, sweatshirts – whatever I could do with him. We did books, calendars, magazines ... I made every product possible available, anything that people wanted, we did everything that was possible to justify Cantona as a marketing product" (pp. 198–9). On field, Cantona also made an impact: in his first season, 1992/3, the club won the Premiership; in 1993/4 and 1995/6, the club won both the Premiership and the FA Cup.

The marketing apparatus built around Cantona was well in place when the player unexpectedly announced his retirement in 1997. So much so that, as I indicated earlier, his departure made little difference to sales of merchandise. The momentum had, by this time, acquired its own dynamic that kept driving it along. By the time Beckham was a first team regular, marketing operations were geared to turning him into the same kind of merchandising figure as Cantona. No one, at that stage, could have imagined that Beckham would far surpass Cantona as a marketing phenomenon.

During Edwards's tenure, Manchester United came to represent about 30 per cent of the net worth of the entire Premiership and almost one-fifth of the league's total turnover. Its annual profits were typically three times that of its nearest rival. Its salary bill was usually the biggest in the league, though, as a percentage of its turnover (usually £118 million+), the smallest. In 2001/2, the club generated £24 million from television, just £1 million short of the total the Football League's seventy-two clubs received from tv for the whole season and £10 million more than the whole turnover of Premiership club Southampton. In two hours on any given match day, 15,000 people spend about £10,000 in the Manchester United megastore. The club has the largest membership of any British football club – 40 to 50 million worldwide – and even a tour in Asia was watched by 200 million viewers. In terms of sponsorship, United has few peers: one deal alone with Nike is worth £230 million to the club.

Edwards was generously assisted by Freedman, whose idea for the club magazine was "the key to driving the Manchester United brand". But, as Bose acknowledges, the idea "may never have got off the ground but for the support Martin Edwards gave" (p. 196).

None of this served to fortify Edwards's attachment to the club. If anything, United's financial gigantism seems to have hardened his resolve to capitalize on his accomplishments. His actions betray a dispassionate bearing: at various intervals in the 1990s, he disposed of shares, netting a total of about £30 million. He was deep into negotiations to sell the club to Murdoch's BSkyB for £625 million before the Monopolies and Mergers Commission blocked the sale. Implicit in that figure was the value of the Manchester United brand, a creation fostered principally by Edwards. Even then, United's share price was considered undervalued: a report by the Japanese finance company Nomura in July 1998 stated that the stock exchange categorized the plc incorrectly as a sports club or leisure group rather than a "media asset". If we consider that the whole Premiership had a capital value at the time of £1.3 billion, Manchester United was effectively worth 36 per cent of the league.

The sale doomed, Edwards came under fire from all sides, particularly the fans. "If he really does want to make £80 million [the amount he stood to have made from the disposal], he must sell his shares to the people that care – the fans', said Steve Brisco, the chair of the club's supporters' association. "He has made it obvious that he wants rid of the club. I fail to see how Edwards can command any respect from within the football industry and especially from the shareholders." A cross-party coalition of MPs also deplored the mooted sale, which, it argued, would distort the British football market.

The affair disclosed Edwards as something of a mercenary. If the money was right, the plc could go. From that point on, sales of tranches of United shares suggested that Edwards was no longer interested in controlling the club and was happy to let other interests take over. It also showed him to be a businessman first and foremost and a soccer fan, well, perhaps not even a distant second or third. This is not a criticism: the thing about

Edwards is that, in the late 1980s/early 1990s, he was exceptional; today, he is typical of football chairs and owners. Edwards was a harbinger, one who announces the approach of others. Most other chairs of professional football clubs now share his mentality: clubs *have* to be run as businesses; there is no alternative. The process he and his coteries of like-minded colleagues who plotted the formation of an independent league unfettered by more modest clubs is irreversible.

Abuse following the abortive sale may have contributed to Edwards's decision to recede into the background, leaving Peter Kenyon, as chief executive, to take a more public role in August 2000 (Kenyon later left to take up a position at Chelsea). Over the next several years, groups such as Cubic Expression, owned by J. P. McManus and John Magnier, upped their shareholdings in the club, further diminishing Edwards's influence. But, Edwards's part in the making of David Beckham should not be overlooked. In steering Manchester United away from a prominent, but not top, club in England to perhaps the most ubiquitous name in world sport, Edwards provided Beckham with a platform, a stage and a theatre. His name was linked unbreakably with that of ManU. Of course, this was of great benefit to Edwards: the same fans who might formerly have identified with the likes of Darlington, Exeter City, Torquay United (all featured in the Deloitte & Touche report), or whatever their local club might be, now cheered for a club lying miles away. Why? Because Beckham played there. What was once a one-way relationship became reciprocal, Beckham eventually ripening into a brand of his own.

There is, of course, one obvious gap in my account of Martin Edwards's influence: success on the field. Edwards's task in establishing his club as the pre-eminent team in England and the best known in the world was simplified greatly by the fact that Manchester United was an unconquerable force. In the first ten years of the Premiership, it lost only two titles and those only by narrow margins. It also won the prestigious European Champions' League. It's entirely possible that the commercial operations pioneered by Edwards would have been set up anyway; but there is no reason to suppose that they would have met with comparable success had United's competitive successes been limited to, say, a couple of titles. If this had been the case, it's also possible, if not probable, that Beckham would have been a famous player, even a celebrity, like Michael Owen or Wayne Rooney, both regulars in the tabloids and well-to-do endorsers of all sorts of products. Neither became a phenomenon like Beckham: his status derived from the fact that he was part of not just a perennially successful club, but an international brand.

"We shouldn't believe that our only competitors are other football clubs", Kenyon told the *Guardian*'s John Cassy in 2002 (30 March). "Kids today have PlayStations, multichannel televisions and a multitude of other sports they can play and watch." The club has moved on from its conquest of football: the fertile crescent of popular culture is the next destination in its imperialist expansion. Beckham is already there, of course. His appeal may once have been limited to fans, but now it's been stretched far beyond. His image is on the very computer games that Kenyon saw as competitors. He's on many of the tv channels, either endorsing products, attending openings or doing the many other things he does besides playing football.

"Manchester United" resonates like a thunderclap in the collective imagination as a club, a culture, a corporation, a business, an industry, a trademark, perhaps even, for some, a philosophy. Could any other club have showcased Beckham more effectively, more memorably? Probably not this side of Madrid. The words "David Beckham" and "Manchester United" were twinned for so long, that it was almost unthinkable that he could pull on the shirt of any other club. That we think in these terms has much to do with the potency of the ManU brand.

Michelangelo's masterpieces wouldn't have been possible without the people who built and maintained the Sistine Chapel. In an imperfect world, it often needs an artisan to make an artist. Yet, the masterpieces are the master's and, after a while, he's liable to strike for independence and create his art wherever he wishes. Manchester United put on a brave face when it transferred Beckham inexpensively. Given the marketing dynamo he had been at United and the signature he brought to the brand, a fee of €50 million wouldn't have raised eyebrows. True, United didn't fight too hard to keep him at the club and, with the value of the transfer market in decline, it might have sensed Beckham had hit a peak, either in playing or in marketing terms, or in both. Whatever the motives, the suspicion lingers that Beckham had become bigger than the club. Unreliable and anecdotal as it is, some indication of this arrived in the immediate aftermath of his move to Madrid when Manchester sports shops reported that white number 23 Real shirts with "Beckham" across the back were consistently outselling official Manchester United replica shirts.

There were times when clubs were unchallengeably bigger than players. The age of celebrity put paid to that. Beckham might be a herald, a forerunner of a generation of celeb players with status and power sufficient to make them independent of any one club. But, while he marches on transcendingly, we should remember that, had his original club not turned itself into a global brand, he would have been an artist painting on a smaller canvas.

five

THE WORLD IS JUST ABOUT ENOUGH

When the 11-year-old Beckham won a football skills competition at Old Trafford in 1986, English football was slithering towards what many felt was its grim fate. By 1992, when he débuted for the United first team, football was fast becoming the lavishly upholstered wing of showbusiness it now is. If the game had continued on its road to ruin, Beckham might still have been playing in the pros – but in front of twenty-odd thousand people a week instead of the global audience he now entertains. While he'd be getting write-ups in the *Manchester Evening News*, he wouldn't be commanding the attention of analysts, scholars and an assortment of other luminaries. Q: What happened to change all that? A: Rupert Murdoch.

In his book *Virtual Murdoch*, Neil Chenoweth reckons Murdoch's mission in the 1990s was to become "the uncrowned sports czar of the world" (p. 232). Mission accomplished: Murdoch started the twenty-first century as the most powerful person in sport. There were other contenders, such as Michael Eisner, head of Disney, and John Malone, chief of Tele-Communications. But no one really came close to Murdoch; his worldwide influence in almost every facet of sport was undoubted. And yet, he had no particular passion for sport. "Murdoch had hated sport as a boy", according to Chenoweth. But, "as a young man he worked in the newspaper industry and quickly realized how sport stories sold newspapers" (p. 231).

In time, he recognized that sport could do much more than this. Addressing the 1996 annual general meeting of his corporate mother lode, News Corp., Murdoch announced that sport "absolutely overpowers film and all other forms of entertainment in drawing viewers to television". Comforting shareholders with the news that the company held long-term rights to major sports events in most countries, he revealed future strategy: "We will be doing in Asia what we intend to do elsewhere in the world – that is, use sports as a battering ram and a lead offering in all our pay television operations." It was a widely quoted remark and, as it turned out, an honest one. Murdoch's grasping quest for leadership, if not ownership, of the sports markets, reflects both sport's crucial role in generating television rating and television's equally crucial role in the financial health of sports.

Beckham never experienced what big-time football was like pre-Murdoch. The influence of Murdoch was barely felt when he first signed with United in 1989, but, over subsequent years, the impact was undeniable. Just about everything in football changed, even the rules. When Beckham surfaced, football was in a state of transition, its chrysalis breaking apart as the sport emerged as something quite different from the stolid, traditional working-class game of yore. Think of this: the young Beckham can never have known what it was like for footballers to live in the same kinds of house as fans, shop at the same stores, perhaps drink at the same pubs or drive Rovers. He has no experience of a time when indoor heated swimming pools were things you only saw when you went to the chairman's place. Or when agents were people you contacted when you wanted car insurance or a new home.

Football was created anew thanks largely to Murdoch. Had the changes he instigated not happened, football would almost certainly not have transfigured into the seething, fiery, dramatic fresco that television reveals every day. It wouldn't be an overblown spectacle capable of holding its own with music, film or any other form of entertainment. And it wouldn't have been an abundant source of money, capable of attracting the world's top players in search of the world's top salaries. It may even have remained an ailing sport surviving on money from the contracting sport budgets of terrestrial tv companies, shrinking gates and the slight if well-intended contributions of supporters' clubs. Maybe its practitioners wouldn't have become the highly valued celebrities they now are. If this had been the case, would Beckham, the player, be Beckham as we know him? It may be a disturbing thought to many, but Beckham wouldn't be the being he is without Rupert Murdoch; well, at least, without the profound changes to football wrought by Murdoch's BSkyB television network.

There are two key moments that comprehensively and probably irreversibly changed the value of contemporary sport, both in a financial and a cultural sense. Murdoch was present on both occasions. Not physically perhaps, but present nevertheless. One was in 1991 when Murdoch's subscription television channel BSkyB secured exclusive rights to screen "live" games of soccer from England's new competition, then known as the Premier League. The other was in 1993 when Murdoch's Fox network in the USA acquired broadcast rights for the National Football League (NFL). In both cases, the sums paid seemed exorbitant: £304 million over four years for the soccer and $1.58 billion (£1 billion, or €1.44 billion) for the NFL, again over four years. Murdoch's companies had grabbed Britain's and the USA's national sports and, in the process, incorporated the respective tv channels into mainstream broadcasting. (BBC television paid only £5,000 per year to show regular highlights of English soccer in 1965.)

There were several byproducts. As the owner of extensive media networks throughout the world, Murdoch was able to promote both leagues in his newspapers and magazines as well as television stations everywhere. Interest in the Premiership and NFL flourished in places where they didn't even play either sport. The astonishing amount Murdoch was prepared to pay – astonishing by early 1990s standards, anyway – also changed the rules: any bidding war for top sports events was bound to involve a substantial bid from one of his organizations, so rivals would need to adjust their budgets. Not least of the consequences was that both leagues' governing bodies were foaming with money. Much of the new revenue made its way to clubs, which duly converted this into players' salaries. Players weren't exactly underpaid before Murdoch's hidden hand signed the cheques, but after, they were rolling in it. In Britain, the flood of money created a class of nouveau riche: Aston Martin DB7-owning, Ozwald Boateng-suited, Louis Roederer Cristal-swigging athletes with need of accountants, agents and lawyers to handle their affairs.

Footballers came to epitomize glamour and celebrity. The media was saturated with stories of their triumphs and follies, their indulgences and further indulgences. In 1992, few people would have cared whether a married footballer was having an affair; ten years later, it made national headlines, kept off the front pages only by the death of the Queen Mother (though admittedly only after a court case to try to stop publication of the player's identity). And when models had babies sired by footballers, there was probably interest, but still not quite enough to embolden an internet company to bid to screen the actual birth "live".

"Out of control!" screamed the headlines when players got drunk, snorted coke, abused women, wrecked cars, fought in nightclubs or became involved in other sorts of depravity. Who needed the likes of the Gallaghers when you had equally famous and comparably disreputable footballers? Even the monstrously burlesque series *Footballers Wives* (the omission of a possessive apostrophe somehow distilling the illiteracy of the subculture it was meant to depict) began to look like reality tv after a while.

Such is the change in status of footballers. Their lives became like a new reserve currency for the media. They created the kind of attention once reserved for only actors and singers, especially the wayward ones.

In the days of George Best, discovering a wild child who happened to be a good footballer and had pop star looks must have been like the Danny Boyle movie *Shallow Grave*, in which a group of flatmates stumble across a suitcase full of money. A totally unexpected windfall. Post-Murdoch, the media was much more proactive in their search for footballer copy. New celebrities were found, cultivated, closely observed and, some-times, demolished. Footballers were perfect raw material. As interest in the sport grew, so did interest in the players, their wives, their mistresses and anyone else with even the most tenuous connection to them.

Murdoch-owned tabloids, as might be expected, led the way. The *Sun* and the *News of the World* regularly ran stories about the inconsequential details of footballers' lives. This would have been unthinkable before the 1990s. Footballers were just not that newsworthy. Football was only a sport. Murdoch changed that.

———

Few people in football would have been interested, in June 1988, when Murdoch announced his intention to start up a satellite television service for Britain called Sky. The government had already approved a competitor, British Satellite Broadcasting (BSB), so Murdoch was in for a fight. Still, his track record suggested that he relished such a prospect. His decision to buy both *The Times* and *The Sunday Times* and move both, along with his tabloids, to a state-of-the-art plant at Wapping in 1985 had precipitated a long and fierce conflict with trade unions and resulted in one of the great class conflicts of the decade.

Although it wasn't widely known at the time, Murdoch was using the profits he made from his newspaper operation in Britain to finance colossal and often complicated television ventures in the USA. Murdoch's defiance of union power may have drawn the admiration of Margaret (now Dame) Thatcher, then Prime Minister, and those who assented to her policies. But, for many others, he cut an odious figure whose presence in Britain was as unwelcome as it was malevolent. One shudders at what dyed-in-the-wool football fans would have thought if they'd foreseen the fallout from Murdoch's Sky television initiative in 1988. Four years later, the unloved Murdoch had absorbed BSB, seen off the challenges of the traditional British tv networks, subverted age-old sporting traditions and begun changing the character of football.

The concept of showing football "live" on a subscription satellite network would have seemed laughable in 1988 when Murdoch proclaimed "the dawn of television's new age and the most dramatic innovation in broadcasting since the launch of commercial television in Britain more than three decades ago".

Britain's only commercial television stations were ITV and Channel 4. Like US channels, these were driven by advertising revenue and their programmes were, of course, free-to-air. Although his original plan was to beam his programmes for free, Murdoch later proposed charging viewers a monthly subscription, much like US cable services, as well as an initial installation fee. They would also have to sit through commercials. This was two years before Martin Edwards's portentous meeting with Greg Dyke at London Weekend Television's studios. It was three years after the Heysel disaster and a year before Hillsborough.

Even from Murdoch's own perspective, it would probably have seemed a stretch. He had no experience, nor it seems any personal interest, in sport, or in subscription television. He had owned a shell European company called Sky since 1982, which was haemorrhaging money, and he intended to follow its existing entertainment menu, adding a separate news channel, a Disney channel and a sports channel. Collectively, it may have been a respectable entertainment package, but the British viewer had been getting a total of four choices of channel for nothing (well, apart from the premium that advertisers add to the retail price of their products, of course).

Complications meant he would have to charge a monthly subscription and this, in turn, meant that he had to scramble his satellite's signal and issue decoding set-top boxes to subscribers. It all seemed improbable. An encryption programme was devised, but only after the launch of Sky in February 1989. Eventually, it was crucial to the success of the company: it meant the tv network could control access to its programmes and fix whatever rates it thought appropriate. Eventually, viewers who wanted to see "live" games of soccer from the newly established Premier League either had to pay for the privilege or hope that their local pubs had subscribed. We can't be certain how Murdoch arrived at the idea that football could become the saviour of his British tv enterprise. He would no doubt have gleaned plenty from his newspapers, both tabloids, the *News of the World* and the *Sun*, featuring plenty of football news and gossip. The quality papers didn't stint either. It's also possible that he found Alan Sugar persuasive.

In June 1988, Sugar and Murdoch made a deal whereby Sugar would make the receiving dishes needed to get a signal for Sky. "Murdoch and Sugar liked each other, they were both obsessive bottom-line Eighties men with scarcely a single interest in life outside their businesses", writes David Conn in *The Football Business* (p. 18). Later, in 1991, Sugar and his then business associate Terry Venables bought 57 per cent of Tottenham Hotspur Football Club for the sum of £57 million. They then declared a rights issue. It was a controversial move, but one largely supported by Murdoch's papers. Maybe Murdoch began to spy the potential in football when he witnessed his business associate ploughing his money into what appeared to be an ailing industry.

Sky was also ailing: losses averaged almost £15 million per month until October 1990 and the total cost of the Sky project was probably £550 million. BSB was taking a comparable pounding. The crisis resulted in a merger and the arrival of Sam Chisholm as chief executive of the new channel known as BSkyB. Chisholm had previously been head of Australia's National Nine Network, owned by Kerry Packer, who had, in the 1970s, broken up cricket's establishment by luring away top players and featuring them in a television-friendly competition. He antagonized cricket's traditionalists, but turned Nine into Australia's leading network.

In 1992, two years after Martin Edwards had met Greg Dyke, chair of ITV Sport, and his co-conspirators with the intention of creating an elite league of clubs, he attended another meeting, this time at London's Lancaster Gate. Also present were the chairs of the other twenty first division clubs. They were gathered to vote on which television companies would be granted rights to screen the newly minted Premier League competition. For months before, Chisholm had been testing the waters, trying to determine how much it would take to secure the rights. BSB had made it known earlier that it was ready to invest heavily in football, though the Dyke-sponsored meeting that engineered the breakaway Premier League put paid to its hopes, and it struggled. Two hours before the vote, Chisholm called Murdoch in New York asking for permission to up the

BSkyB bid by £30 million to make sure of beating ITV's improved offer (he later claimed that he would have gone even higher).

As the champagne corks popped, there must have been a few residual doubts in Chisholm's mind: football was going to cost BSkyB £76 million a year, less BBC television's payment to screen its late-night highlights programme *Match of the Day*. Those doubts were assuaged within a month: despite predictable resistance from traditionalists who claimed that football, as the national game, should be screened free-to-air, BSkyB signed up a million subscribers, all of whom paid £5.99 per month. In other words, the seemingly ruinous outlay was anything but: the deal virtually paid for itself. On top of that, sceptical advertisers suddenly became believers, introducing another stream of revenue and enabling BSkyB to turn its losses into a £62 million profit in 1993. Chisholm called football the "turning point". Profits rose year on year, turning BSkyB into a blue-chip company.

By the end of the twentieth century, BSkyB could claim five million viewers and there were a variety of packages and ways of receiving the games. The importance of having English football in the portfolio had been affirmed. So much so that Murdoch was prepared to crank up his bid to £743 million for the next four years and over a billion when the time came. Losing the Premier League wasn't an option for BSkyB. And, as if to underline its intention to be the leading purveyor of high-quality sport, the channel also added rugby and rugby league to its register, instigating a complete revamp of the latter by converting to a summer schedule and integrating it into the world's first genuinely global club competition, Superleague.

———

Murdoch's acquisition of the Premiership rights signalled his arrival as a key player in European sport. But, for many years before, he had been steadily building his interests elsewhere. He had already assembled a bundle of British newspapers to add to his collection of Australian titles. Having been thwarted in an attempt to buy London Weekend Television, he turned to the States where he had been impressed by the achievements of cable channels, especially ESPN and MTV. In 1983, he bought a struggling satellite operator, Inter-American, which he turned into Skyband. The purchase proved a disaster, and Murdoch lost $20 million within six months. In the same year, he tried unsuc-cessfully to buy Warner, the Hollywood studio (later to merge with Time).

20th Century Fox was then struggling and, in 1985, Murdoch took advantage to buy first a 50 per cent stake and, later, full control from its owner Marvin Davis. Fox was insignificant in the tv market, but Murdoch grew it into the fourth major US network. Buoyed by the results of his first foray into sport, Murdoch repeated his British tactics in the US in 1993, bidding what seemed a suicidal $1.58 billion (£1 billion) for the rights to screen NFL games. Murdoch's Fox Broadcasting Company pushed CBS out of the picture; it was already losing money on American football and wasn't prepared to lose even more. Murdoch, however, was: in the 1994/5 season alone, Fox dropped $100 million. Undeterred, Murdoch signed further deals with Major League Baseball (MLB) for $575 million and the National Hockey League (NHL) for $155 million. Fox's follow-up deal with the NFL cost no less than $4.5 billion over eight years. It also paid $2.4 billion to MLB for a six-year con-tract. Cast against these, the various Premiership deals, even the £1.1 billion one (over three years), do not seem so huge.

The logic in this apparent lunacy was that, by wresting the Sunday games away from CBS, Murdoch established Fox as a media force. Many local stations changed their affiliations as a direct result of the coup and, of course, advertising revenue soared. Solid audience ratings helped Fox advertise its other shows in the commercial spots, thus increasing viewer aware-ness of the station's menu. While the rival networks howled in disbelief at the sums offered by Murdoch, he persisted with sport.

The allure of winning big audiences has always been power-ful in the USA, where advertising income is precious fuel. Murdoch seems to have been prepared to pay over the odds in the confident expectation that advertisers' money would follow the big audiences that sport attracted. As the British tv market opened up in the 1990s, the need to grab audience share was more important than ever.

Then, Murdoch changed the formula: he beat off Ted Turner's challenge to buy the Los Angeles Dodgers, admittedly one of sport's astral franchises, but not worth $350 million (£217 million) in the estimation of most market analysts. His attempt to repeat the strategy in Britain was stymied when the £600 million bid for Manchester United, though accepted by the owners, was blocked by the Monopolies and Mergers Commission, an official body set up to guard against antitrust arrangements. Manchester fans were incensed by Murdoch's audacity in trying to buy a club that they believed was theirs rather than the board's.

Martin Edwards was, by all accounts, surprised by Murdoch's bid. The story goes that, on 1 July 1998, he went to lunch with Mark Booth, the chief executive of BSkyB. Booth opened the conversation with a jaw-dropping question: would Manchester United be for sale at the right price? The leverage promised by owning the league's leading club and, as we have seen, one of the leading sports brands in the world was plain: BSkyB would virtually ensure it retained broadcast rights and, even if it didn't, it could break away and start its own separate competition. The merchandising possibilities were also attractive: imagine the boost to sales by marketing through not only the BSkyB airwaves and cables, but through any number of other Murdoch-owned channels around the world.

Murdoch wasn't the only media owner to have sensed the advantages in owning clubs: in the early 2000s, media companies owned at least 20 top clubs in baseball, football, basketball and hockey. The process was known as vertical integration. Italian media magnate Silvio Berlusconi owned the AC Milan soccer club of Serie A. The French cable television company Canal+ owned the Paris Saint-Germain club. In Britain, ntl had interests in Aston Villa, Leicester City, Middlesbrough and Newcastle United. Granada was interested in Arsenal, Liverpool and MUTV. Media–sports cross-ownership was also common in North America.

Apart from the scale of Murdoch's empire, which frightened many, his methods of construction were also alarming. With his cross-ownership of several media, he would typically sacrifice profits from one medium and underwrite costs from another. An example was *The Times*. Murdoch also owned the *Sun*, which he had bought cheaply in 1969 and, within nine years, converted into the nation's best-selling daily. Profits from the *Sun* allowed Murdoch to use *The Times* as a sort of loss leader by dropping its cover price to about two-thirds of that of its rivals.

Any club owned by Murdoch was eligible for *The Times* treatment. In other words, it could become the beneficiary of cash from other outposts of the empire. The consequence of this would be to weaken rival clubs and media groups by driving up wages. Such possibilities gave rise to the suspicion that Murdoch's goal wasn't ownership of clubs or media companies, but of sport and the communications industry. His track record suggested that, if he wanted something, he was prepared to pay over the odds for it. This is why *Big League, Big Time* author Len Sherman, writing before Murdoch clinched the LA Dodgers deal, trembled at the prospect: "Murdoch could, if he gained control of the Dodgers, deploy his newspapers and TV networks to forcefully thrust baseball into the international arena, forever upsetting the power structure of Major League Baseball, remaking the industry and the sport from top to bottom" (p. 35). The same goes for British football.

In the end, Murdoch wasn't allowed to buy United. All the same, it's tempting to speculate about what might have happened to Beckham had Murdoch's bid been approved by the Monopolies and Mergers Commission. Murdoch's Byzantine network of media interests around the world would have made it possible for him to create all manner of opportunity for the world's leading sport celebrity. For instance, Beckham might have been eased into the role of the host of a chat show on a Murdoch-owned tv station, or feature in a movie made by the Fox studios. We can imagine how Murdoch's publications could promote any Beckham enterprise with laudatory stories and photospreads; how David Beckham cookbooks, travel guides or gardening manuals could be published by any of Murdoch's imprints. And what about a reality tv show modelled on

Celebrity Wife Swap, with Beckham spending a week with the likes of Christine Hamilton, or Ann Widdecombe, perhaps?

Something like this could still happen. Superstar athletes are "made to be cross-promoted", according to Naomi Klein, who, in her *No Logo*, reminded us: "The Spice Girls can make movies, and film stars can walk the runways but neither can quite win an Olympic medal" (p. 57). Substituting Beckham for Klein's own example (Dennis Rodman – her book was first published in 2000), we might say it's more practical for Beckham to write two books, star in two movies and have his own television show than it is for Irvine Welsh or Ricky Gervais to play midfield for Real Madrid, just as it's easier for Michael Owen to release an album than it is for Geri Halliwell to play for Liverpool. This is a slight amendment of Klein's argument, which holds that only animated characters are more versatile than sports stars.

———

"It was money from satellite TV that turned English football from a cheap-and-cheerful ferry service into a no-expense-spared luxury liner", declare Ian Bent and his co-writers in their book *Football Confidential* (p. 23). Not only English football, but European football (25 percent of people in Europe who describe themselves as football fans subscribe to pay tv, according to Uefa; reported in Craig McGill's *Football Inc.*). Throughout the 1990s, money has poured into sport in general and football in particular. No one doubts the accuracy of statements such as Bent's. The question is, why did television – not only Murdoch's stations, but all the main networks – think sport was a good bet? Football at the start of the decade must have seemed an especially doubtful proposition, "cheap and cheerful" though it might have been. Within two years, the manufacture of the luxury liner was well under way.

Here's a clue. By the early 1990s, "Sports had arguably surpassed popular music as the captivating medium most essential to being perceived as 'young and alive'." That was the view of Donald Katz in his *Just Do It: The Nike Spirit in the Corporate World*. According to Katz, sport had "so completely permeated the logic of the marketplace in consumer goods that by 1992 the psychological content of selling was often more sports-oriented than it was sexual" (pp. 25–6).

The rules were essentially the same as before and the players still had two hands and two feet, but the institution had changed, not because of anything internal, nor because it grew more exciting or became consistent with the spirit of the times – though in fact it did. It changed because big business woke up to the idea that products can be sold on the back of sport, just like they had been sold using celebrities from film, radio and, later, television. This led to a new form of exploitation; not the kind that would leave athletes in bondage, but one that would release them to start demanding money and aspiring to a status previously associated only with the entertainment industries.

This may have been the single most important change in sport since it developed governing organizations to regulate and run sports in the late nineteenth century. No one bright soul had a "Eureka!"-style idea and shouted: "We can sell products by linking them with sport, even if the products themselves have nothing to do with sport!" But the gradual realization that commodities as diverse as razors, cars and pizzas could all be marketed using sport promoted colossal changes. Murdoch may have been urgently in search of viewers while BSkyB struggled, but those viewers were not ends in themselves: they were the means through which to attract advertisers.

Companies such as Nike, Coca-Cola and McDonald's hitched their wagons to sports stars, and profited enormously as a result. Car firms, clothes makers, food manufacturers and other organizations with no particular interest in sport apart from its ability to sell their products began to express interest in the early 1990s. This took the form of signing up athletes to endorse products, advertising in the commercial spots that punctuated televised sport competitions and sponsoring entire competitions, such as the World Cup or the Olympic Games.

On reflection, sport was a "natural". While the intemperance pursued by other forms of entertainment made them effective but unreliable partners in the mission to promote the kind of images and values that move products off shelves, sport was ostensibly different. This was a pursuit that disdained and

95

discouraged drugs, inhibited revelry and actively promoted clean living. It was wholesome, healthy and, as such, radiated with the kind of meanings that appealed to manufacturers. To associate one's product with sport implicated manufacturers in an equation. It meant that their commodities could be identified with an enterprise unclouded by the kinds of ambiguity of established areas of the entertainment industry. While the number of rock and movie celebs involved in *causes célèbres* multiplied (Michael Jackson, Charlie Sheen, Kurt Cobain, Rob Lowe were among the legion), sport stayed transparently virtuous, worthy, perhaps even exemplary.

Many of the values apparently embodied in sport were actualized in Beckham. He was, for commercial purposes, salutary, avoiding the drugs, booze and other types of trespass so fiercely – if ritualistically – condemned by sport's authorities. As such, he appealed to advertisers eager to render their products synonymous with all-round rectitude. In time, he also became a national symbol, leading the England team triumphantly to the Word Cup Finals. To differing extents, the environment of which Beckham was a part advanced the kinds of principle favoured by advertisers. In truth, professional sports have for long been virtual breeding grounds for assorted types of deviance, study after study affirming that the actual practices of many athletes contravene the supposed ethos of sports. Revelations of widespread corruption and drug use multiplied, particularly in the late 1990s. But the image of sport was, and remains, an agreeably serviceable one, and one that was exploited by virtually any company or individual with something to sell.

Sport sells. More specifically, athletes sell. In the past, heroes came from the ranks of great political figures, military leaders, explorers, scientists and even philosophers. Now, they have been replaced by celebrities, described by Len Sherman as "the most watched, admired, privileged, and imitated people" (p. 189). Celebrities are, by definition, famous; but, in the twenty-first century, they also have a kind of exemplary authority, an influence that they do not usually use to facilitate social change or promote good causes, but to sell commodities.

A cynical public, having abandoned and been abandoned by old institutions, "gladly seizes upon this substitute, a substitute that might not provide a lot of benefits, but doesn't require a lot in return either" (p. 189). Apart from money, we should add.

"British football and its stars have become an integral part of the landscape of the media entertainment industry", write Raymond Boyle and Richard Haynes in their book *Power Play* (p. 103). In fact, most professional sports are constituents of the entertainment industry. The changes wrought in that industry by the twentieth-century revolution of media of communications are all about us. The coming of television, the proliferation of film, the advent of digital technologies, the creation of cyberspace: these are some of the key developments that have changed the way we get our entertainment, the way we consume it and the lifestyle patterns we make out of it. We now consume sport in much the same way as we consume drama, music and other forms of amusement: by exchanging money for commodities. Purists once abhorred the way film and, later, television corrupted live theatre; connoisseurs deplored the phonographic cylinders that were used to reproduce music. Traditionalists were more ambivalent over the conversion of sports into packaged goods, though many probably lamented the passing of times when being a sport fan involved more than buying a replica shirt and sitting at home with a Whopper and a widescreen tv. It meant actually going to see competitive action; and, no matter how you analyse the statistics, younger people have tended to go to events less and to watch tv more.

The media plays a crucial role in directing sport. Global corporations like Coca-Cola, Kodak and Panasonic – which sell products with no direct relevance to athletic competition – revved up their interests in sport in the early 1990s. The zest with which Rupert Murdoch bought television rights attested to his confidence in the cultural power of sport to deliver its followers to his programmes and, by implication, his customers – the advertisers. Murdoch's master plan was never confined to one country, or indeed one continent. Moving to Britain from his native Australia, then the USA, he recognized that markets had no natural boundaries: unlike nations, corporations, especially media corporations, were not confined by government and the limitations of any single polity.

The postcolonial world was one in which old empires had disappeared and new forms of interdependency had grown: nations relied on each other's support, not only militarily, but also politically and, of course, commercially. Advances in telecommunications, particularly in satellite and fibre-optic technologies, enhanced the capacity and flexibility of media networks to carry services (data, video or voice) around the world. No other phenomenon possessed this unique capability.

While no entity could actually own a nation's political system or economy, it was perfectly possible to own a telecommunications network that encircled the earth. The power this conferred on the potential owner was unequalled. Owners of the means of communications could exert influences in any number of countries. By the end of the twentieth century, the technologies that could make this theoretically possible were well advanced. They included: digital methods of encoding, transmitting and decoding; multimedia cable and satellite networks to carry and disseminate information; and a single international collection of computer networks from which users could access information from computers anywhere in the world – the internet.

One of the many consequences of the global expansion of the mass and multimedia has been the sharpening of awareness in other cultures. "Awareness" probably understates the case, because there's been a convergence of tastes, consumption patterns and enthusiasm for lifestyles, many of which have origins in the United States. Witness the eagerness of young people all over the world to follow the NBA, wear replica clothes and devour any artefact connected with basketball. Yet it's soccer, a sport largely ignored in the States that has become the first truly global game, capturing the interest of every continent, especially at the time of its World Cup championship. Neither of these sports would have occupied their current status without television. There would still be Beckham, of course. Maybe he would be quite famous. But as a footballer, not a global celebrity. To understand the unique position he holds, we need to reckon with all the developments that have reshaped the relationship between sport, the media and the entertainment industry.

These developments have changed the way we live, the way we see the world, the way we determine who is and who is not important. Celebrities like Beckham clearly are. We haven't arrived at that conclusion unassisted. The culture in which we operate has invested celebrities with special values, values that we respect. This may strike some as sad, others as realistic and many others as admirable. Whatever your moral stance on the subject, it's reality is indisputable: footballers are part of an elite; their lives are meaningful to us; we give them priority over politicians and maybe over pop stars. There's no natural reason for this: it's been created by a series of commercial developments that have helped position football as a member of the select ensemble that qualifies as the entertainment industry.

——— six ———

VICTORIA'S MACHINE

Cupid can be a rascal. His pairings sometimes teem with inspired parallelism. Yet there can be mischief in his matchmaking. In 1997, when Beckham's involvement with Posh Spice became known, they looked a faultless item. His career was in its ascendancy: he'd captained the national Under-21 team, made headlines with his dramatic goals and drawn rare praise from football's insiders, including Matthew LeTissier, who prophesied: "He will dominate football for the next ten years." She was already dominating her own expanding province. The Spice Girls had just returned from the USA, where they had registered their first number one hit to complement the three in Britain. Talk of "Girl Power" gave the Spice Girls a not altogether new quality, but one that had not yet been exploited commercially. When the endorsements were added to the royalties and the personal appearance money, Posh had made several million pounds from her initial ventures in showbusiness. Beckham, then into his second contract with Manchester United, was limping by on a mere £10,000 a week.

Five years on. Beckham was the England team captain, an exquisite sporting character, a fully-fledged celebrity, an endorser of several commercial products and, literally, the stuff dreams are made on. The Spice Girls had split up, leaving Geri Halliwell as the only former member to achieve consistent success with her records. Posh, or Victoria Beckham as she preferred to be addressed, released her début album in autumn 2001, but it sold only 20,000 copies and failed to recoup the £5 million it cost to produce and market. Her first single release with Dane Bowers, formerly of boyband Another Level, "Out of Your Mind", sold respectably, however, 180,000 units, enabling it to reach number two in the British charts. The hugely publicized follow-up single fared worse, peaking at number six. Posh fired her manager, Nancy Phillips, whom she once described as "the lady who makes the Victoria Beckham machine run".

While her solo sales were decent, her career was burdened by expectations formed by her prodigious performance with the Spice Girls: the group had nine number one singles in Britain and sold more than thirty-five million and counting albums worldwide. Her fortunes declined further in early 2002, when the *News of the World* revealed: "Posh Spice Victoria Beckham is being axed by her record company" (17 February). Six days later, Virgin denied this. In the interim, news of her second pregnancy had broken.

"Posh and Becks" were different from other celebrity matches, a genuine case of $2 + 2 = 5$. Individually, they would both have chivvied out handsome, lucrative careers and enjoyed the status afforded top singers and athletes, respectively. Together, they expressed elemental properties of the times. "The sense of invulnerability and omniscience that fame confers is magnified in both Victoria and David Beckham by the potent chemistry produced by the bonding of the worlds of pop and sport", writes Andrew Morton, author of *Posh & Becks* (p. 20). Even Victoria herself acknowledges that, while she had been in the Spice Girls, she "was always the one in the background". Once it was known she and Beckham were an item, "it was like a snowball, it got bigger and bigger and bigger until really it was out of control".

In 2003, as Beckham stepped up to collect his OBE, Victoria reflected: "I think I wouldn't be as famous if I wasn't with David. And I don't think David would be as famous if he wasn't with me." As her husband commanded the attention of the world, it was easy to neglect Victoria's importance in his occasionally troubled trajectory from the accursed soul he was in 1998 to the god-like being he became.

The Spice Girls were never going to be like the Slits, the all-female punk band that supported the Clash on the "White riot" tour of 1977 and which, as Pete Frame puts it in his *Complete Rock Family Trees*, "splattered onto the scene like a bursting boil" (p. 29). Nor were they even going to resemble the bimbo-esque trio Bananarama, which triumphed with its splashy-sweet music in the 1980s. The time when bands emerged as if by happenstance from the ranks of disaffected art students and unemployed ne'er-do-wells was over by the 1990s. But the contrivance that lay behind the Spice Girls wasn't new.

In 1961, Berry Gordy, the creator of Motown, signed three Detroit teenagers known as the Primettes, changed their line-up, installing a 16-year-old Diane Ross as lead singer, gave them singing and dancing lessons, choreographed every stage move – right down to seemingly spontaneous gestures – even polished up their elocution before launching them as the Supremes, later to become Diana Ross and the Supremes. No detail was ignored in the industrial process that produced what became the biggest-selling girl band in the world, at least until the 1990s. And, lest sentimental clingers to art-rock values forget, the Monkees were no Gorillaz.

In March 1994, Victoria Adams responded to an ad in the theatre trade journal *Stage*. It started: "RU 18–23 with the ability to sing/dance?", then gave details of auditions for a "choreographed, singing/dancing all female Pop Act". Heart Management, a music industry management consortium, had run the ad. Adams had trained for three years at the Laine Theatre Arts school and performed in the short-lived musical *Bertie*, but was having to make ends meet by working as one of those store assistants who approach you with an atomiser and ask you if you would like a spray of whatever fragrance is being promoted. A month later, Adams, then 20, was recalled. She was already rehearsing with another band called Persuasion, but Heart Management was a proven commodity in the music industry and the auditions augured well.

Once the hundreds of aspirant singer/dancers had been pared down to five, Adams was, with the other four, taken to a guesthouse just outside Windsor where they rehearsed together. Still on the dole, Adams agreed to a further period working with the others, this time going into newly converted recording studios. After a month, she and the others approached their mentors who agreed a weekly wage of £60 each. Bob and Chris Herbert claimed they had "discovered" the band Bros. The financier, or backer, of the project was Chic Murphy, who also professed credentials, having managed the Philadelphia trio, the Three Degrees.

When one of the prospective band members lost favour, she was jettisoned. Another stage school-trained female, who had been in *EastEnders*, was drafted in as a replacement. The band's working title was Touch, though this was changed shortly before the showcase. A showcase is a four- or five-song set in which acts perform before an invited audience comprising a & r (artists and repertoire) people, record producers and writers or representatives of publishing companies. The showcase for Spice, as the band was christened, took place in studios in Shepherd's Bush, London.

Two writers in the audience, Matt Rowe and Richard Stannard, were impressed with the set and invited the young women to participate in writing some material. The demo tape that resulted from the collaboration had on it "Wannabe", which was to be the band's first single. While the Herberts and Murphy had brought the five together, they had not secured their services contractually. The five sought out Simon Fuller, who had managed Annie Lennox and Cathy Dennis and whose company was called 19 Management. By May 1995, they had a manager, though it was another year before "Wannabe" was released. The band signed for Virgin Records, which had been taken over by EMI a few years before. At that stage Virgin's managing director was Paul Conroy. Each member of the band was given £250 per week plus expenses. Virgin appointed Alan Edwards to take care of the Spice Girls' publicity, in much the same way that Pepsi appointed the same man to look after Beckham's. Edwards wasn't alone in handling the affairs of both Posh and Becks: in 2003, Fuller's 19 Management replaced SFX as Beckham's agents.

Such are the wiles of the record industry that "buzz" typically announces the arrival of a new product. So, at the 1996 Brit Awards, Virgin invited the band, but let the word circulate without any formal notification, apart from the name. Who, or what, is Spice? The policy of priming expectation is, of course, tried and tested and can work like a charm. The six months following the award ceremony helped create an interest in the single "Wannabe", the final six weeks before its release in July 1996 being especially important as the band stepped up promotion. An appearance on the popular *Surprise, Surprise* show, which was screened, on national tv, was particularly useful. The single entered the charts at number three then went to number one, where it remained for seven weeks. By Christmas, the band, which had added Girls to its name, had scored two further number ones, "Wannabe" selling three million copies and topping the charts of twenty-seven countries.

Having labels like Posh, Baby, Ginger, Scary and Sporty was clever marketing, but, according to Adams, not of their own creation. A pop magazine editor dreamt up the names and, of course, they stuck. It helped consumers remember and identify the women, without having to think "which one is she?" In Adam's case, it might have been, in the absence of the Posh label, the moody one; she never smiled at the camera. Her face had a permasneer. Victoria showed how attitude itself can be product – and I'm using "attitude" in the sense of exhibiting a disrespect, scorn or contempt for authority, convention or established values. Victoria didn't so much oppose anyone or anything as turn the expression of 'tude into a commodity subsumed by the music industry and processed into something cool. Nothing and no one was ever questioned, less still challenged. But, it moved cds and merchandise like nothing in history. "We were so hot we were on fire", reflects Victoria in her autobiography *Learning to Fly*.

Celebrity status suited all of the band members: the media pursued them and they responded with pranks and any kind of stunt that would get them in the news. Of course, consumers want more of celebrities: they want to know what they are "really" like. How did they get to be so famous? What did they do before they were famous? Where did they come from? Replies to these kinds of question were not readily forthcoming: they were usually submerged under an avalanche of rhetoric about "girl power", itself a bit obscure.

These kinds of question must, theoretically at least, be answerable, even if the answers are not available. But it wasn't until one of the band's members broke ranks that anything resembling an authentic human being manifested. By this stage, suspicions that the band had been manufactured were not only rife, but seemingly well founded. Answering advertisements out of a magazine and rehearsing behind locked doors suggested something out of line with usual expectations of bands – a bunch of mates buying equipment with their savings, gigging at pubs and downmarket clubs for beer money, waiting to be discovered. Throw in the image of a shadowy Svengali figure pulling the strings and the end product is ... an end product, not a gathering of creative artists.

Closer analysis of the popular music industry reveals that the distinction between manufactured and natural bands is far less distinct than typically imagined. There is no organic process through which bands emerge. Of course, the Spice Girls were among the least spontaneous of assemblies: they were strangers brought together with a definite project in mind. But compared to later developments, particularly the televised industrial process that led to the formation of Hear'Say or Girls Aloud and the fabrication of Gareth Gates, the Spice Girls were created on an impulse.

Even sport, especially football, is subject to the industrialization process that has shaped other areas of entertainment. Gone are the days when clubs reared homegrown talent, scouting the environs of their grounds and gradually integrating youth with experienced members of their teams. Today, clubs buy or loan players, often for contracts lasting less than one season. Clubs are more likely to assemble teams rather than nurture them. In the same way, the Spice Girls were assembled, though, in their case, there was a good deal of nurturing involved before they actually became commercially viable.

Success brought with it the usual endorsement contracts. Adams was a Diet Coke drinker, so a big deal with Pepsi caused a ripple of embarrassment. Also embarrassing and costly was a contract with Asprilia scooters, which culminated in a court case. The band did deals with, among others, Benetton, BT

Phonecard, Cadbury, Mercedes, Polaroid and Walkers Crisps and lent its name and image to all manner of merchandise, including Spice Girl dolls, cameras, books, videos – everything imaginable that would bear the name "Spice Girls". The blizzard of marketing tended to conceal the fact that the band, for all its commercial success, did not actually perform "live", not even on television, until almost a year after its launch, on the US comedy show *Saturday Night Live*. The band's first actual "live" performance in front of a real, as opposed to a studio, audience was saved for Istanbul and even that was a commercially driven affair. Pepsi, one of the Spice Girls' sponsors, wanted the show to take place in a country in which it was the market leader (Coca-Cola is the leading soft drinks brand in most countries).

The phrase "licence to print money" might have been coined for the Spice Girls during the mid-1990s. For personal appearances the band would charge upwards of £50,000. For one promotion alone, to launch Channel 5 (now, Five), the band was paid $500,000. Record sales, typically the mainstay of pop acts, provided just one of many sources of income for the Spice Girls. *Spiceworld – The Movie* was only a matter of time. It was less a work of art, more an extended piece of merchandise. By 2000, Victoria's personal wealth was estimated at £24 million (the other Spice Girls were worth slightly less).

The Spice Girls' rise to "power", if we can call it that (they did), was at a time when any vestigial notions about popular music's equation with youthful resistance or rebellion was gone. The resistance may have been freighted with much more symbolism than actuality, but it was important symbolism and it served to maintain continuity with recent history. Rock 'n' roll music and its progeny pop emerged from the gathering storms of generational conflict and youthful postwar insurgency. The fans who bought not just Spice Girls cds, but also lunch boxes, dolls and magazines, flocked to their movie and logged on to their dozens of thousands of internet sites, had probably never witnessed a "live" performance. They were, to use Barney Hoskyns's phrase, "bred like *Invasion of the Bodysnatchers* pods to be passive consumers of lifestyle accessories, digesters of fads and images living in Warholian dream-state" (from his article "The Brits: pop you can and should get out of your head").

In August 1996, two completely unrelated events affected the destinies of Beckham and his wife-to-be. First, the famous goal against Wimbledon, which set everyone talking and ensured the name "Beckham" was widely known in football and its penumbra. Second, the death of Princess Diana. Beckham and Victoria were to enter "the sentimental terrain once occupied by Diana, Princess of Wales", according to Morton. "They are the new royalty for the common man." Other writers have tended towards the same conclusion, though with a slightly different inflexion. *Inside Sport* writer Mike Pattenden believed, "the Beckhams have replaced the late Princess Diana as the main source of celebrity gossip in Britain". As support, he noted: "It was their wedding, not that of another royal, Prince Edward, that gained blanket coverage in the tabloid – and broadsheet – newspapers." Julie Burchill also saw the comparison, though in her book *Burchill on Beckham*, she interprets Beckham himself, rather than the couple, as having "shades of Diana".

With the paparazzi quietened after Diana's death, the tabloids had to content themselves with meagre pickings. A pop star and a footballer were no substitute for royalty, certainly not for enchanted royalty. But there was potential in the combination of the two. Footballers had been seen with pop stars before, though they didn't make a habit of socializing with the likes of Elton John or attending Jade Jagger shows, or wearing silk bandannas and other garments that football fans might ridicule. The now-famous shot of Beckham in a sarong coincided with Paul Gascoigne's omission from the England World Cup squad. Gascoigne had, for long, been the footballer most pursued by the media, his every utterance and movement being worthy of a story. Now, it seemed, his England days were over. Time for a new game. Beckham's timing could not have been bettered, from a media perspective at least.

Beckham became a new type of game for the media. "He has never kicked a fan, hit his partner, been pictured pissed the night before a game, let off a fire extinguisher, trashed a hotel, been involved in a fight outside a night-club or written off his Ferrari in a drink driving incident." Pattenden's observations are accurate, yet they tempt the question: so what else is left? Beckham has, as Pattenden pointed out, "done nothing to cause real offence, avoiding all the pitfalls that footballers usually stumble into after a few shandies." The point missed by Pattenden, in his article "A Cross to Bear", is that the "pitfalls" are exactly what make most footballers into celebrities. With Beckham, the media had something completely novel to report: a gormlessly handsome fellow who dressed effeminately and hung out with showbiz types.

No sooner had the media latched on to him, of course, than he committed the heinous sin of getting sent off and despatched from the World Cup Finals. Fleeing to the USA where he met his fiancée (they had announced their engagement in January 1998), then in the middle of spending a tax-efficient year outside Britain, he kept his distance and remained silent while the British media roasted him.

The Spice Girls had already made their impact in the USA, indeed in most parts of the world. They were in the middle of their most fertile period commercially, with hit records replicating themselves at a rate not witnessed since the days of ABBA. The success of his fiancée's band, combined with his fashion predilections and showbusiness companions, helped intensify the reaction against him in Britain, where effigies were burned and even a politician contributed to the odium.

Victoria had earlier disclosed a business-like efficiency when she and the other band members dismissed Fuller. In brushing aside anything that resembled an obstacle to progress, she may well have supplied Beckham with a philosophy for dealing with troublesome episodes. She was also known to have a formidable work ethic. "What I lacked in talent I made up for with hard work", she acknowledged, citing determination and self-belief as the secrets of her success. These were highly compatible with Beckham's own industrious values. As a youth with Manchester United, he would usually stay back after training to hone his skills. Alex Ferguson praised him for this persistence.

She was also, by this stage, used to dealing with the media, having had a couple of years of living in camera range: the paparazzi would use helicopters and long-range lenses to capture her image. And image was, of course, central to the Spice Girls. They had one famously fractious incident in Barcelona (and similar fracas in India and Sweden) when photographers tried to take pictures of them during rehearsals. The Spice Girls, being avid merchandisers, were ever protective of their image and ejected the photographers. It seems reasonable to conclude that, having gone through comparable – if perhaps not so invective – treatment from the media, she would have been well placed to advise him on how to negotiate it. In other words, Victoria would surely have had some answers to Beckham's questions about how he should approach the upcoming season when the hail of abuse was about to become torrential.

Being engaged to the maligned footballer brought Victoria a new legion of enemies: the vulgar chanting involving her was once, in the absence of a more appropriate term, playful. It soon became nauseating. Beckham eventually subdued it by knuckling down to play hard and auspiciously well. It was all business for Beckham as he narrowed his attention to the games and gated out the crowd – as far as humanly possible. He also gave short shrift to the media, spurning requests for interviews, strenuously avoiding photographers and limiting his public comments to an absolute minimum. All the media were left to feed off was his football; and it was sublime. Beckham contributed appreciably to Manchester United's most successful season ever.

Brooklyn, their first child, was born in March 1999 and it's some measure of the Beckham's rehabilitation that he and his wife were able to take the baby onto the Old Trafford pitch and receive a resounding welcome. By the end of the 1998/9 season, memories of Beckham's *faux pas* had all but disappeared. The phrase "zero to hero" is sometimes used to summarize Beckham's return to favour, though, in reality, he had probably never lost the devotion of his wider circle of followers. Football fans and the sports media may have demonized him and, by association, Victoria, but it's unlikely that the majority of his by-then expanding fandom was interested in his footballing exploits. He was part of a distinctly appealing pairing that brought together the glamorous world of pop music with that of the exciting world of sport. There were other fashionable couples, of course, but none with the populist sentiment embodied by Posh and Becks.

Ask any person under the age of 16 to list their interests, and pop music and football are bound to feature as priorities. There have never been forms of popular culture that invade our lives as pervasively as pop and footie. In the Nineties and the Noughties, they became inescapable. The young person that likes neither is unusual indeed. So, the singular fusion brought about by Beckham and Victoria drew new fields of fans. Beckham profited most from the liaison: the guy who dates, gets engaged to, then fathers the child of one of pop's leading lights is someone to be admired, envied and perhaps even venerated. Beckham was. But maybe this is all a bit too idealistic. Maybe there were more prosaic processes at work.

———

When Beckham started to see his future wife, he entered an adjacent culture, that of pop music. He never left football culture, of course, though it was occasionally possible to think he was drifting. Certainly, that was the view of Alex Ferguson, who, in his *Managing My Life*, revealed that he was worried by what he calls the "showbiz element in [Beckham's] life".

In July 1999, Ferguson reacted to what he must have seen as the disruptive effect of that element. He ordered Beckham to return to training within days of his wedding. Whether or not it was the audacious pomp and fake regality of the wedding, the unbearable media interest in it and the meticulous stage management of it that reminded Ferguson that his charge's lifestyle was becoming too excessive for an athlete, we don't know. Maybe he just wanted to ground him with a bump. Or maybe he was offended by the request for extra days off that was made by Beckham's agent, Tony Stephens, not to him but to Martin Edwards. Whatever the precise motivation, the outcome was the same: Beckham was back in training sooner than he preferred.

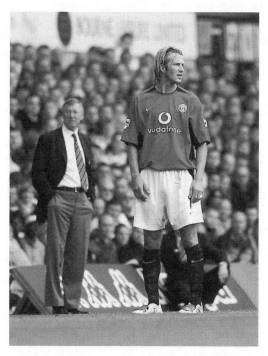

Figure 6 Alex Ferguson was a virtual surrogate father to Beckham in early years, but was made to look on as Victoria assumed more influence in the player's life.
Source: Getty Images

The wedding may have been the high point of Victoria's global popularity. Always, and on her own admission, the least known of the Spice Girls, she had maintained a high profile during her relationship with Beckham. Her wedding completely eclipsed that of fellow Spice Girl, Melanie B, around the same time. The extensive and elaborate arrangements befitted a royal wedding. And, as if to whet the appetite of the media further, a deal was signed to authorize *OK!* to take and use the wedding photographs. The magazine, incidentally, enjoyed a surge in sales for the two issues in which it featured the photographs. Even the Vera Wang wedding dress was kept under wraps for fear of letting rival publications get photos of it. The day was themed as if by Disney; Luttrellstown Castle, an eighteenth-century house outside Dublin, was transformed into a fairy kingdom. As if in acknowledgement of the inspiration, the theme from *Beauty and the Beast* was played. The couple commissioned fanfares, a flag bearing their own crest, a lush purple carpet. The royal jeweller, Slim Barrett, who had worked for Diana, lent Victoria a diamond and gold coronet for the day. It was a royal wedding without royalty.

The truncated honeymoon at a house owned by Andrew Lloyd Webber in Nice ended with Beckham back in training. It was by no means the only conflict Beckham had with his manager. Ferguson's irritation with Beckham's priorities is well documented. Few, if any, managers in any sport have had to deal with, supervise and advise a player like Beckham. Phil Jackson, the head coach of the Chicago Bulls basketball team in the 1990s, had not only the iconic Michael Jordan, but celebrities like Dennis Rodman and Scottie Pippen to manage. Jackson summarized his task: "I had to convince Michael that the route to greatness was in making *others* better," according to his biographer Roland Lazenby. Ferguson's approach appears to have differed.

Whatever Ferguson suspected about Beckham before the wedding would after the event be confirmed: he had a luminary presence in his ranks. Beckham and his new wife may have been the functional equivalent of royalty for many. And, for many, many others, they were 22-carat celebrities. For some, perhaps, they were demigods, at least partly divine. There is one documented case of a woman who claimed, in allusion to Beckham's god-like powers, that he had spoken to her personally. The woman rode by taxi from Edinburgh to Cheshire where she broke into the building in which the Beckhams had a flat; she was detained under the Mental Health Act.

The Spice Girls didn't actually split up: the individual members simply made their own records, mostly with success, though not on the same scale as the band's. Victoria, perhaps distracted by becoming a mother and getting married, didn't seem to pursue her individual career with the same vigour as the others. Yet, she emerged as the most celebrated post-Spice band member. This was because of her association with Beckham, as she acknowledged – the "snowball" effect. Her fame grew proportionately with his. "Posh and Becks" became a potentially marketable brand in its own right.

The Spice Girls effectively over, the other members engaged with other projects, Victoria's career was in flux. She failed to get a part in the first *Charlie's Angels* movie, but hosted her own television show, *Victoria's Secrets*. Her first single away from the band was commercially successful, selling 180,000 copies, which is good, but nothing like the 1.25 million copies of "Wannabe" sold in the UK alone. But the first album foundered and her single "Not such an innocent girl" suffered the misfortune of being released on the same day as Kylie Minogue's "Can't get you out of my head". Even against a background of declining singles sales in Britain, there was no mistaking a downturn in the fortunes of Victoria. Despite her renown – and she became the most illustrious of the ex-Spice Girls – she was unable to translate fame into actual achievement and drew perilously close to, or perhaps reached, the dreaded point where fame becomes its own dynamic.

The suspicion arises: had Posh not become Mrs Victoria Beckham, she may have tottered on her beloved Gina stilettos and perhaps fallen completely out of public purview. Fame comes with no guarantees of longevity and one crucial thing she must have learned in her Spice years was that it has to be worked at. A cold, callous, inveterate observer might conclude that, while she clearly married her husband for love, it wasn't a bad career move either. Without the lavish photospreads and screaming headlines elicited by her piquant romance, she may, to use her own phrase, have remained "the one in the background".

So, how does this square with my earlier argument that it's easy to neglect her importance to Beckham's trajectory? The first point to remember is that, when the two elements combined, they produced the potent chemistry, as Morton calls it, or the out-of-control snowball, as Victoria prefers. "Posh and Becks" as an item was much more than the sum of its parts: it was a phenomenon in its own right. Even allowing for the restraint of the media in the aftermath of Diana's death, there were still plenty of paparazzi willing to play at being big game hunters and plenty of editors happy to publish their spoils.

The theory that Posh and Becks sauntered into the "emotional territory" once held by Diana is a popular one, though not one I find compelling. Diana's entrapment and escape from an unhappy marriage, her indefatigable work for humanitarian causes and her efforts to shield her children from a prying media secured her a unique position. She was revered throughout the world as an idealistic, philanthropic yet tormented spirit engaged in a quest that would always be futile. Like Diana, Posh and Becks occupied the media's incessant attention, more so after her death; but whether their deeds evoked a comparable intensity of emotion is doubtful.

Certainly, the scandals and rumours that shook public confidence in the royal family in the aftermath of Diana's death helped create an environment in which people were liable to affix their faith to new symbols. The same period also saw the rise and rise of celebrity culture, with people no longer satisfied with staring at pictures of or seeing movies featuring stars. Instead, they wanted to feel intimate with the celebrities they followed: they wanted to know their innermost secrets, share their private passions, engage with their personal selves. The media, wherever possible, met the demand and, in truth, generated much of it.

Posh and Becks may not have tapped the wellsprings of affection in the same way as Diana. They had one thing in common though: every move they made was not only documented but propelled by the media. Beckham actually ended up in court after speeding in an effort to evade a paparazzo. His successful defence suggested a kind of US-style celebrity judgement: that the famous should be judged by different standards on account of the unusual media pressure they have to endure. Death threats, kidnap threats, dubious affairs: these made great copy and contributed to a self-perpetuating spiral of interest in Posh and Becks.

There were four other specific ways in which being involved with Posh contributed to Beckham's ascent. First, at the time their relationship was made known, in 1997, he was a promising footballer with Manchester United, known for his 57-yard goal and for his captaincy of the Under-21 team, but not yet established as an international player, nor the owner of the number 7 shirt – which belonged to Eric Cantona, who was shortly to announce his retirement. She, on the other hand, had earned her celebrity credentials: best-selling records around the world, a bunch of endorsements and enough merchandise to fill Harrods. As part of the world's leading female act, Posh had a teen fandom rivalled only by the likes of Take That or the New Kids on the Block. The Spice Girls' film was in the offing.

Beckham, by sheer association, was plugging into a complete new circuit. As the beau of one of the most celebrated women around, he became a figure of curiosity. Of course, high-profile women always cause a buzz when they find a new escort; but it's usually short-lived. With Beckham, it was different: he was a public figure in his own right; not yet a celebrity, but known and closely watched by the sports fraternity. Becoming involved with Posh meant that he would be closely watched by multitudes.

Victoria's second important contribution was her knowledge of the celebrity production process. Apart from odd jobs to pay the rent, she was committed to working in the footlights, even before she left school. Her training and initial experience in theatre equipped her for a life in showbusiness. At the time she met Beckham, she was an old head on young shoulders. Barely 23, she had plotted her way through the minefield, avoided the explosives and, at one stage, dumped a manager whom she felt wasn't guiding the Spice Girls appropriately. While the other band members were probably enjoying the moment, Victoria was taking notes. So that, by the time the Girls finished, she had filled a folder.

Victoria was skilled in the celeb industry. Beckham was not. One can easily imagine how she tutored him in the importance of controlling his image, getting the best value for his labours and rationing his exposure. Up to December 2000, Beckham allowed only four interviews, his careful selection of publications indicating a branding exercise in operation: *GQ*, the *Sunday Times* Style section, *Time Out* and *The Times*.

This leads to the third contribution: branding. Surely, one of the most critical lessons learned with the Spice Girls was how to build a brand rather than stay as a group. The trade magazine *Advertising Age* introduced the Spice Girls into its "Top Marketing 100" in 1997. *Forbes* ranked the band number six in its "Celebrity Power 100" in May 1999. These ratings weren't based on fame or numbers of records sold, but on the value of the brand. In the absence of "live" performances, the band created a reputation at first on the back of records and tv appearances, then through lending its name to a series of products, including its own merchandise. The film sealed the Spice Girls brand. (The wonder is that there wasn't a Spice Girls cartoon series.)

Beckham was part of a brand: he was, after all, playing for Manchester United, one of the world's leading sports brands. By default, he became part of another brand in the Spice Girls. In the years after he met Victoria he developed a brand in his own right, licensing his name and image, and converting himself into a commodity in much the same way as the Spice Girls had done. Advice on how to match himself to his market, manage impressions through public appearances, adapt to changing circumstances (such as those following the Red Card in 1998) and so on would have been valuable to a player making his mark on and off the field. Beckham, of course, had his agent, Tony Stephens, to look after many of his business affairs; and he was later to acquire a publicist in Alan Edwards. As his fame grew, so too did his team of advisers and courtiers. But his most valuable strategist was probably his wife.

By the time Posh was reaping the rewards of stardom, it would have been no surprise to her that the music business isn't a meritocracy. Talent may or may not be a factor. Work always is. And this is the fourth factor. Victoria's autobiography is punctuated with meditations like, "I was always down in the rehearsal studios an hour before class began, and when the favourites had packed up for the day, I was always the last to leave", and "it's all about hard work, determination". Graft was more important to becoming one of the biggest acts in the world than anything airy like talent. Maybe Victoria knew little of football when she met Beckham; maybe she knows a little more now. But, for sure, she knew showbusiness and realized that success needed to be worked-at. Beckham is himself famed for his work, not only during competition, but also in training. So, they were kindred spirits as well as lovers. If there were ever suspicions in his mind that he could be as globally celebrated as he is by natural talent, she would surely have removed them.

At some point, probably around late 1999, Victoria was probably admiring her handiwork of the previous few months. She and her husband had dominated the celebrity gossip magazines, tabloids and even the serious papers. They had been on tv and were regularly parodied – a mark of distinction for celebs. Far from falling from grace, she had become the most famous member of the Spice Girls. A couple of the others were pursuing solo projects, but she had come across an altogether different project that could help enshrine her in the celebrity pantheon. Let's suppose she glimpsed in Beckham the source material for a new kind of undertaking, part-athlete, part-fashion model, part-rock star, part-movie actor, a being that could seamlessly integrate all parts into one whole. Such a being could dominate the world. She dug out her folder to refresh herself on the mechanics of the celebrity-production process and began to apply them, not to a budding pop star or a wannabe actor, but to an athlete. After all, football, as we've seen, had effectively been turned into a division of showbusiness, so there was a kind of elective affinity already in place.

Her husband was to be the man who would become the world's first celebrity for all seasons. Remember, she had the knowledge and the contacts. A few strategically placed calls and DHL was at the door bearing gifts from the likes of her friends at Dolce & Gabbana, Ermenegildo Zegna and Versace. Another few calls and the hairdresser was waiting, along with the tattooist and body piercer. Yet more calls and the journalists were lining up waiting to be screened. It's easy to imagine the advice: "Do the interview for *GQ*, but not the *Daily Mail*. Do the photo-shoot for that gay magazine *Attitude*, but not with that photographer who took the bad shot of me ... and I want to see a

Figure 7   Beckham's appearance began to change dramatically after he met his future wife. His hairstyles and clothes seemed to reflect his changing status.
Source: Rex Features

contract sheet before anything goes to press. Oh yeah, and tell them you want to keep the clothes and the jewellery."

No detail was overlooked. It was like a media conference at which only digital cameras were allowed. This way, all the shots could be checked and either approved or prohibited. Or a daily comb-through of the newspapers, counting how many stories Beckham or she herself featured in and checking them for accuracy. Unlike many footballers who spurn journalists, or, worse, abuse them with foul language or gestures, Beckham began to featherbed them all, just as his wife did.

Any man in a relationship expects his partner to exert an influence over his life, hopefully a good one; otherwise he

Figure 8   Even without a hit cd in years, Posh commanded the attentions of the paparazzi wherever she went, thanks entirely to the presence of her husband.
Source: Rex Features

wouldn't be in the relationship in the first place. Beckham quite naturally listened to his more celebrated wife as she unveiled her ingenious plans. Why wouldn't he? Everything she did worked not so much like clockwork as one of those autokinetic watches that are powered by the movement of the body and can set themselves to exactly the right time. Even Victoria must have been agog at the results of her endeavour. A celebrity athlete emerged alright: a celebrity athlete, the likes of which had never been witnessed.

Beckham's star waxed as his wife's waned, though, given the alternations of celebrity life, this was probably no more than she expected. She was already a genuine celeb, part of a global brand and an habitué of pop and fashion galas, launches and premieres; she'd seen celebs come and go – and come again. She probably realized that while her husband at the top, her place was secure.

The important thing was to remain in the public consciousness. Far from being annoyed, she would have been gratified to discover that the tabloids were preoccupied with stories about a rift caused by the move to Spain. Even when her much publicized collaboration with rap producer Damon Dash, of Roc-A-Fella records, failed to turn around her recording career, she attracted more coverage than the most successful divas. What she did for Beckham extended far beyond introducing him to Lenny Kravitz, taking him to Johnny Depp's birthday party, procuring him invites to Gucci fashion launches or spending time with him at the vacation homes of Elton John and Andrew Lloyd Webber – although she did all these things. Most of all, she may have mapped out a strategy that changed him from a footballer into a demigod.

———— seven ————

MANCHILD IN PURGATORY

There are defining moments when a life can change unexpectedly. An action, a gesture, even a remark – all have the capacity to transform someone in a way that they can barely understand. Let me pick a most dramatic example from mountaineering: Joe Simpson and Simon Yates are climbing the Siula Grande in the Peruvian Andes. After climbing the west face, Simpson shatters his knee in a fall. The descent begins to go grotesquely wrong and Yates is faced with a choice: his only chance of survival is to cut the rope between him and Simpson. The instant Yates slices the blade of his knife through the rope, he is consigning his partner to certain death at the foot of an icy crevasse. Well, not quite certain: Simpson somehow manages to stay conscious and crawl for miles over glacier and rocks. He lives, writes of his experiences, has his work, *Touching the Void*, translated into fourteen languages, sells more than a million copies, sees it made into a film and becomes a celebrity mountaineer/author.

Paul Gascoigne's defining moment wasn't nearly so incredible, though it certainly influenced his career in a way that few could have imagined. On 4 July 1990, playing for England against West Germany in the semi-final of the World Cup championships in the Stadio delle Alpi, Turin, Gascoigne clumsily made contact with his German adversary, a challenge later described by the then England manager Bobby Robson as "mistimed" rather than malevolent. The referee raised a yellow card to Gascoigne in an act that served as the functional equivalent of Yates's wielding of his knife. The ramifications of the caution quickly sank in: Gascoigne's face contorted and tears started to

121

dribble down his cheeks. The caution meant that, if England prevailed in this game, he would be suspended for the next – the World Cup Final. In the event, England didn't prevail, but Gascoigne's very public display of emotion was caught on camera, sent around the world and repeated frequently in the hours, days, weeks, months and even years that followed. Athletes rarely dissolve into tears, save for those of happiness after a triumph. Tears of self-pity are another thing entirely, of course. No matter that they signified a self-centred immaturity consistent with that of a spoiled child, the tears changed Gascoigne's life.

Pictures of Gascoigne weeping as he tried to come to terms with his fate featured in newspapers in Britain and around the world. The fact that athletes express themselves so infrequently made the shot all the more memorable. "As symbolic moments go it stands as potent as any in sport", write Ian Bent and his co-writers in *Football Confidential*. "So potent that Gazza's tearful performance in the game against the Germans in Italia 90 transcended sporting interest and became a shared cultural event for the whole nation. Suddenly it was respectable for academics, highbrow novelists, agony aunts, sociologists, commentators of any conceivable hue and, of course, politicians to go slumming it in the workingman's game. Football was more than merely rehabilitated from the horrors of hooligans, Heysel and Hillsborough, it was fashionable" (p. 5). Even allowing for some exaggeration and the unfortunate pairing of hooliganism and Hillsborough, Bent and co. have a point. They load Gascoigne's moment with symbolic and practical cargo.

Gascoigne's is less a career, more an odyssey: one tempestuous episode after another. Revered as the true heir to George Best, reviled as a wife-beater, respected for ingenuous sincerity, ridiculed for childlike misdemeanours, Gascoigne elicited the whole spectrum of emotion, not just from football fans but from the nation and beyond. While the comparisons with Best are compelling, comparisons with Beckham are more revealing. As personalities, Beckham was an alkali to Gascoigne's acid. Despite his occasional show of passion, Beckham is a study of monastic self-control – certainly compared with Gascoigne. But

Figure 9   Paul Gascoigne's tearful departure from Italia 90 effectively ensured him the status of football's first celebrity.
Source: Getty Images

there were more significant differences in the contexts in which they operated. Gascoigne emerged at a time when footballers were just beginning to attract the kind of attention typically reserved for showbusiness performers. He played a large part in the process by which footballers were converted into genuine celebrities.

Best had been a rare bird: a singular talent with a lifestyle that pulled in media interest. As with Gascoigne, one event served as a green light for the media. "Following the win against Benfica [1968 European Cup Final]," writes Best in his *Blessed*, "I got my own column in the *Daily Express* and people wanted to know everything about me. Not just my football views but what clothes and music I liked and what clubs I went to" (p. 94). In another book, Joe Lovejoy's *Bestie*, Best reflected that he was engaged in some extracurricular activity "nearly every day". No other footballer of the time got remotely the same kind of attention as Best. He was too unusual, too exceptional, too ectopic to be a symbol of the times. Gascoigne was also exceptional, though not so out of the system that the media needed an entirely new vocabulary to make sense of him. He foreshadowed the coming of the celebrity footballer, whose affairs, habits, even mannerisms were minutely documented by a media rapidly wising up to possibilities offered by sport.

As Gascoigne cried, football was poised to turn into a new sport, one in which the players were to become the hares to the media's hounds. Gascoigne lamented that, while countless other players got involved in the same type of Bacchanalia as him, "none of them gets a photographer up his backside. None of them has photographers hassling his wife and kids outside school." (Beckham, in his autobiography, uses almost the same phrase as Gascoigne when describing the attention he receives from the media, though he expresses incredulity rather than disgust.)

Gascoigne's biographer Paul Simpson argues that there was "a certain amount of truth" in this, though blaming the press for the convolutions of his career was tantamount to evasion. The picture he often painted of himself as a persecuted innocent wasn't convincing, especially when set against the background of his excesses, on and off field. Every indiscretion was the sardine that fed the shoal of tabloid trawlermen (*pace* Cantona).

Gascoigne's relationship with the media was intricate. Without an entourage of photographers and journalists, he might not have played to the gallery so often but, instead, might have concentrated on his football. Without them, he might not have become the most eminent player since Best, had his own lines of merchandise, appeared in tv commercials, endorsed his own videos, made hit records, authored joke books, owned his own trademark or amassed a personal fortune. With them, he became the first British athlete to offer consumers the chance to participate in his life. Gascoigne's audience consisted not simply of football fans, but also of impassioned voyeurs, all eager both to witness and help create the spectacle of Paul Gascoigne.

After the tearful exit from the World Cup, Gascoigne's life was changed. He didn't change, at least not at first: he continued his oafish, often endearingly immature, but always captivating exploits. But, with a massive audience. Within days, the famous image of him sobbing was plastered over newspapers, magazines, tee shirts, coffee mugs, even underpants. It was an image that defined the tournament. And it made Gascoigne a celebrity.

He was invited to meet the then Prime Minister, Margaret Thatcher, at Downing Street, switched on the Christmas lights at London's Regent Street, made records and was routinely tracked by photographers. While Gascoigne was never totally comfortable in the culture that turned him from the most ordinary of ordinary people into a celebrity who numbered Rod Stewart among his drinking partners, his excesses combined with his sporting talent made him ideal material for the media. Sensationalist story writers, doorsteppers, plain hacks and gossip columnists were drawn to him. But so too were serious analysts trying somehow to unlock the secrets of this haphazard talent that was curiously prone to self-destruction. From 1990 to 1998, he was England's principal footballer. He was also the first footballer to be forced to perform under the almost continuous glare of the spotlight. At first, he luxuriated in it; later he writhed in pain. Still later, he seemed relieved that another player had assumed not only his status as a player, but his position as the focus of the media's fascination. In the end, he didn't destroy himself and actually extended his playing career, holding his own in the Premiership until the age of 34.

At the time of his tears in Turin, Gascoigne was playing for Tottenham, having been transferred from Newcastle United in July 1988, two months after his twenty-first birthday. Apart from having patent talent, he was known to play physically: he was prone to what Simpson calls "volcanic rages". In one game in 1988, Wimbledon player Vinnie Jones – himself a physical player of note – devised a plan to subdue Gascoigne for an entire game. Jones marked him tightly, bringing him down by fair means or foul whenever the opportunity presented itself. Cue a famous moment when Gascoigne squirmed as Jones clenched his testes. The image was captured on film and became one of the most famous shots of the time.

Within months of moving, Gascoigne was brought on as a substitute for England in a game against Denmark – his first international cap. A native of the Northeast, Gascoigne never truly left, and his frequent returns to his old domain usually ended with a nightclub brawl, a drunken binge or an emphatically rebuffed advance on a young woman. Without the ballast of his Geordie mates, Gascoigne seemed needy and, at times, implosive. Evidence of this came in the FA Cup Final of 1991. Having enjoyed arguably his best season with Tottenham, which included a sensational semi-final goal, he was stretchered off the Wembley pitch following an unjustifiably dangerous lunge on Nottingham Forest's Gary Charles. The challenge served no practical purpose: it appeared to have been motivated by one of Gascoigne's volcanic eruptions more than anything. Its result was a cruciate ligament injury.

By this time, Gascoigne was already established in the public consciousness: a restless, combustible, yet peculiarly vulnerable manchild capable of acts of wanton vandalism and brutality, yet himself fragile. The fragility wasn't just of his body, though his career was punctuated by long injury-enforced absences, some of them brought on by his own carelessness. It was his mind too: as a high-profile footballer, he was able to embrace or fend off the media, either playing up to expectations or rudely dismissing them. But after the tears he was no longer just a footballer: he was a figure of national interest and, as such, had to contend with the paparazzi. At first, he wallowed in the adoration, which was known as "Gazzamania", perhaps as a child delights in attention. Later, it seems, the attention became like one of those lights the cops in the movies shine in the face of a suspect during an interrogation. Gascoigne reacted like a suspect: he couldn't flee, so he could either cooperate or clam up. He did both, in a ratio of about 9:1. At times, he clowned. Quite literally on one occasion, when he appeared on television's *Stars in Their Eyes*. And at times, he withdrew; at least, as best he could.

Whether Gascoigne's move to the Italian club Lazio in 1992 was an attempt to avoid the glare that had become so integral to his life is open to question. The transfer fee was £5.5 million (it was reduced from £8 million following his injury), of which he would have taken a slice, and the salaries in Serie A were superior to those in the English Premier League at the time. So, there were obvious financial advantages. But, if he thought he would escape the media, he was mistaken. A paparazzi versed in the global approach to celebrity spotting, having pursued Diana around the world, had little trouble keeping track of Gascoigne.

On paper, the idea of the Geordie with a liking for a drink, a taste for kebabs and a reputation for revelry relocating to a then modest Italian club, whose players' idea of indulgence was a second bottle of Pellegrino, was curious. Gascoigne lasted for three years, after which he moved to Glasgow. During his time in Italy, he managed to amuse or offend the media by belching or farting in their presence, went through a series of outlandish hairstyles and colours, and suffered a spate of injuries that were characteristic of his career. His drinking foibles continued unabated, but he seemed to enjoy engaging with the media: he had a playful shoot-out with journalists, using water pistols, at one interview. He paraded around an Italian nightclub with a condom stretched over his head. At no time, did Gascoigne ever disappear, even briefly, from the public view. It didn't matter what he did or said. *He* was news. His pranks were headline-ready.

This was a time when the media lapped up even the most nauseating rebukes from celebrities. Members of the band Oasis, like Gascoigne, would be more likely to answer media questions with an expletive or a gesture than a coherent response (although some gestures are perfectly coherent). Destroying hotels, annoying other guests and getting rat-arsed may have been pioneered by rock stars, but Gascoigne showed himself adept at replicating the deeds. It was a time also when the vaunted Girl Power, symbolized, of course, by Beckham's wife-to-be, implored young women to drink, swear, domineer and, generally, do everything that coarse men were supposed to do.

Young women of the early nineties sought a symmetry with their male counterparts. They were the Ladettes. There was no doubt that Gascoigne was a Lad. He gave the world irrefutable proof of this during the England team's tour of East Asia immediately prior to the 1996 European Championships.

Planned as a series of warm-up games away from the scrutiny of the British media, it turned into a *débâcle deluxe*. As well as being involved in wrecking the cabin of the Cathay Pacific plane and insulting a steward, Gascoigne got into a full-scale drinking session at a Hong Kong nightclub, which culminated in what became known as "the Dentist's Chair incident". The chair in question was customized so that it tilted back, enabling two bar staff to stand over the incumbent and pour shots down his or her throat. Having relaxed with a few cocktails known as Flaming Lamborghinis, some of the players sampled the unusual piece of furniture. It might have been called "the Electric Chair" as far as Gascoigne was concerned: the press was ready to administer capital punishment. "Disgraced fool", the *Sun* cried, singling out Gascoigne as the biggest buffoon of the party. It also reinforced his credentials as the Leading Lad among Lads.

The wonder is that, during the actual tournament, Gascoigne was inspiring. Suspicions that he was past it were vanquished by superb performances against Switzerland, Scotland and Holland. After the tournament, which was played in England, writes Simpson, "he had been securely reinstated as the reigning, undisputed genius of English football" (p. 128). At this stage, Gascoigne could not have helped but notice that English football had undergone what some called a gentrification – made fit for nobility. The terraces had gone, replaced by seats. The prices had gone up far beyond the rate of inflation. The fans didn't fight – well, not so much as they used to – and they wore the same shirts as the players.

Over the next couple of years, football's transformation would continue, New Labour values would diffuse and Lads would recede. The recession was commemorated in August 1997 by Noel Gallagher's visit to 10 Downing Street to meet Tony Blair. Gallagher wore a suit, his wife a floral dress. At some point around that time, the big music corporations must have asked themselves: are the days of obnoxious, drug-taking, piss artists with a fondness for insulting journalists and starting fights over? What's the alternative? Submissive stage-school graduates, who are prepared to take orders on how to sing, dress, diet, even talk and will at no time cause offence. Somehow, the mood shift away from Lad culture towards something altogether less raucous, less adventurous, but more controllable signalled the passing of Gascoigne's era. And the coming of an era more accommodating to Beckham.

Janus-like qualities became evident while Gascoigne was playing for Rangers. The tireless practical jokes (at least, he never tired of his own jokes; others often did) and occasionally ill-natured repartee (he mocked Celtic fans by playing an imaginary flute as if in a Loyalist march) remained. But there was what his manager at Rangers and, later, Everton, Walter Smith, called his "deeper, darker side". After the European Championships, in which Gascoigne was effective and, at times, outstanding, he resumed club football with Rangers. He had, at various stages of his professional life, shown a careless disregard for other players and, at times, a malicious impulse.

This came to the fore in a European Champions League game against Ajax when Gascoigne kicked Winston Bogarde, an offence for which he was sent off. In most contexts, this might have sparked another bout of finger wagging. But this time it coincided with the publication of a picture of his wife, Sheryl, her face bruised apparently by his punches. It appeared on the front page of the *Daily Mirror*. Later, in November 1999, she revealed, through a series of interviews, an image of Gascoigne as a dangerously irrational and suspicious husband, prone to aggressive outbursts and intent on monitoring his wife's every movement.

Gascoigne offered neither excuses nor explanations: just an expression of deep regret. "It will live with me forever", he stated, later linking his "domestic problem" with the Bogarde incident. He was 29 years old at the time; the immaturity argument would not convince anyone. Long seen as a wayward, boozy prankster with a puerile sense of humour, he now became something different: a bully – someone who used physical intimidation to try to impose his own will against those he considered weaker. Remember: he had not struck back against Jones back in 1988, even when Jones teased him with "Don't go away, fat boy". There was also the episode recounted by Simpson, in which Gascoigne asked the airline steward of the flight bound for East Asia in 1996 for a drink and patted him on the backside. The steward punched Gascoigne in the face and, despite being wound up by team mates with "You're not going to take that from him, are you?", Gascoigne just said: "If Jim ['Five Bellies' Gardner, his close friend] and my dad were here ...". His colleague on the flight, Stuart Pearce, recounted how he looked as he had on the memorable Turin night. Maybe those weren't tears of sorrow after all; maybe they were the tears of a bully who had discovered that he couldn't get his own way.

The revelations about Gascoigne's domestic life gave sinister dimensions to his public image as the great jester. He was absent when his wife gave birth to their son Regan. In fact, his wife claimed that, at one point, he went missing for twenty-nine days, during which he was "refuelling", as some called his drinking. A woman claimed he slapped her across the face. This period of his life bears similarity to that of Mike Tyson's following his conviction for rape in 1992: a Pandora's Box of accusations opened up and virtually everything Tyson did after that point was interpreted in terms of his purported bestiality. Gascoigne, like Tyson, was contrite. In 1998, he checked himself into the Marchwood Priory Clinic, Hampshire, in an effort to rid himself of his drink habit and, presumably, to rehabilitate himself in more ways than one.

While his football at Rangers was decent, his virtuosity seemed to sparkle only briefly, raising doubts about his ability to withstand ninety minutes of football. As the World Cup approached, the England manager Glenn Hoddle needed to make harsh decisions. Gascoigne's cavorting can't have endeared him to the straight-laced Christian Hoddle, who may not have needed much of an excuse to omit Gascoigne from his squad for France. Ostensibly, the reason was Gascoigne's lack of match fitness, though the obvious clash of temperaments may have been a factor. Gascoigne was crestfallen as he returned to Britain, though, paradoxically, much of the previous bad feeling was neutralized. Portions of the media felt he was hard-done-by, being so obviously the most technically skilled English player yet excluded on the grounds of fitness. The suspicion was that, given fifteen minutes of playing time, Gascoigne had the ability to change the momentum of a game. Indignation over his exclusion soon evaporated. By the end of the tournament, the media had displaced all their antipathy onto a new hate figure.

Gascoigne had left Glasgow shortly before the World Cup started, transferring to Middlesbrough for £3.45 million, the size of the fee (in 1998) indicating that he was still regarded as a valuable player. The culture at Middlesbrough was rumoured to be less than disciplined, Italian player Fabrizio Ravanelli complaining that he needed to have his training instructions faxed over by a former coach. Gascoigne did not prosper in such a milieu. His value fell to the point where he was offered a free transfer to Everton, where he was reunited with his old Rangers manager, Walter Smith.

Smith, it was thought, could handle Gascoigne. He didn't subscribe to the kind of philosophy best summed up by David O'Leary when interviewed by Sue Mott of the *Daily Telegraph*: "I think every manager would love to be able to park them [players] up in a cage and just take them out every day" (26 January 2002). Smith adopted a, let's say, humanistic approach, treating his players as mature adults and expecting an appropriate response. Gascoigne performed respectably at Everton, avoiding the usual pratfalls, but without recapturing his old form. Still, he strove for it. Even at the age of 34, he still talked about regaining his England place. But the talk sounded like that of an old pro boxer who keeps promising to win back his former title: it never happens.

Smith's departure in early 2002 was a cue for Gascoigne to leave Goodison, and he signed for Burnley, then in the first division. It was an ill-advised move and, soon, Gascoigne found himself coaching and playing in China, but with no more success. After a period of rehab in Arizona, he returned to England where, in 2003, he found some sort of sanctuary in Wolverhampton Wanderers' reserves. With his headline-making days at an end, his drinking no longer news and his England exploits a thing of the past, Gascoigne gently disappeared from the limelight, though perhaps not completely. The very name "Gazza" was enough to elicit images of days when footballers not only played, but played up. But it was a name with historical significance, an anachronism that somehow didn't belong in the twenty-first century.

The chalk-and-cheese contrast between Beckham and Gascoigne is all too obvious. But, pause to think of the similarities. Gascoigne surfaced during a period when the tabloids were locked in a circulation war. The more prurient the stories, the more startling the headlines, the more intimate the details, the better the sales. The *Sun*, in particular, which, as we saw in chapter four, was bought by Rupert Murdoch and turned into the best-selling daily, seemed to substitute the estate agents' three criteria of a property's value with three criteria of a newspaper's value: football, football, football (and perhaps page-three girls). For a period in the early 1990s, Gascoigne was the most newsworthy footballer in the world.

The rise of magazines specializing in celebrity tittle-tattle meant that Gascoigne also had an audience of gossip-hungry readers, primed by his tears and eager to learn more about this odd combination of red-blooded manhood and infantile fragility. Despite carping about the meddlesome media, Gascoigne was never slow to capitalize on their interest. He, or rather his wife Sheryl, struck a deal with the *Sun* immediately after being released from the England World Cup squad in 1998. Like Beckham, Gascoigne sold the exclusive rights to his wedding photographs in 1996 to a magazine, in his case *Hello!*, and for only £150,000 compared to Posh and Becks' £1 million. But, of course, the market had quickly moved on by 1999 and the football celebrity had caught onto the fact that he was as precious as any pop star.

Gascoigne was, it should be said, very close to realizing a status even more colossal than the one he had; it wouldn't be a status he desired. He was photographed on drinking sessions with his friends, the tv presenter, dj and record station owner Chris Evans and Rod Stewart, neither of whom is known to favour temperance. Beckham's well-documented associations with pop stars and fashion designers were influential in transforming him from a well-known athlete to an all-purpose celebrity. So Gascoigne was moving in the right circles, or at least the ones that maximize the chances of staying in the headlines.

Critics might say that Gascoigne was usually in the headlines for "all the wrong reasons", meaning reasons unconnected with football. Let's be clear: in the celebrity stakes, there are no wrong reasons; anything that gains exposure sustains consumer interest. Gascoigne could have used a few more headlines like the ones that followed his heroic performances in the World Cup Final games against Belgium and Cameroon in 1990, or against Scotland in the 1996 European Championships. They would have cemented his reputation as an athlete. But these jockeyed for space with the more lurid ones.

The most interesting similarities between him and Beckham lie away from the field of play. Gascoigne didn't go in for self-promotion. He didn't need to do photoshoots for magazines or pose in stylish glasses. This isn't a criticism of Beckham; it merely suggests a cultural change, away from the spontaneous to the managed. Gascoigne's efforts at promotion were mostly unwitting: getting smashed in a nightclub and sundry hell-raising will get many elite footballers into the headlines. Gascoigne, it was generally agreed, was the leading player of the early 1990s. Anything he did was news. The play-ups were manna from heaven.

Even when the alcoholism stories had dried up and the antics became too commonplace to be newsworthy, there was the hurtful side of his character to inspect. Gascoigne's celebrity was less the product of wilful endeavours to stay in the spotlight, more the outcome of a mass media's appetite for information on a figure who was both in and out of his time. My earlier description of Gascoigne as an anachronism is true in more than one sense. By the end of the twentieth century, he was an ageing player who had perhaps drank his best years away and had begun to look vaguely pathetic in his insistence that he could still play for England. But, even during his peak years, he was a throwback.

Football up to the late twentieth century was a sport in which fans and players coexisted in the same small world. Players were often drawn from local talent and they would stay with their club for their entire playing career. It would not be unusual for fans to know personally the players they watched and with whom they would share a drink after the game – perhaps even get the same bus with them to work. The players would not be paid more than the maximum wage (lifted in 1961) and could afford only the same kind of lifestyle as their fans. The players and fans, in other words, were organic parts of the same community. By the early 1970s, this had all but disappeared: players' salaries, the transfer system and the development of an industry devoted to football and its artefacts put paid to the wholeness that once characterized football.

Judging by the exploits of Gascoigne, it was almost possible to forget that he was earning maybe eighty or ninety times as much as the people with whom he drank. Not one for uprooting himself, Gascoigne returned to the Northeast at every opportunity, socializing with his old pals, in particular Jimmy "Five Bellies" Gardner, who became a minor celeb thanks to his friendship with Gascoigne. The player was simply an ordinary guy who happened to be able to play extraordinary football. He never ensconced himself away from prying eyes and only rarely surrounded himself with security guards. While he revelled in the lavish publicity he got in early years, the media clearly corroded him in later years. "I do not have respect for any journalist", Gascoigne told *Match of the Day* magazine. "I absolutely hate them. I detest them."

It's simply not imaginable that Beckham would utter anything like this. Like it or not, he needs the media attention. Without it, he is a player, a great player perhaps. But only a player. Gascoigne, one suspects, would have been content with being just that. The celebrity status is something he could live with or without. Either way, he would have been earning more than his friends back in Gateshead and he would have spent sixteen or seventeen years of his life doing what he did best. Perhaps he would not have made records with Lindisfarne, or given his name to a line of boxer shorts, or dolls. In fact, these and the many other commercial activities in which he became involved, may have been the distractions that stopped him becoming an even greater player than he was.

———

Richard Giulianotti and Michael Gerrard have argued that around Gascoigne there was a "myth" created as if to consolidate football's "reinvention". In their essay "Evil Genie or Pure Genius?" Giulianotti and Gerrard reckon that images of Gascoigne crying at Turin in 1990 "were an open goal for those powerful forces within the UK game who were seeking to re-package and reinvent English football" (p. 133). The game had a global free-to-air television audience, which included the sought-after ABC 1s and women. The BBC's "high-brow packaging", as Giulianotti and Gerrard call it, of the World Cup tournament, complete with Pavarotti's plaintive rendition of Puccini's "Nessun Dorma" as its signature music, was part of football's appeal to new consumers. Gascoigne's tearful departure elicited "human interest": from that point on, his words and actions were the subject of intense scrutiny and evaluation. And there was interest from everywhere, not just football's fandom.

Giulianotti and Gerrard liken Gascoigne to Stanley Matthews, who "validated working-class respectability, sociability and industry", and George Best, who "celebrated the new working-class dream of individualism, easy consumption and spectacular mobility" (p. 135). Gascoigne symbolized the movement away from football's "blighted past" towards the "brave new future". As he left the playing field, he symbolically walked away from a past that included, as Giulianotti and Gerrard put it, "traditionally masculine fans and players, colourless playing styles, a pervasive distrust of foreigners, financial problems among clubs, dilapidated stadia, and a generalized atmosphere of cultural entropy" (p. 133).

Gascoigne functioned as a walking affidavit of a new age in football, one in which the game changed not just structurally but culturally. The branding afoot at Manchester United, the new-found media power procured by BSkyB and the financial jackpot promised by the Premier League were all parts of the big changes. So were the new fans, introduced to the sport via advertising, music, even literature, many perhaps alerted to the drama of the sport by Gascoigne's exploits, or more specifically, the media's coverage of them.

By the time Beckham arrived, football's fandom had a different demography to the one Gascoigne witnessed when he first played for Newcastle's first team in 1985. The fans had a different social make-up and different tastes: they weren't content to watch footballers; they wanted to know all about them. Gascoigne remains a repellent character to many. To his all-round boorishness we could add a catalogue of other sins. But he was interesting. Why else would the media hunt him down and report even the most minor transgression? People just enjoyed reading about, talking about and seeing him. He was, to use a sporting euphemism, colourful.

———

"JESUS SAVES", proclaimed the famous poster. "Gascoigne scores on the rebound", someone had daubed across it. It was a famous graffito. OK, Gascoigne didn't exactly generate religious fervour among fans, but there was no more celebrated player in the early 1990s. He was the man of his times. His time ended in 1998.

It's tempting to conclude that, as Gascoigne left the England training camp dismissed from the 1998 World Cup squad, Beckham crept into his kingdom. Then, the media found a new figure in their lenses. In a sense, this is accurate: Gascoigne never really recovered his full stature, while Beckham, despite the torment of the Red Card incident, went on to replace him as the nation's premier player and the media's favourite target. The point to remember is that, although their careers overlapped, the context in which they played was fast moving. Gascoigne obviously struggled through the often-wearying attentions of the media. He learned his sport at a time when footballers were just footballers. There was only one George Best and, by 1985, when Gascoigne made his first team début, Best was 40 and making the news only when filing for bankruptcy or getting caught for drunk driving. Football looked to be in decline, anyway.

Eight years separates the ages of Beckham and Gascoigne, who joined Newcastle United as an apprentice in 1983 when he was 16. At the time, Britain was in the middle of Prime Minister Margaret Thatcher's reforms. Class conflict seemed to melt away after the miners' strike that finished in 1985, leaving several industries denuded and millions unemployed. British industry was believed to be leaner, hungrier and fitter. Football was, as we have seen, struggling: gates were down, tragedies were ahead. The transformation began as Gascoigne moved to Italy in 1993. By the time of his return to Britain, in 1995, changes in England had gathered momentum. But, of course, he didn't play in the Premiership until 1998, two months before his thirty-first birthday. He was left out of the England squad around the same time. His reputation both as an athlete and a celebrity was earned either playing abroad, in Scotland or in the national team.

Beckham, by contrast, appeared to the public gaze with a club that was in the throes of becoming a world brand, in a league that was being remade into one of the most lucrative and exciting competitions in sport and at a time when television had started to dictate not only the terms of the sport, but the entire nature of it. The tabloid wars were still raging, though, by his time, the chat magazines had joined the battle. While Gascoigne may have loathed and, in his words, detested, the media, Beckham acquiesced; he may have had to come to terms with the more invasive elements of the media, but, there again, he would have grown up as a footballer knowing no alternative.

The media were everywhere by the late 1990s. Gascoigne had probably witnessed the progressive ratcheting-up of press and tv interest. In 1987, when he made his début for England's Under-21 team, football was dank and glamourless, still recovering from the shock of Heysel in 1985. By the time of his move to Lazio in 1992, there was renewed interest, much of it from Murdoch-owned newspapers, which gushed with news of a game supposedly reborn and restored. And, by the time of his own rebirth at Euro 96, the sport was well on its way to becoming a new division of the entertainment industry.

By contrast, the figure who supplanted him was part of what Giulianotti and Gerrard call "a bland generation". Beckham came across as well mannered and virtuous. Perhaps that blandness is the key. Perhaps the seething, bellicose masculinity embodied by Gascoigne and reflected in his outrageous fortunes were simply played out by the late 1990s. After all, one can hardly imagine Beckham being hailed by fans carrying banners with "Beckham's men are here to stay. Shag women. Drink beer." Substitute "Beckham's" with "Gascoigne's" and you have the picture Gascoigne saw as he met his rapturous fans in Italy in 1992. Gascoigne and Beckham were, in their own very different ways, models of masculinity. Each gave off clear and, in Gascoigne's case, obtuse signals about how they understood their manhood. Perhaps Gascoigne's most memorable statement was a silent one. Returning home to Luton airport after the 1990 World Cup to thousands of exhilarated fans, Gascoigne stepped off the plane wearing a lewd Benny Hill smile and a plastic creation that incorporated a huge pair fake of breasts and a potbelly.

Beckham in the same outfit is simply beyond imagination. In fact, you couldn't easily credit Beckham with anything that Gascoigne got up to, apart from playing good football. Yet, in their own completely different ways, they represented masculinity. Gascoigne's exaggerated, perhaps even caricatured, version of masculinity may be transparent. But Beckham's needs some examination.

——— eight ———

SEX, MASCULINITY AND THE TEMPTATION OF GAY MEN

"If a man wears a skirted garment you become immediately aware of him as a sexual presence", writes Andrew Bolton in his 2003 book *Men in Skirts*. When Beckham appeared in a sarong, he silently communicated the first of his many messages about sex. Men have worn undivided clothes since ancient Egyptian and Roman times; even today, they wear jellabas, kaftans and kilts – *à la* Jean-Paul Gaultier, as well as like Scotsmen. Beckham, though, was neither a Gaultier model nor a Scot. He was a footballer. But, a footballer with a sexual presence.

Sex was one of those qualities Beckham implied without ever making it explicit. After the sarong shot in 1998, his sexuality was a matter of serious, as well as lighthearted discourse. In subsequent years, he would appear in nail varnish and, of course, his famous Alice band, and would speak openly about his manicures. He also appeared to have his eyebrows shaped. Spurning the conventions of football culture, he sent out signals – some clear, some ambiguous – about his version of sexuality, without actually saying anything. It was this capacity to announce without speech that sparked endless debates about Beckham's sexuality and kept alive interest in the transgressive male who was committed to a woman but enjoyed the adoration of men.

Beckham was no innocent in these matters. Nor did he pretend to be. He didn't become an accidental sex symbol any more than he fortuitously discovered a freakish gift for taking free kicks. He worked on both. Take for example, the fashion shoot he did for *Arena Homme Plus*, number 14, in Autumn/Winter

2000. "Beckham posed most assuredly as a bit of rough; a rent-boy whose masculinity was available – at a price." At least, this was writer Colin McDowell's interpretation.

Beckham's expression was unsmiling, even slightly grave with a hint of a pout. The clothes looked as if they had been torn off a US soldier; green, brown and black fatigue-like garments, not scruffy, but certainly not elegant; the look was hard. He posed incongruously in a rather ordinary-looking bedroom. It appeared "to be engineered specifically to excite the gay reader", according to McDowell in his article "I'm (not) too sexy for Milan".

The engineering must have been of the highest tolerance. Beckham acknowledged his following, publicly confirming that he knew he had gay admirers. His clear and evident heterosexuality didn't stop him becoming, to use an over-used term, a gay icon. Many showbusiness performers have either cultivated or just acquired gay fandoms.

Asked about this element of his following on national television, Beckham confirmed to chat show host Michael Parkinson that it didn't embarrass him. There's no reason to doubt that he was being anything but honest. Why should it embarrass him? This is, after all, the twenty-first century, the age of New Men, a time when males are meant to be touchy-feely, in tune with their feminine side and attentive to women's sensibilities. Actually, there are quite a lot of reasons, the main one of which is obvious – he is a footballer, not a ballet dancer.

My contrast is deliberately concocted just to make a point. There's a moment in Stephen Daldry's film *Billy Elliot* when the boy's father learns that his son has been slyly dodging boxing training in order to attend ballet lessons. "I could understand it if it were football or wrestling", he despairs. Billy's brother agrees: "ballet is for poofs". This is the mid-1980s: the film is set amid the epic miners' strike that many believe was the last great show of working-class solidarity. Defeat for the miners effectively emasculated a working class that had been assailed by Margaret Thatcher's reforming, rightwing government. The shrinking macho values of the miners provide the tradition for Billy's generation to question and confront.

As an undergraduate student in Newcastle-upon-Tyne in the 1970s, I shared a flat with an economics student who came from Hull and whose mother took in lodgers. My fellow student's father was a carpenter, incorrigibly working class to the point where he banned wholewheat bread from the house on the grounds that it was "too bourgeois". When one of the lodgers revealed that he was a ballet dancer, my friend's dad made him as welcome as the wholewheat bread.

Could any of this happen now? Does this kind of prejudice still persist? Do stereotypes still circulate? Maybe not. Ballet's men have become progressively more craggy and muscular, more unequivocally masculine on stage. And footballers? Some of them – Beckham included – have played with hair accessories that were once unmistakably effeminate, and David Ginola promoted L'Oreal hair care products, in one commercial prissily whispering "because I'm worth it". Yet the prejudice and stereotypes are still around, and, indeed, the culture of which they are part may have changed, but not too dramatically. There has been continuity amid the change. The traditional macho values, including an unremitting hostility to any suggestion of effeminacy and an earnest respect for things homophobic, still characterize football. There are openly gay athletes in swimming, tennis, even rugby. But not in football.

Beckham could be mistaken for a ballet dancer, of course. His physical appearance on and off the field of play gives no hint that he plays football for a living. His androgynous good looks could mislead the uninitiated into thinking he was an actor, like those in tv commercials for Mach 3 razors, or a model you might find in cK ads, or a flamenco dancer in the style of Joaquín Cortéz. A ballet dancer isn't so different. Even when Beckham speaks, he does so with an almost innocent openness that would make most other footballers blush. For instance, on an LWT documentary, *Being Victoria Beckham* (telecast in March 2002), he exchanged views with his wife on the appeal of Tom Cruise.

DB: He's good looking.
VB: Alright, babe. Keep that to yourself.
DB: I'm just saying, he's good looking.

Victoria replies that she thought he looks better when he has his hair cropped. Beckham himself wore his hair famously cropped at one stage. He responds: "He was good looking, anyway."

The surprising part of this eavesdropped conversation is that it wasn't surprising at all. It's exactly the kind of interaction consumers expect from Posh and Becks. They probably talk about fashion, their children, music and football; and about other famous people – what they're wearing, how they're doing their hair, how good they look. Later in the discussion, the subject of Angelina Jolie comes up. "She *is* really pretty", opines Beckham. All this seems perfectly normal. But, pause: would an offguard Robbie Savage be expected to phrase his evaluation of Jolie in terms of her prettiness? Would he even mention Cruise's looks, especially in public? Forget Savage: would any other footballer?

In the same programme, Victoria reveals how her husband flapped when preparing to present his new baby to the media, fussing over his outfit and asking his wife to assist him when styling his hair. Presuming the couple had retained the right to approve the end product, they would have been aware that this revealed him as self-aware to the point of being vain. And, yet again, this didn't seem revealing: just Beckham strutting his stuff. Beckham has the kind of ambivalence that makes him beguiling to a wide audience. Yet, he performs in an arena that openly despises and actually punishes any deviation from the straightest of straight sexual orientations.

Beckham's New Man or New Age family-first side appeals to housewives and grandmothers alike, but also to a whole new generation of young people tired of traditional sex-typing. Beckham, for a while, seemed to be pursuing what *Sports Illustrated*'s Grant Wahl calls "non-traditional sports demographics" (p. 65). This coincided with the first phase of his relationship with Victoria. He ran the risk of alienating hardcore football fans, but he probably figured: "Who cares? They already hate me. How much worse can it get?" This was around the time of the 1998 Red Card. Before the sending-off, the media poked fun at him and his strutting peacockery. After, they, along with the rest of the nation, mauled him, throwing his masculinity into question.

142

The football fans were, however, just a small segment of the target market Victoria had in mind for her construction of Beckham's image. Her project was more embracing. She launched "Out of your mind" at the G.A.Y. club night at London's Astoria, where she had once performed with the Spice Girls and where she yelled provocatively to the audience: "Do you think David's an animal in bed?" Victoria herself retained a strong gay following in her solo career, though it was minor compared to her husband's. Not that she minded: in fact, she seemed to revel in it, perhaps knowing what an important lever it could become in elevating his status, not just as an athlete but as an all-round celeb.

In this respect, the Beckhams were challenging football's core values: the main one of which is that it is, has always been and always will be a man's game. It was invented by men, for men and, according to some writers, for the express purpose of validating masculinity. A detour into history will show us why.

England's Football Association was formed in 1863, at the same time as the Rugby Football Union, each governing organization framing the rules, regulations and procedures that were to shape the sports and give each a distinct identity. Around the same time, the factory system was replacing human labour with machines: automation of industry meant that many tasks that relied on physical strength and robustness were performed by machines. Physical strength and allied attributes were thought to be characteristics of men. The traditional ways men used to exhibit their superiority over women were under fire. The onslaught of industrialization effectively meant that men were given fewer opportunities to demonstrate their own physical prowess and the excellence of their gender. In the absence of war, men had no chance of proving their worth through military means – even if they were built to be warriors.

Competitive sport was a substitute: it offered an opportunity for men to show their worth physically, going head-to-head in demanding, often brutal – and early sports were far more violent than today's – competition and stretching themselves to whatever limits their bodies imposed. Football, no less than rugby, boxing and athletics (all of which took shape around the same time), was a means of publicly proving or authenticating masculinity at a time when it appeared under threat.

Sport was also a trusty training ground, making men from boys. Even today, when computer games keep young men indoors, male adolescents who show no interest in physical sports are still teased. There are even remnants of the creed of muscular Christianity that emerged in the Victorian period: playing sport was, and is, thought to help develop a young male's moral character as well as his physical health.

By the start of the twentieth century, there was *Fußball* in Germany, *fútbol* in Spain, *voetbal* in Holland and *futebol* in Brazil and, everywhere, the game was played by men. The English had taken the sport to all these and many more parts of the world (though Italians insist the game we now call football has sources in the fifteenth-century game *calcio*). Some say its original purpose was lost once taken out of its context; others insist that all football that emerged at the time embodied a style of masculinity. One thing is certain: English soccer manifests an aggressive, almost virulent conception of masculinity that, it seems, it just can't shrug. Despite the global influences that have affected the way football is run and played since 1992, the essential manly character of the English game seems impervious.

Three examples illustrate this. Graham Le Saux, an international player, married and with children, acquired a reputation among professional footballers: apparently less interested in tabloids than were his colleagues and a connoisseur of life's finer things, he became known as something of an aesthete. In football, these reputations can quickly mutate or become indicators of other characteristics. While playing for Chelsea against Liverpool in 1999, Le Saux was subjected to abuse from opposing player Robbie Fowler that centred on his sexuality. According to Le Saux, during the game, he pointed out to his opponent that he was a married man, only to be further subjected to slurs about his wife's sexual proclivities. Fowler was censured. Le Saux continued to play, though his disinclination to indulge in the same kinds of pursuit as his colleagues ensured that he would never be totally accepted by fellow pros.

144

Le Saux was probably offended by a fellow player's apparently unsolicited aspersions, but the consequences were not dire. For Justin Fashanu, a public declaration that he was gay precipitated a chain of events that resulted in his death. The son of a Nigerian lawyer, Fashanu was abandoned as a child and raised with his younger brother John (who also became a soccer pro) by white foster parents. A decent heavyweight amateur boxer, he considered turning professional, but opted for football instead. After playing for Norwich City from 1978 to 1980, he moved to Nottingham Forest for the then costly transfer fee of £1 million. He was the leading light of a small number of black players who were breaking through to the highest levels of British soccer.

Fashanu's conflicts with his manager Brian Clough were legion. Clough recalled with some arrogance how he responded to rumours of Fashanu's sexuality. He asked the player where he would go if he wanted a loaf, to which Fashanu answered, "the baker". Clough barked: "So why do you keep going to that bloody poof's club?"

Clough's sentiments were probably typical of the aggressively macho sports culture of the 1970s. But no major footballer after Fashanu has dared proclaim his homosexuality. Fashanu's symbolic expulsion from the ranks of soccer served as a warning. He himself struggled for ten years after he left Forest before coming out. In the interim, gossip and innuendo were rife and his career went into freefall. Turning to religion, he became involved in Charismatic and Pentecostal assemblies, believing that some sort of divine intervention would prove his salvation. In fact, the church deepened his sense of inner conflict, as homosexuality was strictly proscribed. His sojourns to the USA and Canada amounted to little, and he returned in 1989, still only 28. Presumably believing that Britain would by then provide a more enlightened and accommodating environment, he chose to volunteer the truth of his sexual preferences and start afresh. The decision prompted brother John, by then a high-profile player with Wimbledon, to repudiate him.

Justin Fashanu played for several clubs, including Heart of Midlothian of Edinburgh, from which he was dismissed in 1993 for "conduct unbecoming a professional". The incident that initiated this was bizarre: Fashanu tried to sell stories of alleged sexual encounters with Conservative Party politicians to the tabloids. After moving to the United States, where his reputation was not so great, he worked with several youth projects in Atlanta, Georgia, then with the Atlanta Ruckus soccer club and, finally, the Maryland Mania, for which he worked as a coach. It was during his employment in Maryland that he became involved in a purported offence that preceded his suicide. A 17-year-old male alleged that he had been to Fashanu's house with five others. They'd all consumed alcohol and drugs, according to the man, who claimed he slept on a sofa and awoke the following morning to find Fashanu making forcible sexual contact. Fashanu voluntarily gave himself up for questioning about the incident (there were two specific allegations), but later fled. He was found hanged in a garage, a verdict of suicide being recorded.

The third example concerns Beckham himself. In February 2000, Beckham failed to report for training a few days before his club was due to play Leeds United. He was in London and his baby son had gastro-enteritis. After a fitful night, Beckham left his home for Manchester at 6.00 a.m. After half an hour he had second thoughts, turned round and returned home. An acceptable reason, one might have thought, especially as it was the first time in nine years that Beckham had skipped training. The next day, he drove to Manchester to find United manager Alex Ferguson mightily displeased. He may have let it pass had he not heard that Victoria was at a reception at London Fashion Week at the time. Victoria herself, in her autobiography, doesn't deny she went to the reception, but only after Beckham had left for Manchester. Victoria believes that "Ferguson had been waiting for any excuse to have a go ... 'The Gaffer' was angry at all the travelling he [DB] was apparently doing, saying it was affecting his game" (p. 282).

Apart from Beckham and Ferguson, no one knows what words were passed, but we can safely assume that the famous Ferguson hairdryer was blowing on maximum setting. While there is no mention of this in Ferguson's account of the episode,

Victoria's reveals that Ferguson said: "That no player was bigger than the club and that he wanted him [DB] to leave" (p. 283).

Unthinkable as it was to drop Beckham, Ferguson did it. This revealed a quixotic streak in the "old school" Ferguson: short-term losses in the interests of long-term gains. It also revealed a conflict of cultures. Twenty-first-century New Man versus traditional football man. New Age versus old school. Postfeminism versus patriarchy

Ferguson was shaped by growing up in a Scottish working-class family in the 1950s. His world was not one in which wives or womenfolk had much of a say in their men's lives. Coming from Govan, on the south-western side of Glasgow, where his father worked in the shipyard, Ferguson left school, worked as a toolmaker, becoming a professional footballer for Dunfermline only at the age of 22. After a spell managing St Mirren, he managed Aberdeen from 1978 to 1986, before moving to Manchester. "Old school" is a phrase made for Ferguson. He is steeped in the kind of values that characterized British football for most of the second half of the twentieth century.

Any disharmony between Beckham and Ferguson disappeared over the following years, though the missed training incident must have put their respective priorities into clear perspective. One can imagine Ferguson's exasperation at the attention afforded Beckham, his irritation with the showbiz lifestyle, his annoyance at the obvious influence Victoria brought to his life. He may also have suspected that Beckham had become a law unto himself. But, the idea that even a family man could skip training without permission to attend to his child while his wife was somewhere else was too much to bear. It must have contradicted Ferguson's definition of manliness.

When the errant boot flew across the changing room and came to rest on Beckham's head in 2003, it was interpreted by the media to mean the beginning of the end of the two men's friendship – and the spark that lit the fuse, exploding on Beckham's departure. But it was also a symbolic moment: two versions of masculinity clashed. Perhaps it was the release of pent-

Figure 10 While the picture painted for the media was one of harmony, tensions simmered beneath the surface.
Source: Getty Images

up anger. Ferguson can't have been pleased to read some of Beckham's remarks, such as: "Being a gay icon is a great honour for me" or, as Wahl quotes him: "I'm quite sure of my feminine side and I've not got a problem with that. These days it's the norm, and it should be" (p. 65). Ferguson doesn't appear to have been in touch with his own feminine side, nor, on the evidence of his behaviour, does he believe that being in touch is the norm.

While the rest of society has changed, English football's idea of masculinity has been preserved, as if in Vaseline petroleum jelly. We can almost imagine conducting a questionnaire survey among football players in 1864, asking questions about the rightful place of men, women and children, natural sexuality, the essence of manliness and so on. Administer the same questionnaire 140 years later and the results would probably not differ markedly. They might suggest what Robert Connell, in *Masculinities*, calls "hegemonic masculinity". He argues that while there is no single all-encompassing meaning for masculinity, they do not all hold equal sway. The hegemonic, or foremost, version is the one that prevails. At least, that's the orthodox view. Beckham's encroachment onto the previously hallowed ground of masculinity presents us with an alternative interpretation, one that suggests there's room for more than one version of masculinity in and out of football.

So, for instance, in sport, there might be an ideal concept of masculinity. In her essay "Masculinity", Andrea Abbas captures it: "Homophobia, an indifference to the pain of one's own body and those of others, a win-at-all-costs-philosophy, and an inability to form intimate relationships with and a disrespect for women" (p. 619).

Football amplifies all these. Attitudes and behaviour that contribute to football's idea of masculinity might include: Tony Adams's drinking, which sometimes stupefied him to the point where he would urinate in his pants; Dwight Yorke's apparent fathering of supermodel Jordan's child; Paul Gascoigne's farting resoundingly in the presence of a gathered media; Stan Collymore's striking Ulrika Jonsson in public; Jonathan Woodgate's involvement in affrays outside nightclubs in Leeds and Middlesborough; Alan Smith's lobbing a plastic bottle into a crowd of fans; rough group sex activities, known as "roastings" in five-star hotels. These seem to chime perfectly with the notion of masculinity enshrined in football. There are echoes in Port Vale fan Robbie Williams's declaration to biographer Mark McCrum that, being followed continuously by the media means: "You're being watched. And it takes your masculinity away, because you want to go and break legs and you can't do that" (p. 214).

Football's dominant type of masculinity is only one of many other varieties, none of which is "natural", all of which depend on historical and cultural contexts. Given the torrid time given to Justin Fashanu, it is small wonder that so few gay players have chosen to make their sexual preferences public. There must be dozens of gay players in the English leagues who live up to the traditional ideal notion of masculinity. They must survive with this deception. Others, who may not subscribe to the masculine ideal, must also survive.

Beckham, of course, has survived and prospered: his hetero-sexual credentials are not in question, though virtually every-thing else about him hums with ambiguity. It's difficult to imagine any other footballer being asked about his views on anal sex on national television, with his wife sitting beside him. Yet, somehow, Ali G's guileless interrogation, on Comic Relief night, seemed cheeky but not heinous. Beckham cushioned the question like a high ball. Victoria was unfazed by the bilious wit.

Even Beckham's marriage wrongfoots football fans. Allowing that the traditional husband-as-breadwinner/wife-as-home-worker model has gone, high-profile footballers are still expected to tower over their wives or partners. With the exception of Harry Kewell's marriage with actor Sheree Murphy, there are no other coequal relationships involving high-profile British-based foot-ballers. When Beckham started his friendship with Posh, she was an established celebrity, earning millions and with a global fandom. He was very much the junior partner. Even after he rose through the celebrity ranks and – assisted by her – became an international figure in his own right, his words and actions never hinted at precedence. If anything, she remained the more assertive of the two. Beckham never appeared discomfited by this.

He was far more discomfited by newspaper reports of his alleged encounter with another woman during his wife's first pregnancy. His response was an emphatic refutation. Many footballers are more likely to brag about, rather than deny, their promiscuity. Beckham's reaction was one of disorienting maturity. After all, this was a handsome young multimillionaire, a champion of one of world's most popular sports, in short a man who, in different circumstances, wouldn't go short of female companionship. His reply to admittedly erroneous stor-ies of his infidelity was not to shrug them off, but to become upset and make his feelings known. It must have struck fans brought up on a diet of footballers' sexual incontinence as a case of pathological monogamy.

Oliver Bennett has speculated that fans have warmed to this. "Stability is admired, particularly in marriages – if only because it comforts us that the celebrity has less sex than we do", writes Bennett in the *Independent on Sunday* (31 March

2002). "The Beckhams have maintained their public standing and Paul McCartney has survived well, as if trying to disprove Montaigne's dictum that 'fame and tranquillity can never be bedfellows'."

Undermining this even more, Beckham used parenthood as an occasion for the most conspicuous demonstration of paternal pride. Beckham and Posh dressed their son in a Manchester United shirt and took him onto the Old Trafford pitch. Another player might meet with derision. Beckham drew applause. These behaviours are very New Mannish and quite out of the usual orbit of footballers. They're simply not expected to do such things. Le Saux drew gibes just for being an art lover and a *Guardian* reader. According to Whannel, he was " 'suspect' from the perspective of the constricting limits of working-class terrace subculture masculinity" (p. 148).

In his first autobiography *My World*, Beckham reflected on his own father, Ted, a man he believed loved his mother, but had "never been affectionate to her in front of my two sisters and me". Beckham calls him "hard-faced" and occasionally sarcastic. His mother Sandra, by contrast, is portrayed as softer and more prone to tears in stressful situations. The couple broke up after thirty-two years of marriage in 2002. It sometimes happens: a son, having witnessed what he sees as shortcomings in his father's demeanour, makes a point of not repeating them. But my task isn't to discover the sources of Beckham's bearings: it's to understand why, in a context bristling with hard-bitten, hard-drinking yob-macho types, he was able to introduce an alternative that was at once extraordinary and ordinary.

———

How is Beckham able to subvert all football's conventions about masculinity, sex and carnality? Where does his faintly boring purity fit into a context where rabid heterosexual values rule? One answer comes from Julie Burchill in her essay *Burchill on Beckham*. "It is largely to do with the homoerotic desire of the fans for the players", writes Burchill. "There is something very gay indeed about football fans; not gay in a good, healthy out-there kind of way, but gay in a closeted, self-loathing, woman-hating sort of way" (p. 90).

This is obviously a mischievous, even outrageous, statement, but one which is complemented by a welter of scholarly writing on the subject of sport and sex. Allen Guttmann's volume *The Erotic in Sports* is packed with examples of how sport is a sexually charged environment throbbing with sublimated attraction and desire. Think about it: lightly clad competitors clash with each other, touching, pushing, pulling, grabbing or patting each others' bodies, having worked themselves up to a state of high arousal. "The neurological centers governing sexuality and aggression are in such close proximity within the human brain that arousal of one influences arousal of the others", Guttmann points out (p. 10). "Testosterone facilitates both sexual and aggressive arousal." In other words, when playing or watching sport, we experience a similar kind of thrill as we do when preparing for or engaging in sex. It's almost inevitable that there is some slippage between the two. All sports, even those dating back to the ancient Greeks, have an erotic element. Maybe this is a clue to why sport is enduringly popular.

There is no reason to doubt that there is something homoerotic in a heterosexual fan's responses to athletes of his or her own sex. "The frenzy of the mostly male spectators at a boxing match must be more than the excitement occasioned by the demonstration of the manly art of self-defense", writes Guttmann (p. 146). Similarly, the delight experienced by a mainly female crowd watching a female skater can't be just aesthetic.

This seems a provocative way of understanding our fascination with sport, though not nearly as extreme as Burchill's. She reckons that the reason why so many fans taunt Beckham about his wife's purported interest in anal intercourse is that "a good number of the geek chorus dream of taking it exactly that way from the beautiful Mr Beckham" (p. 91). Of course, Burchill may just be mistaking envy for lust.

Another possible reason that Beckham has been able to break with tradition with impunity is provided by Garry Whannel, in his "Punishment, Redemption and Celebration in the Popular Press". By the time Beckham had asserted his credentials as a celebrity, the environment in and surrounding football had changed. "Men's interest in fashion, style narcissism and the possibility of being objectified have all been nurtured by a decade of the style press", writes Whannel, citing the likes of *Arena*, *GQ* and *FHM* (p. 148). So, Beckham's ascent coincided with a shift in masculinity, not so much in soccer but in the rest of culture.

Levi's might want to take some credit for this. The 150-year-old San Francisco denim jeans company arrested declining sales with a tv commercial for 501s that featured Nick Kamen getting down to his boxer shorts in a launderette. The campaign, which ran in the mid-1980s, showed how a male body could be turned into a sex object just as effectively as a female's. So did Peter Cattaneo's *The Full Monty*, though in a different way: the movie, released in 1997, was a comedy about unemployed workers with a minor cultural flashpoint, so to speak. Men taking their kit off to entertain women – and getting paid for it.

Not that we should read too much into this. In their *Power Play*, Raymond Boyle and Richard Haynes caution: "The shifting patterns of young men's consumption, with heavy emphasis placed on 'the look' and style of appearance may not, however, suggest a wider transformation in sexual politics" (p. 136).

Still, sport in general and football in particular play critical roles in shaping masculinity and the rapturous reception of someone as singular as Beckham clearly indicates that there are changes going on. Shuttle back in time to, say, 1995, and try to imagine what the reaction might have been to a sarong-wearing, Tom Cruise-admiring blond, who was conspicuously devoted to his wife and who doted on his child. Then imagine him posing for glossy magazines and professing no embarrassment at cultivating a following of gay admirers.

We can't be sure, of course; but an educated guess tells us that the reaction would probably have included ridicule, derision and vulgar mockery on a regular basis. In the twenty-first century, Beckham is lauded. This tells us something about how times have changed. Maybe there hasn't been the "wider transformation in sexual politics", but there has been change. How else would it be possible for Beckham to have escaped the bombardment that would surely have come his way had he surfaced a few years before he did. As I said at the outset of this book, the way to understanding the Beckham phenomenon is not by looking at him but at the way others consume him.

"Phallic anxiety." Germaine Greer uses the term to describe the condition of footballers, though she never actually defines it. In psychoanalytic theory, there is a phallic *stage*, in which there's a preoccupation with one's genitals. There is also phallic *character*, which describes male adults who regard sexual behaviour as a display of power and potency. And there is *phallocentric* behaviour, referring to the tendency to see the development of females as a reaction to males. Phallic anxiety, then, should be an affliction involving distress over properties of manhood. Male athletes are, in the rest of the word's eyes, associated with their bodies – what they can do with them, the skills they perform, the ways in which they bring inanimate objects under their control. This implicates them in a process of feminization: women are identified with bodies, men with minds. There are few worse profanities to scream at a footballer than "tart!"

Like glamour girls, writes Julie Burchill, "they must at some level realize that it is humiliating to be valued for one's physical package, like an animal, rather than one's essential, unique self, however handsome the remuneration". Footballers are particularly sensitive, it seems. Perhaps this is why they beat their wives and partners, sometimes in public, even when they know the consequences will be dire. Why they choose supermodels as companions, then slide off to bed prostitutes behind their backs. Why they rarely marry or date women who are transparently more intelligent and more successful than them.

Burchill reckons that this type of behaviour is typical of "only a man painfully aware of his own sexual shortcomings" (p. 57). In other words, someone who is insecure about his sexuality needs to play a dominant role at all time, expressing this publicly and, perhaps, violently. On this account, Gascoigne would be aware of his shortcomings, while Beckham wouldn't be. So, presumably, the latter would suffer less than the former in the phallic anxiety department. Rather than resist the feminization implied by playing football for a living, Beckham has embraced it, at the same time spurning conventional ideas of blood-and-guts, hegemonic masculinity and opting for a softer, caring approach.

Beckham's inclusive popularity prompts a question that exercises the male mind, every so often: what's the essence of masculinity? Is it Travis Fimmel, the boyish Calvin Klein model with the redoubtable packet? Sylvester Stallone? Jaye Davidson (remember him? The chanteuse-cum-chanter in Neil Jordan's *The Crying Game*)? All of them epitomize some element of masculinity, yet none distils the essence – there's no such thing. What Beckham is portraying, whether he knows it or not, is a version of masculinity that contradicts, confuses and conflates a notion that is almost synonymous with football. Here's the headline: "BECKHAM ATTACKS FOOTBALL'S ALPHA MALE."

Absorbing values and images once associated with only the homosexuals and under-the-thumb husbands, Beckham has the look of a gay porn star and the attitude of Niles Crane (brother of *Frasier*). Hard and soft – respectively. For Beckham's fandom, sexual orientation is somehow irrelevant. Traditional insecurities over sexuality melt away. The traditionally rigid male/female divide disappears. Football won't change its hegemonic masculinity as a result of Beckham. No one is going to see players turning up at press conferences in mink tank tops, sequinned shirts, *diamanté*-encrusted jeans or the kind of attire favoured by Graham Norton (OK, maybe the jeans). But changes are afoot. Masculinity will never be the same after Beckham.

——— nine ———

CUSTODIANS OF THE IMAGE

It came as a shock, not least to Tony Stephens of SFX. Beckham had no sooner acquainted himself with the words *hola* and *gracias* than he announced (in English) that he was parting company with his agents and entrusting more of his business to 19 Management, owned by Simon Fuller, who is popularly credited with turning the Spice Girls into an international phenomenon.

Stephens had worked closely with Beckham over the years and they enjoyed a sound personal relationship. They had known and, presumably, trusted each other since Beckham was a teenager. Stephens was on a sort of sabbatical at the time, voluntarily rendering himself incommunicado after an exhaustingly long period negotiating the transfer from Manchester to Madrid. After that he apparently took his family on an extended cruise. But his partner Jon Holmes expressed surprise; as far as he was concerned, Beckham and SFX were still in business together. In fact, only weeks before, the agency had delegated one of its accounts managers with the responsibility of tending to Beckham's business. He was sent to Madrid with this brief.

Beckham himself declared, somewhat implausibly, that he wanted to take time off from his commercial ventures and spend more time concentrating on his football. But there appeared to be no let-up over the succeeding months: if anything, Beckham's image seemed to proliferate on the advertising hoarding, in the print media and on tv commercials.

The relationship with SFX had been an extraordinarily productive one, perhaps the most productive in football history. All professional footballers sooner or later, usually sooner, find themselves an agent to handle their business affairs. The agents take their cut of 5, 10, sometimes as much as 15 per cent of whatever the player earns, but the arrangement usually presents good value. Players rarely criticize them and, when there's business to be done, players let their agents do the talking. Beckham was no different in this respect. Agents, though, are but one aspect of a complex business that works behind the scenes to keep Beckham's image in the public eye. In this chapter, I'll examine the business.

Tony Stephens played football for a team called Martini International, based at the pub in West Bromwich. In 1983, he was appointed as commercial manager of Aston Villa, leaving three years later to become the marketing director of Wembley Stadium. While it was conventionally portrayed as the home of football, Wembley was also the venue for a great many rock concerts in the 1980s and Stephens gained valuable experience of the music business, experience which stood him in good stead when he decided to start up his own agency. Tony Stephens Associates, as it was called, began in 1988 with one "name" client, David Platt, who played with Villa, then transferred to three Italian clubs before moving to Arsenal in 1995 (where he was one of the first players to negotiate image rights). After ten years of operation, Stephens sold his agency for £2 million to the US marketing company Marquee.

A year before, in 1997, Marquee had merged with another American sports agency, ProServ, which had started life in 1969 as the marketing division of the Dell, Craighill, Fentress and Benton law firm in Washington DC. The "Dell" was Donald Dell, the captain of the US Davis Cup-winning teams of 1968 and 1969, who had extensive contacts in pro tennis and was a cofounder of the Association of Tennis Professionals (ATP). Dell's concept was to duplicate the successful strategy of Mark McCormack of the International Management Group (IMG) agency, but with tennis rather than golf players. IMG was the first and, at that point, biggest sports agency in the world with a client list that boasted Arnold Palmer, Gary

Player, Jack Nicklaus and practically every other golfer of significance.

ProServ lived in the shadow of IMG for many years until it signed a promising basketball player from North Carolina and handled his affairs as he moved to Chicago Bulls and beyond. The acquisition of Michael Jordan assured ProServ's future as a major sports agency. The precise conditions of Jordan's contract with ProServ were not clear, but typically the agency would be entitled to 4 per cent of a player's annual salary from his or her club and between 15 and 25 per cent of other commercial deals, including endorsements. In the 1990s, Jordan's yearly earnings would ordinarily exceed $30 million (£18 million, or about €26 million). ProServ's annual billings topped £150 million. When the agency merged with Marquee, the new organization had annual billings of $400 million, exceptional though still less than half of IMG's estimated billings. The takeover of Stephens's agency was part of a planned strategy to expand into Europe and even up the competition with IMG (which already had many interests in Europe).

Shortly after the takeover, another merger took Stephens into the fold of the SFX corporation, which is part of the Clear Channel Communications media group, currently valued at $56 billion (about £38 billion, €55 billion). The SFX Athlete Representation division (and there are several others, including SFX Music, SFX Television, SFX Theatrical) operates as an autonomous subsidiary of SFX and represents such luminaries as Andre Agassi, Kobe Bryant, Jerry Rice and hundreds of other athletes, including Jordan.

Stephens, by then in partnership with Jon Holmes, became part of a new agency called the SFX Sports Group (Europe) which represented footballers like Michael Owen, Steven Gerrard and Robbie Keane, as well as ex-players such as Alan Hansen and athletes from other sports like Greg Rusedski and Jonah Lomu. Stephens, who assumed the title of Marketing Director, continued to specialize in advising and negotiating for footballers, while Holmes, the Managing Director, managed the professional careers of clients and the origination of television shows, like *They Think it's All Over*. The firm employed other licensed football agents, each of whom was delegated responsibility for the affairs of particular players.

Stephens represented Beckham when he wanted to negotiate an auxiliary clause in his contract that provided for Manchester United's right to exploit his image. It was Stephens who, according to Draper, in his *soccernet* article, was "of the opinion that Beckham's extraordinary global image helps to drive United's multi-million pound merchandising operation".

There are two possible responses to this. First, the contribution of Tony Stephens and the SFX Sports Group (Europe) to Beckham's status has been considerable, perhaps even invaluable. Beckham's agents have steered him assiduously clear of all pitfalls and brokered the kinds of deals, especially endorsement contracts, that have provided him with control over his image, its distribution and, to a lesser degree, its consumption. They have positioned his image in the market precisely and strategically, associating it with products that resonate with the right kinds of value: Brylcreem – youth; Police – style; adidas – vigour; and so on.

Second, his agents have been largely inconsequential. Beckham has such sublime talent and natural looks that he would have become a soccer great and top shelf celeb anyway. He would have become recognized for his athletic skills rather than his chic qualities, and his commercial ventures, whether endorsements or merchandise, would have added only supplementary value, in much the same way as breakfast cereal ads did for Owen, or credit card commercials did for Roy Keane. In other words, Beckham would have prevailed with or without his agents.

I favour the first response. Beckham's image is pivotal to his status. In a sense, it actually *is* his status. Yes, he's a footballer of immense proficiency and there's little doubt that, in any era, he would have been widely accepted as such. But only in the present milieu would he be the singular celebrity athlete. The particular constellation of factors that appeared in the early 1990s made it possible for a new type of celebrity athlete to emerge. The factors are now plain to see: the revolutionizing of football, largely at the hands of BSkyB and the chairs of England's leading clubs; the renewed interest in advertisers and sponsors, sensing a burgeoning market among the demographically desirable young enthusiasts; the ramping up of merchandising as a new form of revenue; the expansion of interest in television-spawned celebrities and the admission of footballers into this class of beings; and the combined effect of all these in bringing forth a novel product still called a sport, but with all the accoutrements of an entertainment industry.

Not that anyone could have simply strolled into the offices of Tony Stephens Associates, slammed their fist on the desk and commanded, "The time is right. Make me a star!" Beckham was in the right team, had the right partner and, of course, the right "look". He could also play, though that particular factor is less important to his status than it might appear. The creation and manipulation of his image *was* important and, in this respect, the retinue led by his agents that explored and exploited the Beckham image has played an estimable part in the production process.

In contrast to Stephens, who was a football man through and through, Simon Fuller was a total showbiz man. In July 2003, Fuller welcomed Victoria back to 19 Management with a promise that he would revive her ailing singing career and project her as part of a newly minted Beckham brand. Of course, by that time, the brand itself was less driven by Victoria and more by her husband. The only plausible explanation for Beckham's decision to part with his long-time friend and associate Stephens was that Victoria had mapped out a joint commercial future for them that didn't include Stephens. There was no reason to doubt the soundness of her judgement. As we've seen previously, she proved herself astute in, well, pretty much everything.

Fuller had only limited experience in sport: he once handled the affairs of Steve McManaman but was more comfortable with the music business. He started out running discos, then became an a & r man for Chrysalis Records. Branching into management, he guided the career of Paul Hardcastle in the 1980s. Hardcastle's Vietnam-themed track "19" was an international hit that effectively established Fuller as a player. He started his management company, using Hardcastle's title as his inspiration.

In chapter six, we saw how the Spice Girls were impressed enough by Fuller to approach him after they'd split with their original management team of Bob and Chris Herbert. It's unlikely that he tried to manage the Spice Girls as legitimate singers – probably a good job too. His mission seems to have been to create a marketing phenomenon, a brand capable of moving everything, from Pepsi to dolls and all things between, including a few million cds.

Once established as both a global band and global brand, the Spice Girls inexplicably turned against him, opting to manage their own affairs. As Fuller had the band under contract, he continued to pick up his commission, in his case 20 per cent, from all earnings in which he played a hand. The result was ironic: while he sat back and let the Girls do their own negotiating, he earned more than any single one of them off their earnings.

Unbowed by the ungracious dismissal, Fuller simply set about constructing another sturdy, hit-making, product-promoting unit, this time called S Club 7. When S Club disbanded, its members were reported to have claimed that he paid them £2,000, or about €2,900, a week, while making more than £50 million from them. Fuller justified this by pointing out that he conceived and developed the whole project. In effect, the individual S Club members were characters in a drama he wrote, produced and presented; he could have changed the cast without damaging the dramatic effect of his creation.

Fuller's *pièce de résistance* was the tv show *Pop Idol*, the format of which was recycled elsewhere in the world. Essentially, the weekly programme showcased young talent, the best of which were signed to – no prizes – 19 Management. Again, the suspicion arose: the likes of Will Young, Gareth Gates and their overseas counterparts were like Dyson washing machines, or Sinclair vehicles – creations, rather than creators and of varying quality.

In Victoria, Fuller had a ready-formed product with proven capacities. Any other artist would have disappeared into oblivion after such a long barren spell without a hit record, tv series or movie. Being the wife of Beckham meant that she lived by different rules. She was one of the most photographed, most talked-about, and, generally most celebrated women in the world, a status that owed almost everything to her husband. It's unlikely that Fuller would have been so enthusiastic about her return to his stable if she had not brought with her such a sumptuous gift.

If the alignment with 19 Management said much about Victoria's intentions, it said even more about her husband's. Fuller's knowledge of the football business may have been slight compared to that of Stephens and Holmes, but he knew about popular music, commercials and fashion and, as David Thomas pointed out in his story "Three-minute wonder": "Beckham ... is not so much part of the football world as of the fashion, hair-gel, computer game and pin-up world – and that's something Fuller does understand" (*Independent*, 12 November 2003, p. 23).

At the age of 61, Pelé signed a deal with Pfizer to endorse Viagra. He neglected to say whether he personally used the drug. You might imagine that enlightened consumers would have been curious. There again, you might also imagine that they'd figured out that the celebrities who publicly pronounce their allegiance to a product do so not out of brand loyalty or because they honestly believe the product in question is the best on the market or because they use it. They do it for money. The fact is: consumers don't seem to mind.

Perhaps they're enticed by what Robin Andersen, in her book *Consumer Culture and TV Programming*, calls "a sense of group membership, but membership earned through commodity consumption" (p. 120). Using the same products as the celebs makes them members of the same clique. Even if this is an imaginary clique, the arrangement still moves products off shelves and keeps advertisers alert to the power of certain figures in the public domain.

We don't buy commodities because we need them, of course. We buy them for all sorts of other reasons, like to project a certain image of ourselves, to align ourselves with like-minded others, to remind ourselves who we are and who we'd like to be. "What does your mobile phone say about you?" read the tagline of one advertising campaign. In short, our motivation is much more to do with aspirations and wants than needs. All of which sets up an interesting challenge for advertisers wanting to grab our attention and money. It also sets up a lucrative sideline for any celebrity who can somehow energize our desires.

For Beckham and, perhaps, an elite group of other athletes around the world, earnings from endorsements can, in any given year, dwarf earnings derived from competition, in Beckham's case his salary. His endorsement portfolio is valued in dozens of millions. While most other celebrity footballers remain outside Beckham's league in earnings capacity, most have some sort of deal that provides extra income; which is why the first thing an athlete looks for when he or she signs an agreement with an agent is an endorsement deal.

The Sara Lee Corporation sensed the commercial potential of Beckham in 1997 when it signed him to endorse its hair care product, Brylcreem, and, later, initiated the Brylcreem David Beckham Soccer Academy. The links between Brylcreem and football date back to the 1940s when Arsenal player (and Middlesex cricketer) Denis Compton became the "Brylcreem Boy". Now Beckham was granted the title.

Brylcreem's sales had slumped from the 1960s, when young men turned away from hair preparations; later generations favoured gel rather than cream. Brylcreem's market image was summed up in research by the Sponsorship Research Company: "greasy old man". The US company Sara Lee bought Brylcreem in 1993 and prepared for market war with the likes of Shockwaves and Studioline. Its target market was 15–16-year-old boys. Beckham, then 22, kept his hair groomed without being too kempt (perhaps habits learned from his hairdresser mother). He'd drawn much attention to himself after his outrageous goal against Wimbledon the previous year. He was also the England Under-21 captain and in the process of becoming a full international player. So his profile was decently high, though still a long way off its zenith.

Basically, visuals of Beckham appeared in Brylcreem's tv and press advertisements and information about him was included in a brochure, which also had copy about Brylcreem's styling products. This accompanied samples of the products, which were distributed in schools. Also in the sampling bag was a competition entry form for those who wished to attend the Brylcreem David Beckham Soccer Academy. The contract was worth about £1 million to Beckham, according to some estimates; only £200,000 according to others.

While Brylcreem was no doubt dismayed initially when Beckham sheared off his hair, the constant references to his Brylcreem deal, if only in irony, would have strengthened the brand's link with sport and enhanced its recognition. There was also a bonus: his companionship with Victoria Adams, then at the height of her renown with the Spice Girls. They met in March 1997 and he proposed in January 1998. The Beckham promotion yielded results: according to Brylcreem, sales increased by 8.5 per cent year-on-year up to June 1999, justifying a further deal, this time worth £4 million. Beckham's endorsement credentials were established.

Over the next several years, Beckham became something of an industry in his own right; both producer and product. He effectively turned himself into a perfect commodity that could be bought and sold just like any other article of trade. As we know, footballers are not usually the kind of people who feel obliged to dispense of themselves to their fans for nothing, or politely invite them into their worlds. Their attitude seems to be that, if fans really want images of them on their walls, tee-shirts or duvet covers, or if they want the products they endorse, then they'll just have to pay extra for them – unless, of course, they shop down at the market, where there's all manner of unlicensed and unauthorized property ("knockoffs"). When celebs trade their image, they negotiate the best possible price they can.

There's no doubt Beckham's image became valuable property. We're not talking about a faithful reflection of him, here: the Beckham image, in this sense, is a public product, an external appearance or a commercial identity that's constructed for the express purpose of making money. The Brylcreem deal paved the way for a sequence of other endorsement deals. While endorsements are conventionally seen as one way, with the celebrity taking money in return for lending his or her name and image to a product, they are, in many respects, reciprocal – the endorser and product feed off each other. In Beckham's chosen portmanteau, there are products that have not simply benefited from their association with him; they have actually enhanced Beckham's image, adding even greater value to his brand and boosting his cultural stock still further.

There isn't a secret to this: Beckham has an entire industry devoted to cultivating a particular public image. This involves selecting only endorsement deals that involve products befitting the image. "He's a very keen custodian of his self image, or brand", is the conclusion of James Scalpello, the marketing director of Rage, a software company that enlisted Beckham to develop a range of games bearing his name and image. "Although this [the image featured in the games] is new, it's in keeping with the look that he's been nurturing over the years", he told *The Marketeer*. The three-year exclusive agreement, beginning in November 2001, between Beckham, his agents and Rage was worth over £1 million to Beckham, who received royalties for every game sold plus an initial payment.

The "look" referred to Beckham's cultivation of a distinct, recognizable image. In this instance, a portal was positioned in Beckham's cranium and his eyes were those of an android rather than a human being. Previous commercial images of him were less abstract, but consistent with the portrayal.

Beckham was what we might call an aspirational endorser, always looking for a deal that would add to his value as much as he added to its. In 1997, with the Brylcreem campaign gaining momentum, *Sunday Times* writer Lesley White mentioned to him during an interview that she was soon to visit Miuccia Prada in Milan. "Tell her I'd love to do a deal", Beckham joked, though with too much seriousness to be dismissed. Football and fashion, as White pointed out, "are more symbiotic than ever, with magazine spreads on 'footie-chic', players on catwalks, Jasper Conran designing the Leyton Orient strip" (24 August 1997). Beckham's next two endorsements were germane to sport.

A deal with Sondico to wear its shinpads and with adidas to promote its Predator football shoe. How Zinedine Zidane's modelling contract with Christian Dior must have stirred *jalousie de métier*.

———

By 1998, Beckham had announced his engagement and had cultivated a public profile, persuading adidas to offer him a contract worth about £1 million per year. As endorsement contracts go, this was decent – adidas's deal with Tim Henman was worth £750,000 a year – though a long way short of the seriously big deals. Various reports have suggested that Beckham's England colleagues Ryan Giggs (£6.5 million: Reebok) and Michael Owen (£5 million: Umbro) have remunerative tie-ups, but the specifics of these deals are not known. In global terms, Tiger Woods has a multifaceted deal with Nike that earned him $100 million (£70 million) over five years; and Venus Williams had a three-year deal with Reebok worth $40 million (£28 million). But the deal that established the template for all subsequent athlete/sports manufacturer tie-ups and the one that no one, not even Beckham, has yet come close to emulating was, of course, the Michael Jordan/Nike liaison. So important and influential was this deal that it's worth taking a detour to discuss it in detail.

By the time he signed his endorsement deal in 1985, Jordan was already an Olympic gold medallist (in the days when the US sent amateur basketball players, not "dream teams") and had left the University of North Carolina in his junior (third) year to sign for Chicago Bulls in a deal worth $3 million. Both adidas and Converse were interested in doing business, though Jordan eventually signed with Nike in what was then a groundbreaking arrangement. Jordan received a guaranteed minimum plus a percentage of every piece of endorsed apparel or footwear sold. Not just products bearing his name, but all those in Nike's Air range. In the following year, Nike upped its advertising budget from $231 million to $281 million (almost 22 per cent). It seemed like manic profligacy; but the sales justified it. The first year's sales of Nike's Air Jordan range hit $130 million. And, as if to underline the importance of Jordan's tv presence, sales dropped off in the second year when Jordan missed 62 games through injury. Jordan was effectively advertising Nike every time he stepped onto the court.

Nike became brand leader thanks to Jordan. But Jordan took from Nike much more than money. "It was Nike's commercials that made Jordan a global superstar", writes Naomi Klein in her *No Logo* (p. 52). There had been other gifted athletes before Jordan, but none reached what Klein calls "Jordan's other-worldly level of fame". Pre-Nike, sports stars, no matter how great, were athletes who happened to do commercials. They weren't synonymous with a brand, as Jordan was. Nike changed all that, creating lavish tv commercials that became the measure by which others were to be judged. Nike embarked on what Klein calls "mythmaking", establishing an aura around Jordan. "Who said man wasn't meant to fly?" one of the ads asked, showing the gravity-defying Jordan in mid-air. It was almost possible to believe Jordan was actually capable of the unbelievable feats he performed in the commercials. No one's suggesting that Jordan wasn't great, perhaps the best basketball player ever. But, he wouldn't have been a global icon without Nike.

Then again, Nike wouldn't be the market leader without Jordan. In the June 1998 issue of *Fortune* magazine, Roy Johnson analysed what he called "The Jordan effect" which described MJ's impact on the overall economy of the USA. Nike developed a line of footwear and apparel called Air Jordan and, over the 1990s, it was worth, in terms of sales, $5.2 billion, or almost €6 billion. Once you consider those kinds of figures, you begin to understand why the likes of Nike and adidas treasure their endorsers so much: €6 billion would buy you Manchester United, Real Madrid and four or five other top-flight clubs.

adidas's roster of celebrity athletes is almost like a company's capital assets. Since Nike scythed through the market in the 1980s, sports goods manufacturers have been locked in bitter competition to sign the world's leading athletes. It's logical, then, that, once under contract, the corporations take very good care to protect and enhance their assets; in effect, to manage the public image of their charges. Having signed Beckham, adidas arranged for another sector of commerce to be added to his image-production industry. Alan Edwards was familiar with showbusiness pr, having worked as a publicist for the Spice Girls and a media representative of David Bowie. His company, the Outside Organization, had a diversity of interests, including nightclubs, fashion houses and a list of clients that included the likes of Elton John and Boyzone. Edwards was appointed to represent Beckham, his fee for this being paid, interestingly, by adidas. "He handles anything to do with the press for me and David", is how Victoria Beckham described Edwards's role, in her autobiography *Learning to Fly*. As we saw earlier in this chapter, the idea of fusing their commercial interests was to resurface later with the appointment of Fuller.

Edwards pointed out to *FourFourTwo* writer Mark Hodkinson: "In America, whether it be baseball or football, it isn't uncommon to have a team of people around a sports star" (December 2000, p. 54). The appointment signalled Beckham's passage from athlete to all-purpose celebrity and his arrival at this status brought with it a control of his image worthy of Hollywood. As a comparison, let me quote Thomas Harris, who, in his study "The Building of Popular Images: Grace Kelly and Marilyn Monroe" (first published in 1957) noticed that: "The two techniques most frequently used to enhance the Kelly image were (1) an emphasis on her family's adherence to the good life, particularly the drama of her father's achievements in sport and business, and (2) the use of quotes from her co-stars about her off-screen lady-like qualities" (p. 42).

Similarly, two techniques surfaced in Beckham's public image from about 1998. One was rather like Kelly's first: Beckham's commitment to a clean and wholesome life deepened progressively as he became a father, then a husband, dutiful, constant and devout; his ire when a tabloid reported his interest in another woman underlined this. Another revolved around his achievements. Whereas some athletes are portrayed as being in possession of unique qualities available to only the chosen few, Beckham is projected as a model of industry, a mortal who has worked harder and longer at refining his skills and applied them with a diligence that could, in theory, be replicated by anybody. These properties of his image were, in a sense, outgrowths of his "real" self, but they were important in revealing him as earthly rather than completely out-of-this-world. Part of Beckham's fascination lies in the recognition that, yes, he is extraordinary, but, no, he isn't so indescribably, incomprehensibly extraordinary that he lies beyond the imagination – like, say, Madonna; no one could imagine actually being like her. Everyone can imagine becoming like Beckham. After all, he wasn't born a golden child. He was sort of gilded by endeavour.

As we have seen, Beckham's value to adidas was always limited by his affiliation with Manchester United. But, immediately after he moved to Real Madrid, a club that has a contract with adidas, all the promotional shots of Beckham featured him in an adidas shirt. He also appeared in the advertising for a line of winter leisurewear and a sportswear range. There was suddenly a symmetry that had been absent when he played for United. It was as if adidas had been freed from the embarrassment of having the world's premier sport celeb under contract, yet being unable to use him to full advantage. There is a significant difference between Jordan's worth to Nike and Beckham's to adidas: Beckham's impact on the largest, richest market in the world is negligible. Jordan was big everywhere. Beckham is big everywhere except the USA. Of course, the rest of the world is still a huge market and with the economies of the less developed countries set to grow, adidas will still reap considerable benefit. Beckham's original contract with adidas was signed in 1998 and was reputed to be worth between £5 and £6 million (or about €8 million), spread over six years. Jordan's arrangement with Nike changed over the years, starting with a $1 million contract and ending with a share of the profits. Roy Johnson estimates Jordan's typical endorsement contract in the 1990s to be worth between $2 million and $5 million.

The adidas contract is the jewel in Beckham's crown: it will, over time, be the most valuable of his already formidable collection of endorsement deals. Often seen as supplementary sources of income for athletes and other celebs, they are actually much more: they are methods of positioning figures in the market. Often, a celebrity who might otherwise remain unknown or fade in the public memory can maintain a presence by virtue of appearing in popular advertising campaigns. Who would know Gary Lineker had he not featured in Walkers crisps advertising campaigns? It's easy to imagine how he might have been fondly remembered as a fine England player, but would BBC television have been so eager to use the likeable if slightly gauche Lineker as an anchor had his profile not been raised by the popular tv commercials? Possibly. But the ads helped.

Beckham's collection of endorsement deals ensured that his image would be evident literally everywhere in the world. In the event that he suffers a lapse in athletic form, or a long-term injury that keeps him off the competitive field, he will still prevail, if only because his image will continue to beam out of screens and publications. Besides Brylcreem, which got the process started, and adidas, there are other products that have exploited (and I mean in the sense of using for one's own ends, rather than in a derogatory sense) Beckham's image, mainly though not always to great effect.

———

Michael Jackson and Britney Spears are not short of money (at least, Britney definitely isn't). They have no need to do endorsements. Yet they both signed eight-figure sum deals to endorse Pepsi. Why? Because it's almost an honour to be approached to feature in a Pepsi campaign. The Spice Girls didn't hesitate when they were approached (although they didn't seem to hesitate about endorsing any product).

Beckham became one of the elect in 2000, when he signed to do a series of Pepsi commercials, along with fellow football luminaries, Roberto Carlos, Edgar Davids, Raul, Juan Sebastian Veron and elite others. Beckham's contract was worth £2 million. In terms of inventiveness, the tv commercials, which were shown around the world, were right up there with Nike's. In one, a game of table football between Beckham and Davids becomes a surrealistic encounter worthy of Dalí, the players on sticks transmogrifying into real players. In another, Beckham et al. take on a team of Sumo wrestlers at football. Beckham is shown in yet another traipsing off the field of play, presumably having been substituted; as he enters the tunnel, he asks a young boy for a swig of Pepsi, after which the boy appeals for his shirt. Obliging as ever,

Figure 11 Few doubted that, when Beckham was awarded the OBE in 2003, he was not only the most celebrated Brit on earth but had also inherited Michael Jordan's mantle as the world's premier sports celebrity.
Source: Rex Features

Beckham removes his shirt and hands it to the boy who discards it after wiping the top of the Pepsi can. Viewers are reminded that greatness and humility are not incompatible.

Pepsi was behind another humbling experience, though, this time, unscripted. In 2001, Beckham, along with fellow Pepsi endorsers, Rui Costa, Rivaldo, Dwight Yorke and the previously mentioned Carlos and Veron, took part in the inaugural Pepsi Challenge, which tested players' ball skills, like dribbling, shooting and juggling. The virtual unknown, Hazem Emam, of the Egyptian club, Zamalek, unexpectedly won the competition. Worse: Beckham was beaten into third place, the runner-up being Nguyen Hong Son, a player for the Vietnam army.

Beckham was initially selective in the way he allowed his image to be reproduced; and for sound business reasons. Were he, for example, to promote a product that seemed out-of-sync, such as a kitchen cleaner or a beer, it would damage the carefully managed image. But Police Eyewear was ideal: the products screamed with éclat. Beckham fronted Police's British campaign in 2001 for a fee of £1 million. The following year De Rigo, the maker of Police Eyewear, renewed his contract, this time for £3 million. How can the company justify offering such a sum? Silvia Nanni, the managing director of Police, explained it simply to the *Sunday People* newspaper: "The impact he had on last year's [2001's] sales was incredibly strong – we more than doubled the figures for Police sunglasses ... and this is due in no small part to David" (17 February 2002).

Marks & Spencer must have hoped that Beckham could work the oracle for its unhealthy sales. As part of its comeback following the collapse of its share price in 2001, M&S recruited Beckham to help design and lend his image to a range of clothes created by a new company, Zip Project Ltd., which targeted 6–14-year-olds. Beckham's image was, in many ways, the antithesis of M&S's: the retailer's decline was, at least, partly attributable to its reputation for being sombre if not downright fusty. By aligning itself with Beckham, M&S presumably hoped to belie this reputation and were prepared to pay £1 million to do so.

The deal appeared to turn sour when Beckham moved to Real Madrid and swapped his number 7 shirt for 23 (Jordan's number with the Bulls). Presumably, M&S had thought he would either stay at Manchester United for ever (or at least till the end of his contract with them) or take his number with him wherever he went. They had named their range DB7.

When Vodafone entered into a sponsorship agreement with Manchester United, its agenda was barely hidden: having its logo slapped across the United shirts was one thing, but having access to the Beckham image was another. Beckham signed his own separate deal with Vodafone in 2002, which involved his appearance in tv commercials, posters and point-of-sale material. Beckham picked up £2 million for his labours.

When celebrities acquire a global profile, they tend to be choosy about where it is shown. For instance, Asians and Europeans saw Madonna in Max Factor ads; Americans were shielded from the sight. Beckham had already generated a following in Japan prior to his appearances there in the 2002 World Cup finals. But his physical presence served to bolster his popularity and, over the succeeding months, he eclipsed the likes of Leonardo diCaprio. All the same, the excitement elicited by his arrival in Tokyo in the spring of 2003 is harder to understand. During the hectic summer of 2003, Beckham and his wife arranged a promotional ten-day tour of Japan. They had failed to make much impact in the USA but were on more certain territory in East Asia where football aficionados knew all about Beckham and his wife. The brief was unusual: get as much money as possible. Unusual, that is, for Beckham, who usually picked the products he endorsed in a way that complemented, or at least didn't hurt his image. With the Spice Girls, Victoria had seen at first hand how allowing your name to become associated with literally anything can lead to short-term monetary gain, but long-term loss of credibility. So there was some surprise when Beckham and his wife appeared in ads for the Tokyo Beauty Centre and Meiji chocolates as well as a used car dealer, the Japanese equivalent of Reg Vardy. In East Asia, Beckham also cropped up in ads for BP Castrol motor oil, a respectable enough product, though not one readily associated with the A-list. Perhaps the decision was based on the notoriously capricious market: fans go hysterical over people one year and forget them the next. So the tactic was one of grab the money while it's there: £10 million of it was there.

There are perils. Beckham's contract with Pepsi drew criticism when it was pointed out that he was endorsing a product that was harmful to children's teeth. Pepsi itself was embarrassed when, in an unguarded moment, Britney Spears was caught drinking Coca-Cola. Pepsi had paid her $75 million for her endorsement. Martina Hingis may have endorsed Sergio Tacchini shoes and received $5.6 million for her trouble, but this didn't stop her suing the sports manufacturer for $40 million after alleging the shoes injured her feet. Steve Redgrave appeared with Lineker in ads for crisps, a snack high in fat, while at the same time endorsing Flora Pro-Active spread, which was pitched at the health-conscious consumer. Shane Warne was photographed smoking after fronting ads for Nicorette gum. Endorsers risk being seen as exactly what they are: pieces of merchandise that are sold to the highest bidder. All but the most naive consumers already know this, of course: they just don't like their faces rubbed in it.

Much as an endorsement can bring to life a symbiotic relationship in which both parties draw life from each other, it can also bring grief. Athletes who get suspended after doping violations are a classic case: the products they endorse suffer by association. Beckham is about as bankable as a celeb gets: his demographics are wider than most and his apparent commitment to a clean and wholesome lifestyle endears him to many. His benefits are multiple: as well as clawing in the millions, he gains worldwide exposure, guaranteeing that no one has escaped at least a fleeting glimpse of his image.

One question remains: despite all the claims of increases in sales, do endorsements actually work? Common sense tells us that advertisers wouldn't spend gargantuan amounts on securing the services of "brand spokespersons" unless they drew tangible returns. On Beckham's balance sheet, Brylcreem and Police reported sales growth, while Rage sales contracted during his campaigns. In his book *Advertising and Popular Culture*, Jib Fowles quotes a study conducted shortly after the 1991 Super Bowl. An impressive 70 per cent of a sample of the television audience interviewed recalled that Joe Montana, the former NFL quarterback, had appeared in a commercial during the game; but only 18 per cent remembered that the product he had endorsed was Diet Pepsi, prompting the question of who profited most.

Beckham had few rivals in the commodity stakes. Nobody engendered the intensity of emotion, the flood of passion, the teeming fervour of Beckham. And nobody could move goods off shelves like he could. The two are not unrelated. Affix his name to a product and stand back to watch them fly out of the store. We don't buy the products he endorses simply because we think he uses them. Do you imagine he shops at M&S? Or uses Brylcreem? Do you care if he uses the same oil in his Maserati as you use in your Ford? We buy them because, in doing so, we enter into or enrich a particular kind of relationship – a relationship that has turned Beckham himself into an advertisement, a product, a brand. I mean by this that his sheer presence advertises a version of the good life we should all aspire to. We can approach, though never reach, that good life through buying products and Beckham has been turned into not one but several products, all of which, when bought, can take us that little bit closer to a man who rarely acknowledges our existence. His ability to do this is based on his brand. The name "Beckham" now reverberates around the world: by lending his image to a product, a service or, well, anything at all, he affirms its quality. So, it sells.

ten

MADONNA'S PACT

Here's what *won't* happen to David Beckham. He tells Real Madrid that he's taking off to spend more time out of the limelight. Retreating to an obscure island off the coast of Florida, he rents a cottage and fades from view. He tries to wean himself off a well-disguised heroin habit with methadone and Librium but slides towards another dependency by gulping down vodka and the high-octane Italian liquor Strega. Fans only learn of this after he collapses in a hotel. They are incredulous, of course. "Not Beckham, surely? Must be someone who looks like him." But not even he looks like Beckham now. His once twelve stone body has shrunk to nine stone and his well-toned flesh has taken on a pallid, waxen appearance.

Then comes the confession. "It got so bad, shaving became a big problem because I had to look at myself in the mirror and I couldn't stand it", he unburdens himself in front of the media personnel who have flocked to the rehab clinic. "I want to get myself back into shape and play football again. I think I still have a few years left."

I repeat: this won't happen to Beckham. In fact, it actually happened to another improbable candidate, Marti Pellow, formerly of Wet, Wet, Wet, who did, in fact, make a successful comeback. His descent from the sweet charmer with the great teeth to a quivering addict was staggering enough. But a similar decline for Beckham is simply beyond belief.

Beckham's position as a "role model" was often invoked to explain his soaring popularity in the early twenty-first century. He embodied solid family values, loved his wife and kids and generally set a good example for young people. If we assume that a role model is a figure people admire, identify with and seek to emulate, then Beckham might well be exactly that. Most footballers are not: they are young, well-paid men who are told to be single-mindedly dedicated to winning on the pitch. That's all. In view of the fact that most of them have been signed to professional teams since the age of 14 or 15, kept in a highly structured and sheltered environment thereafter and never exposed to such mundane activities as signing cheques or applying for a mortgage, they are the least qualified people to dispense advice to anybody on how to conduct themselves in the real world.

Beckham, though, is different. How do we know? Because we can read him like an open book – we think. Or is he one that's been slammed shut, fastened with one of those locks used to secure private diaries and hidden under a pillow? Sometimes he seems completely transparent. At other times, he's positively inscrutable. That's part of the fascination, of course: knowing yet not knowing for certain, reading yet never quite being sure whether you've figured out the right meaning.

The thing about celebrities is that we think we know them. Actually, we know about three or four key things about them and that's all. About minor celebs, we know even less; just one thing in some cases. Take Jade Goody, the one from *Big Brother* with the big mouth. Or Major Charles Ingram, who "won" *Who Wants to be a Millionaire?* with the help of some judicious coughing. That's all we know about them and maybe all we wish to know. If they were books, we'd skip to the 300th page and read the *dénouement*. But with the likes of Beckham, we want to pore over every page, squinting to see if we can read between the lines.

In his book *Claims to Fame*, Joshua Gamson argues that we've all become practised "readers", with the celebrities and the various stages on which they appear being "texts" that can be encoded and decoded. Texts, in this sense, are not pages full of words or books prescribed for study, but literally anything from which we can take meaning. If it's intelligible to us, it's text. We can make sense of a movie, a tv programme, a rock concert, a football game, a celebrity, even a personal experience; they're all texts.

Gamson's point is that we've become well-read, enlightened by decades of exposure to what was once known as the star system. In more recent years, skilled readers of celebrity texts have demanded more material and been rewarded with a media keyed to providing insider information, not just prurient information, but anything that contributes to the consumers' understanding. Feeding this kind of information into the public domain is part of celebrity production process. Gone are the days when celebrities could isolate themselves in the manner of Greta Garbo or Howard Hughes and expect a fandom to remain fascinated. Fans would now turn to different celebs, who may sustain a similar image of inaccessibility, but who, in fact, have a pr operation responsible for deliberately allowing seepage. Even today, too much information and fans will soon be satiated and grow bored; too little and their interest will wane. Put another way: the text needs to be refreshed occasionally, if only to give fans something new to interpret. In this sense, the Beckham text is little different from the several hundred, perhaps thousands, of other texts that occupy our attention. Still, the suspicion lingers: there *is* something different about Beckham.

Beckham is unreachable in a physical sense. Often distant, occasionally withdrawn, unapproachable by all but an inner circle. Football fans get to see him on match days. Others have to content themselves with his image on television, the internet, in magazines, newspapers or on posters or packaging. Of course, they're rarely short of information: his every move is closely monitored and evaluated and his own pr operations ensure that the dragon of public interest is fed regularly. Yet, the information provided is often about Beckham's image rather than Beckham the man. The inspiration behind a new haircut, the reasons for favouring a certain label jeans, how Brooklyn is progressing at his new school ("alright"): this is the kind of fare on offer.

It would have been unthinkable for Beckham to announce, for example, an opposition to the military attack on Iraq in 2003 or for him to declare an allegiance to Greenpeace or Animal Rights, or sympathy with striking dockers – as Robbie Fowler once did. Certainly, not in a way that could be spilt into public discourse. Yet, those are precisely the kinds of issue that elevated Muhammad Ali not only to prominence but to iconic status. Other athletes have expressed views and opinions, aligned themselves with causes, and protested against what they believed to be injustices. Not only Ali, but Maradona and, most notoriously, Tommie Smith, among many others, used their status as a platform from which to make proclamations on a variety of global issues. Beckham does nothing of the sort. It's this social and political inertia that makes him the all-purpose commodity. He does nothing, nothing at all to disabuse fans of their beliefs about him. Nowadays, an athlete making such pronouncements would be instantly condemned – as was Ali initially, we should remember – and probably ignored – Ali wasn't, of course. The blueprint for Beckham seems much closer to Michael Jordan's, which we looked at in the previous chapter. Hear no evil ...

There's no single, definitive Beckham text that everyone reads in the same way. Rather, there are many, many different Beckhams, all given different interpretations by a motley fandom that draws fulfilment of some sort from its supplication. Think about it: Beckham himself plays football and not much more. He resists making not only controversial comments, but also any kind of comment of depth. He has no known political affiliations, shows no preference for social causes, expresses no views on world affairs and speaks infrequently to the media and then only on matters of football. What the world knows of him is largely based on printed and screen images: we know what kinds of body ornamentation he likes, we can discern his taste in clothes and, of course, we realize he's a family man. At the same time, he doesn't mind posing in a way that is liable to be seen by gay males as rentboyish, as we noticed in chapter eight. This may make him appear a blank page; but, of course, anything can be written on a blank page. There are as many Beckham texts as there as readers.

It's the very absence of definite content in the text that makes it so gratifying. Fans can read into Beckham whatever they want.

I suggested that there was a David Beckham that existed independently of time and space and resided in the imaginations of his fans. In other words, there are multiple Beckham texts, all interpreted in particular ways by fans, most of whom may have little interest in sport but all of whom are gratified in some way by following Beckham. Some celebs issue singular messages about themselves. Tom Cruise, for instance, talks openly about his spiritual beliefs, his marriages, even his sexuality. His actions sometimes betray his beliefs. Cruise marshalled the full might of his legal team to quash an internet-circulated report that he had featured in a gay relationship. Other celebrity actors may not have felt such a rumour to be so repugnant. *Pop Idol* winner Will Young, for example, announced that he was gay within a week of reaching the number one spot in the singles charts.

Beckham wouldn't countenance any kind of revelation. In fact, even the mention that he might disclose personal secrets for a tv show prompted him and his wife to file suit against the publication that suggested it. Not only doesn't he reveal: he doesn't allow others to insinuate he does. Even this, though, becomes futile. "I can't sue", he once told *The Times*, "or I would end up doing it every day." So, the stories continue to go around.

Beckham is open but blank. He lets his fans decode whatever messages emit from either himself or his pr operation. A single photograph will have consumers scanning it contemplatively. In 2000, for instance, I had a series of calls from excited journalists who had just seen a new still of Beckham's back adorned with a fresh tattoo. The journalists sought an "expert" interpretation of the tattoo. "What does it mean?" they asked. When the player fashioned his hair into a mohican (or mohawk, depending how pedantic you want to be about its genealogy), the media were agog, calling everyone from hairdressers to anthropologists to ascertain its significance. Beckham apparently attributed it to his liking for the do affected by Travis Bickle, the implosive de Niro character in Martin Scorsese's *Taxi Driver*. There was one puzzling rumour about falcons. Somehow an untrue story that Beckham was about to buy a bird began to circulate, prompting fans to wonder what the significance of falcons could be. Beckham asked a falconry firm to deny that he was going to buy one of its birds.

Being an all-purpose celebrity athlete for the twenty-first century, Beckham is under no obligation to do or say anything at all. He needs only to engage in *being* David Beckham. The fandom, his audience – consumers – do the rest: that is, the creative work of making a customized icon, something that holds meaning for them, perhaps them alone. As Hornby's fictional, though opaquely autobiographical, character in *Fever Pitch* reminds us, Arsenal is *his* club and the players his "representatives". The players, in fact all players, and all celebrities are only delegates of fans; they do not have unqualified power because it is always conditional on consumers. If fans turn against them, or, even worse, lose interest, the consequences can be fatal.

There may be a Beckham who pulls on a football shirt and plays for his team, but the other Beckham is the product of the fans, the meanings they attribute to him, the fantasies they spin around him, whatever they read in him. They own this Beckham.

———

Sometime after the infamous Red Card incident of 1998, Beckham was opening his correspondence, a mixture of missives, some adoring, others full of bile. The malicious letters were counterparts to the chants that issued from some sections of the stadium whenever Manchester United played. Crude dirges about Posh's sexual propensities had been replaced by open expressions that the Beckham's young son would die with cancer. Riffling through the mail, Beckham came across an envelope containing what might have been an earring, brooch or some similar token. It was a bullet with his initials carved in it. "The note said there was another on the way for Brooklyn [his boy]."

Later, talk of a kidnap plot put the Beckham family on alert, though, in common with many other DB-related stories, this one had no foundation. Still, the family stepped up security and began to encase itself in a protective shield of bodyguards when stepping out in public. Even a walk on the beach with the kids became a group event.

BIG © B|G PICTURES © BIG PICTURES © B|G PICTURES
SCOTLAND No 3, 12 Piershill Square West, Edinburgh EH8 7BA
Tel: 0131 661 1515 E-mail: scotland@bigpictures.co.uk
Byline must read bigpicturesphoto.com
Failure to comply with this request will incur a charge of double
the usage fee in accord with big pictures terms and conditions

Figure 12   A quiet stroll along the beach for father and son becomes a quasi-military operation, with protective guardians surrounding Beckham and Brooklyn.
Source: Big Pictures

Unwelcome admirers, or idolaters, have become almost commonplace for Beckham. At some point, celebrity status is something over which he, or any other recipient, has little control. Once you have it foisted on you, your life ceases to be private property. Occasionally, parts of it can be regained. Amanda Holden and Naomi Campbell both went belligerently to court, indignant that the media had disclosed areas of their lives they wanted left classified. There's no small irony in the spectacle of celebrities for whom media exposure is indispensable not just snarling at, but biting off the hand that feeds them. And yet, they continue to crave publicity. Once you have either achieved celebrity status or had one thrust upon you, the fans take over. Abetted by the media, they become the ones who are able to affect the shape and progress of a person's life.

Despite the carpings of Campbell, Holden and any number of other public figures, this is only right and just. It's a combination of fans and media that conferred celebrity status on them at the start. Once they have that status, they enjoy the plentiful fruits that go with it. So why shouldn't fans assert their limited individual, but potentially great, collective power?

Sometimes this takes a bizarre turn. *Coronation Street* watchers took to the streets in protest at Deirdre Rachid's wrongful imprisonment. I guess their motivations were similar to the ones that guide many newspaper readers to the horoscope page where they read about what fortunes will befall them. "Oh, I know it's all nonsense, but I like reading it anyway", they might reply when confronted with proof that horoscopes are unreliable, inaccurate and based more on superstition than science. They know that, but they still enjoy reading them. Deirdre's fans presumably know she's just a character in a soap, but, somehow, they manage to balance that in their own minds with the pleasure they take from suspending scepticism.

Few Beckham-followers will believe everything they read or hear about him. Living in the twenty-first century means being privy to the ways in which stardom is built and sustained. Most fans know all about the apparatus that we covered in chapter nine. Today's fans possess some degree of knowledge of how they are manipulated, and in more ways than one. An unsolicited letter addressed to you personally and offering you a pre-approved credit card suggests there are limits to the Data Protection Act and that there's a great deal of information on you circulating in places you have never heard of. Access to this kind of information lends itself to manipulation of one sort or another.

Of course, fans can hardly dispute that there is an actual person called David Beckham, though only the extremely gullible will accept all the lurid and occasionally phantasmagoric exposés of him. But, like many of today's celebrity texts, the Becks text makes available its own encoding processes. For example, when the exclusive photo rights to his wedding were sold to one publication, *OK!*, all the others reported it. Immediately, the contrivance was exposed: no one could fail to understand that they were witnessing a facet of celebrity production. Controlling the distribution of images, then making the control mechanism available for inspection was, in one sense, a soulless piece of status engineering that might have been read as disdain for fans. In another sense, it was an inventive and profitable method of ensuring compound publicity: stories about the wedding compounded by stories about stories about the wedding. Fans can't fail to be aware of such publicity-multiplying devices, yet it doesn't mean they will be less engaged in reading the text. In fact, it may well enhance the reading. With a different celebrity text, the result may be different.

Anthea Turner is, or perhaps was, one of those celebrities who triggers the question, "Why are they famous?" Their faces and exploits have run on self-perpetuating energy so that the celebrity is just known for being known. Not an uncommon situation, of course. One of the secrets of maintaining celebrity status for those who fall into this group is never to induce consumers to reflect too deeply. Whereas a figure like Beckham has a ready-made answer to "Why is he famous?" many other celebs don't. Turner didn't. When her manoeuvring of the media in such a way as to publicize not only herself but also her commercial sponsors became known, her celeb stock plunged. She discovered that, while the media are flexible in their use, they rarely stand for being callously and brazenly abused by celebs.

Celebrities who sting the media into such retaliation and who have little of substance to back up their claims to fame may face humiliation on an Emperor's New Clothes scale. Once exposed as being "famous-for-being-famous", they have nothing with which to fire back. Beckham doesn't fall into this category. He has faced the wrath of the media, but answered back, not with words, but on the football field. While his vilification was nothing like that endured by Mike Tyson, his reply came, like Tyson's, through the expression of talent, ability, aptitude and skill – the things for which he became known in the first place. No doubt, Beckham's fans are well acquainted with the battery of devices he, like other celebrities, employ to sustain a profile.

They are also convinced that his celebrity isn't a mere façade: there's genuine substance behind the public image. "Sport is supposed to be about winners, but increasingly there is a possibility for making a living – or a fortune – as a beautiful loser", Simon Barnes wrote in *The Times* in 2002: "He [Beckham] may make the front pages for a stupid haircut, but he also makes the back page winning football matches" (16 January, p. 56).

Here's an important perception in understanding how Beckham's fandom differs from that of other celebrities, whether from sport, entertainment, fashion or elsewhere. He has an additional resource in the public's recognition that he can play football in an uncommon way. Unlike actors or other types of entertainer, who have scripts, props, cameras and a battery of aides, Beckham participates in live, unpredictable competition, assisted only by his teammates. What he does on the field of play is no mirage. He has what David Andrews and Steven Jackson, in the introduction to their book *Sport Stars*, call the "important veneer of authenticity" that distinguishes him from "celebrities drawn from other, more explicitly manufactured, cultural realms" (p. 8).

This is why Beckham's special status upholds itself while revealing elements of its own manufacture. It's as if fans are ready to accept that myth-making and image-management are obligatory in contemporary culture, but that, beyond these, there is a real Beckham, who may at times contradict manufactured versions. Intermittent glimpses of a careless, unstudied character who loses his temper or defiantly jabs a "swivel-on-it" finger to scornful fans confirms this as utterly as the skilful ball player with the sweet right foot.

Few of today's celebrities remain attached to the activity for which they first became famous; and, as I've noted, some became famous without performing any activity at all. In a way, celebrity demands some kind of detachment. Athletes, at the very least, need to do endorsements; rock stars need well-publicized love lives; movie stars need to declare a political, religious or some other form of commitment worthy of exposure. These can run in parallel, or one can supersede the other. Beckham is somewhat different: he hasn't actually pursued any activity that even begins to threaten to supplant sport. He's modelled clothes and accessories, but sparingly. His married life is the subject of discourse, but not exactly an activity that could displace playing football in the public eye. Without actually doing anything, he has transcended his sport, while remaining attached to it. His fans have done it for him.

Again, we return to the simple, yet elemental insight about Beckham: by doing and saying virtually nothing, he never falsifies or undermines what others believe of, or impute to him. He can be anything to anyone. This is the source of his endowment. Such is his status that there is a willingness to believe almost anything, even the most preposterous assertions, about him. And yet, we need to remind ourselves that Beckham plays football and little else. His power lies not in what he does, but in how others interpret him, the importance they attach to him, the meanings they take from him, the authority they attribute to him and the approval they lavish on him – the way they read him.

The unique properties thought to be in Beckham's possession are nothing of the sort: they're held by those who read him so avidly. There are those who dote on him, studying every gesture, analysing every utterance, painstakingly chronicling his life. There are others who see him as a god-like creature, as imposing as he is magnificent. Still others are captivated by his physical appearance or his sexuality, in which they discern an ambiguous quality. And others just believe he is a gifted player who is the best around.

Football hooligans, gay pride activists, teenage girls, middle-aged women: the Beckham text seems to have crossed all the traditional boundaries of taste, class, gender – in fact, everything. The readings are literally limitless. Everyone has his or her own reading of Beckham. What's more, they realize they are bit part players in the drama. At another point in history, this realization may have subverted the whole drama. In the twenty-first century, one of its principal effects is to confirm their participation. It's almost like one of those scenes on the early evening tv news when a reporter thrusts a mike into the face of a senior police officer who solemnly endeavours to answer questions, while surrounded by beaming faces, all trying to squeeze into the shot. Unexpectedly, the audience becomes part of the production. That is what is happening in the Beckham phenomenon: his followers have sensed that, great footballer he might be, but they, his fans, are part of his greatness.

Even then, they doubtless underestimate the parts they play in Beckham's celebrity. Yes, he has an agent, a manager, a pr firm and a team of associates who handle his public image. But celebrity production is nothing if not a democratic procedure. Once the fans stop chasing, believing or even caring, the celebrity status disappears. Remember Boy George? His celebrity status disappeared almost overnight when his fans and the media lost interest. His doggedness in clawing his way back was rewarded years later when he was once again celebrated, though not as a singer this time, but as a dj and chat show regular.

Fans themselves may claim that Beckham has charisma, genius and greatness or *je ne sais quoi*. Yet these are merely characteristics they ascribe to him. They may appreciate that they contribute to his fame without fully understanding just how much. There's no irony in this. In fact, it's part of the celebrity's function that he or she should never acknowledge the full extent of his or her reliance on fans. Celebs thank fans and perhaps salute them; they may even claim that "without them, I'm nothing". Though they probably never believe it. It's literally true, however.

The real irony is this: today's fans are canny enough to know more about the celebrity production process than any other generation. Their reading of celebrities is reflexive, in that they know about their own role. What they perhaps don't reflect on is that the power to make or break celebrities is in their hands.

Whether or not Beckham is a charismatic genius touched by greatness isn't my real concern: this book isn't about whether he deserves such a transcendent label. Nor whether his talent is exaggerated. He creates electrifying football on the field; but he too has been created. Created by a fandom, wide and variegated, and infinitely generous in its acclaim. Assisted by a calculating, efficient publicity apparatus, Beckham has been afforded a status beyond the grasp of the merely talented. The kinds of qualities, perhaps gifts, he's thought to possess have propelled him into spheres unknown to previous generations of footballers and even contemporary players of comparable if not greater technical ability.

It sounds curmudgeonly to submit that Beckham hasn't achieved this status. Yet this is exactly what I'm arguing. His extraordinary status is due less to him and what he does, more to what people attribute to him and believe he does. The special "gifts" some think he owns haven't been granted him through divine revelation, as Mozart's were thought to be. We – those who read him and read about him – are the ones who credit him. His playing abilities are beyond question and his accomplishments are undeniable. Attempting to strip away his mystery doesn't involve denying that Beckham has masterly technique and fearless resolve on the football pitch.

The colossal praise and the disproportionate attention he receives may not even be incommensurate with his technical ability. I stress: I'm not disputing his playing skills. My effort is to reveal what makes Beckham different from any other footballer and, I would argue, any other athlete who's ever lived. To do so we need to appreciate that the fans and consumers, who comprise his audience near and far, are active constructors of the Beckham phenomenon.

As we've seen, Beckham employs a formidable assembly of agents, publicists, lawyers, managers and miscellaneous other advisers. These are just the accoutrements of a sport celebrity in the twenty-first century. Their operations bring them into contact with every aspect of what is now a global sport industry. Much of their time is spent cultivating and protecting a particular image and, as such, their work has an industrial quality – it's geared to production, in this case of a certain type of sports celebrity and the various marketable assets that can be procured from that celebrity. Beckham is an individual; for millions, he is an image.

Back to Gamson: in the introduction to *Claims to Fame*, he asks what happens to a celebrity "when image making becomes visible". What happens when the celebrity fairy tale begins to include the story of its own production? One answer might be that consumers would recoil, disgusted at the manipulation if not outright contrivance involved in the production of entertainers. Consumer resistance might trigger a crisis in the entire industry and a cultural cannibalism could follow.

That isn't what happened. *Pop Idol* happened. This was the title of a television series in which cameras scrupulously chronicled a national competition in Britain, designed to select from a pool of several thousand one singer who would fill the criteria of the perfect Pop Idol. For months in 2001/2, television viewers were privy to the competition, the euphoria, the disappointment, the frustration, the bitchiness and, sometimes, the fuming anger. They were exposed, as were the contestants, to the frequently damning evaluations of a panel of industry insiders, some of whom became minor celebs in their own right for their stinging assessments of the competitor's underwhelming lack of ability.

It was a see-thru exercise, viewers serving as bystanders to a blood sport, the strugglers beaten morally and psychologically, winners emerging in self-congratulatory smugness to hug and kiss each other. The tears flowed, in joy and in sorrow. The losers vanished into obscurity. And the capper was this: the market research didn't cost a bean. The nine million viewers who stayed nailed to their tv screens and phoned in with their favoured choice did it for nothing. Actually, they paid for the privilege (calls were charged by BT). It's no coincidence that the series was the brainchild of Simon Fuller.

In an earlier, similarly structured show, *Popstars*, the winners were hastened away to a secret training camp where they were coached in singing, dancing and handling the media ("Don't ever admit you've taken drugs"). Hear'Say was the deliberately (one hopes) misspelled name by which the band was to be known and, within weeks, it was foisted on the exceedingly suspecting public with a single, followed by an album, both breaking sales records. After this, Hear'Say's fortunes plunged. The point had been made though: pop did not so much eat itself as feast grandiosely on its consumers.

Celebrity pop stars are not discovered, at least not in the sense of revealing, making visible or exposing to view. All these connotations suggest that there's something there, some essential talent or gift, to be revealed. They're produced: brought into existence through a series of carefully planned stages. During the process, raw material is refined into something purer, with more value. This is less like a Philosopher's Stone, which turns base metals into gold or silver, and more like an assembly line, like those in any car plant. Traditionally, the trick is to conceal the manufacturing process, allowing consumers to see only the finished products. Discoveries still happen, though in the same way as specialist research and development firms discover medicines for the large pharmaceutical corporations, which retain them for that specific purpose, or smaller oil companies drill virgin territory and sell out to the oil giants if they strike lucky.

In much the same way, the big record companies, in the 1990s, adjusted their a & r approach so as to respond more quickly and flexibly to unexpected changes in cultural tastes. Rap music, in particular, left the conglomerates panting for breath: no sooner had they brought out an album than they found that tastes had moved on. The smaller, independent labels were much more adept at catching the changing moods. Ears to the ground, the indie labels were able to sign artists and producers, turn around quickly and have their products on the streets, while the juggernauts, like Warners and Sony, were still thinking about it. The solution was simple: the corporations signed up the indie labels, gave them creative autonomy, although within limits, and marketed and distributed the records as if they weren't there. An illusion of small-scale individuality, artistic freedom and, indeed, rebelliousness was adroitly preserved, while at the same time, the major corporate players had maintained their grip on the industry. Of the dozen or so rap multimillionaires who had profited from the tie-ups, none felt obliged to advertise the fact that they were, in reality, in the pay of the corporations. So, the illusion of discoveries was preserved and the reality of corporate manufacture continued.

By the turn of the century, the illusion was no longer necessary. Consumerism had accelerated to the point where prospective end users were actively conniving in the production process: they contributed to the manufacture of commodities that they, in turn, consumed. Early evidence of this connivance came in the form of tee shirts bearing the name and logo of the maker, effectively turning the wearer into an ambulant advertisement for the product. Not since the days of the sandwich board men (who walked streets covered in 4 × 3-foot ad-plastered placards, back and front) had humans functioned as such effective advertisements.

Young people in the 1960s wore tee shirts emblazoned with political slogans, witty maxims or the names of bands. But tee shirts became branded space. Wittingly or not, consumers entered an alliance with the likes of adidas and Nike and, later, with the maker of every other type of tee shirt on the market. There was a time when the maker's name was worn discretely as a tiny emblem on the chest of the garment. Consumers would have been embarrassed to wear an article that bore the name of its maker so boldly that everyone could see. By the early 1980s, they were willing to pay for the privilege of wearing a shirt that bore a logo, but might just as well have been furnished with "THEY SAW ME COMING".

Not that this implies that today's consumers are gullible innocents. Anything but: in fact, they are so clued-up about the entire process in which they are being utilized that the process has actively involved them. Nike, for example, invited customers to design their own word or catchphrase which would then be customized into the new shoes they ordered. One prospective buyer's requested phrase "sweat shop" was apparently turned down as inappropriate.

Today's generation is aware that there are production processes geared to capturing their hearts and minds. The worlds of advertising and marketing are not nearly so obscure to them as they were to consumers of, say, fifteen years ago. The generation's pleasure is in knowing it's being used, yet going along with the game. Returning to *Fever Pitch*, the central character – an avid Arsenal fan – reflects: "The club exploits me, disregards my views, and treats me shoddily on occasions." Author Nick Hornby realizes this and deconstructs the apparent contradiction. *"For alarmingly large chunks of an average day, I am a moron"*, he emphasizes. "There is no analysis, or self-awareness, or mental rigour going on at all, because obsessives are denied any kind of perspective on their own passion." It's Hornby's ability to stand outside his own position, coupled with his obsessive one-eyedness, that makes his work a heady mixture of personal reminiscences and sly observations on the changing character of popular culture. The book is, as the author claims, "about the consumption of football, rather than football itself".

Consumers may once have been disillusioned, affronted or tormented by revelations about their own abuse. Now they embrace it. Far from being untutored dupes, they are mindful of the corporate machinery that allows and encourages their blissful participation in the production process. It's this mentality – of being savvy about your own exploitation – that permits the success of a product such as Hear'Say or Will Young. The same mentality provides for the simultaneous admiration, even adoration, of celebrities *and* an awareness of the machine-like processes through which celebrities are manufactured.

———

After the success of her fourth album, *Like a Prayer*, in 1989, Madonna appears to have seen the future: it was a world in which a new type of celebrity would dominate as consummately as dinosaurs dominated the Jurassic world. The days when people got to be famous and stayed that way just through making movies or hit records or writing best-sellers were approaching an end. In their place, there would be celebs. These would be walking, talking people, but, to return to Gamson, texts to be opened for the inspection of anyone who was interested.

Madge not only epitomized this phenomenon, but helped it materialize. She struck a bargain with the media. It was something like this: "I will tell you more, show you more about me than any other rock or movie star in history; I will disclose my personal secrets, share my fears, joys, sorrows, what makes me happy or sad, angry or gratified; I will be completely transparent to you. In return, I want coverage like no other: I want to be omnipresent, ubiquitous, pervasive – I want to be everywhere, all the time." It was a delicious *quid pro quo*. The media went for it; and the age of celebrity was upon us.

As the 1980s turned to the 1990s, Madonna was, as she wanted to be, everywhere. This was surely the meaning of Blonde Ambition, the title of her 1991 tour. The following year, she bared herself in her book *Sex*, accompanied by the album *Erotica*. Being famous was no longer sufficient: to be a celebrity, you had to strip yourself, make consumers privy to as many aspects of your life as you dare. And no one did it better than La Ciccone. Her ineffable rise occurred at exactly the time in history when the old mass media ceded place to a new multimedia, making possible instant communication to anywhere on the planet. New channels proliferated. The problem then became content. With what could you fill them? Channels like MTV and VH1 gave a clue. Music, gossip and what used to pass as "light entertainment." Now, it was lite entertainment.

The beauty of the age of celebrity, though, was that the consumers weren't hapless chumps: they were educated in the arts of celeb-production by the very channels that presented them. Put another way, they didn't just look at the pictures: they were able readers. They did most of the work. All the celebs did was make themselves available. Madonna was the first celebrity to render her manufacture completely transparent. Unabashed about revealing to her fandom evidence of the elaborate and monstrously expensive publicity and marketing processes that went into her videos, cds, stage acts and, indeed, herself, she laid open her promotional props, at the same time exposing her utterly contrived persona changes.

From Material Girl to Monroe *manquée* to vamp to cowgirl, Madonna made no attempt to conceal the artfulness of her constructions. Her 1991 movie *In Bed with Madonna* (renamed *Truth or Dare* for sensitive American audiences), while ostensibly a fly-on-the-wall documentary of the Blonde Ambition tour, was really a study of a maternally warm, generous, though impulsive woman, prone to occasional but understandable bouts of bitchiness, yet with wit and charm enough to win over her doubters. In other words, a study in celebrity management. The risk wasn't that fans might not be taken in by the film;

they obviously wouldn't be. It was that they might feel cheated: learning only what they already knew.

Today, fans may be in awe of celebrities, but they understand that there's an entire industry at work and that they have been co-opted by that industry. The deal is that the fans will remain awed and curious, while the industry discloses more and more about the celebrities.

Transparency is also apparent in movies, especially ones that employ special fx. Often, television documentaries on "The making of ... ", exposing the technologies that helped create fantastical illusions in the films, are shown either prior to or just after the theatre release of the main item. A blatant promotional device, maybe, but part of the new bargain: let the consumers in on the trick. As recently as the late 1970s, fans would be astonished by movies such as *Close Encounters of the Third Kind* or *Alien*, leaving theatres asking "How did they *do* that?" Such wonderment would not be tolerated today. Savvy fans are up to speed on the powers of digitalization and pixels. They want to know exactly how particular fx were achieved and with what consequences.

By the time Beckham surfaced, there was a knowing fandom already well-read and eager to read more about the new text. Of course, it's possible that they never got to glean more information than team Beckham wanted to release. Well, not too much more. The controlled process of filtering data about Beckham into the public domain was occasionally compromised. Paparazzi have a way of spoiling the best-laid plans. But, in the years since the Posh and Becks wedding – itself a tightly controlled event, of course – Beckham's personnel has ensured that only appropriate words and images escape. This is why his fans have become such adept readers. The Beckham text is constantly being revised, modified, updated, abridged, extended, translated, converted and altered in any number of ways, not by him, but by consumers.

They are creating the Beckham phenomenon; not unassisted, of course. But, Beckham is still their creation, as Madonna was the creation of her fans. He's everything and everyone they want him to be, an idealized figure that belongs to them. Effectively, he is a piece of property. Well, not exactly him – his celebrity image, the public aspects of him. For all the efforts of his formidable assembly of aides, the Beckham phenomenon is, by its nature, beyond the control of any individual.

Fans today are not just gullible consumers of celebrity texts, but enlightened readers too. Yet, the trick of today's celebrity culture is in revealing to fans, devotees or just plain consumers their roles in the production, while keeping them distant enough to observe the process. They become party to a manipulation, rather like the characters in Spike Jonze's *Being John Malkovich* who, once in the portal that led to Malkovich's mind, became both puppet and puppeteer at the same time.

We now know so much about how the celebrity industry works, with its slick pr and marketing operations, that you might think the illusion would be destroyed. It doesn't matter, the joy is in knowing this and celebrating its product simultaneously. The beauty of following celebrity athletes or whatever today is that we know that we're part of the process; we recognize that we play a part and, while it's only a tiny part, it means that their status is always conditional on our attention. Ignore them and they cease to exist.

eleven

AN AD, A PRODUCT AND A BRAND

Being David Beckham is expensive. Quite apart from accommodation, which can cost four or five million (two homes, of course), plus running costs (including security staff), and transport, which runs to close to a million (usually about fifteen cars, including a 5.7 litre, 508 bhp, 575M Ferrari Maranello at a little over £155,000), there are clothes to think about. As every public appearance is bound to be inspected, others' expectations have to be met. Typically, Beckham might wear a coat by Prada, at around £2,500, Evisu jeans at £1,500, a Hermès shirt at £250 and Patrick Cox shoes at £350. Then, of course, there are accessories. Never one to shrink from flamboyance, Beckham ornaments himself with a £50,000 diamond-studded Franck Muller watch, diamond cruciform (£40,000) and ear studs (£20,000) by Theo Fennell, and maybe some other trinkets, such as a ring or bracelet for £5,000, from the houses of Asprey, Van Cleef & Arpels or Boodle & Dunthorpe. He even wrapped his newborn son in a Bill Amberg sheepskin sling – promoting the concept of baby-as-fashion-accessory; his wife asked designer Wale Adeyemi to make a mini version of his graffiti-backed jean jacket and jeans for Brooklyn (£87 and £80 respectively). Total, excluding Brooklyn's attire: £119,600 – and that's before he steps out through the front door. Such are the costs of being a celebrity. Living *la dolce vita* is not enough in itself: Beckham, perhaps more than any other celebrity has to be *seen* living it; he has to look the part. This is how tales are constructed; about how Beckham exists in a kind of parallel universe populated only by celebrities, all of whom are different from us.

We like tales about people like Beckham: Them and Us tales in which the They are so richly large, so showily opulent, so untouchably distant that we can never hope to get near, less still join Them. Up till quite recently, celebrities were locked away in the Them camp: they were remote, glamorous figures and being a fan was based on mystery and ignorance. In recent decades, the mass media have not so much reported on the stars as demystified them: secrets are shared with magazines, close-up interviews are featured on television, biographies spare no detail of personal lives. Videos have made it possible for fans to capture moments of an individual's or a team's life for their own delectation. There is now an entire industry geared to selling proximity to celebrities. This is a relatively recent development, traceable to no earlier than the late 1980s when, as we've already seen, Madonna made her historic pact. In one stroke, she changed the rules of engagement with the media. Famous people existed before then, of course, though they weren't celebs – not in the way we understand them today, anyway.

We have what David Giles, in his *Illusions of Immortality*, describes as a *parasocial relationship* with Beckham; which puts it in the same bracket as "relationships formed with mythical beings, say, cartoon figures, or characters in a drama". Giles explains: "These 'relationships' are illusory, however meaning-ful they be ... because they can never be more than unilateral – internal, private relationships affecting only the viewer" (p. 128). Consumers can see images of Beckham on the screen, they can hear him on the occasions he speaks and they can dote on the countless posters and magazine pictures of him that circulate the globe. They can have what Giles calls "meaningful" inter-action in their own eyes, but the relationship is always unilateral – it only works in one direction. Beckham doesn't actually talk directly to his audience; he might abstractly acknowledge its presence and he definitely has a team to answer his fan mail. But, for all he knows, they might be like characters in the Matrix.

There's an example of this in Gurinder Chadha's movie *Bend it Like Beckham*, in which the central character Jess confides in no one, not even her closest friends. Yet Beckham is her oracle: his face graces a poster on her bedroom ceiling and, at night, she lies in bed pouring out her heart to him, as ancient Greeks would once consult their deities for advice or prophecy. (Despite the title, Beckham was not in the film: look-alikes were used to take the parts of him and Victoria.)

These kinds of parasocial relationship – they're called parasocial because *para* means beyond, as in paranormal – are not new. It's always been possible to feel a bond, or some sort of affinity, with people who don't know you exist. Since the advent of television in the 1950s, however, they've become more and more abundant. That medium, in particular, also took them to a new level: it became possible to sustain a parasocial relationship privately, in the intimacy of your own home. The bond might have been made possible only by the light of a cathode ray tube, but, for the consumer, it was significant.

Beckham would just not have been possible without tv. No other piece of technology has contributed towards his status more than television. It brings Beckham into people's homes in a way that is, at once, remote and intimate. In fact, it's impossible to understand the Beckham phenomenon without some grasp of the manner in which the media generally have transformed our lives and, in the process, set up the possibilities for multiple parasocial relationships.

Some people's wishes come true in the most unexpected ways. Think of Howard Brown: winnowed away from a Halifax Building Society branch in Birmingham, he featured in a popular tv commercial campaign, singing, dancing and, in one commercial, flying on a giant digital swan. A real bank worker one minute, Brown became a nationally known figure the next. Other advertisers, like B&Q, have used real employees in ads, but never so centrally, or with such lavish success. Brown found himself an improbable minor celeb, even if only for the duration of the campaign. He was an unwitting celeb sucked into the media tornado. He was one of those individuals who enjoy celebrity status thanks to intense, though short-lived media attention. Successful quiz show contestants (and, occasionally, unsuccessful cheats), big lottery winners, reality tv show members and mistresses of high-profile politicians also fall into this category. Sport is full of them. Who remembers Jimmy Glass, the goalkeeper whose last-minute goal kept Carlisle in the football league? Or Dave Challenor, the long throw-in specialist who contributed to Tranmere's heroic FA Cup run? Or Roy Essendouh, scorer of Wycombe Wanderer's winner in an FA Cup quarter final against Leicester City? All were nationally famous, but not for long.

They wouldn't have been possible until a few years ago. You need a mass media totally geared up to producing, dispensing and, later, exterminating minor short-term celebrities. Before the age of celebrity, Howard Brown couldn't have been created – obviously. Fame can be gathered from all manner of sources. Brown didn't actually do anything grand to become famous; apart from appearing on our tv screens – which is actually all it takes. Not that deeds alone are sufficient to justify renown. Even deep in history, we can find evidence of a primitive celebrity production process.

Alexander the Great was the first truly famous person. At least according to Leo Braudy, whose book *The Frenzy of Renown* is a historical account of fame in which the author shows how the concept of being famous, decorated, even idolized and, in general, celebrated was not only entertained by the Macedonian king, but actually worked-at. As long ago as the third century BCE, Alexander regarded himself as no other human: more a deity or a hero of Homeric legend.

Alexander may be a prototype of The Famous, but he certainly wasn't a celeb (at least, only when played by Leonardo diCaprio or Colin Farrell). All of his efforts at immortality, and indeed those of the many Roman emperors, who vaingloriously followed his example, were aimed at separating himself from his subjects. Such men deliberately flouted legal and moral rules as a way of confirming their extraordinary status: rules applied to humans, not gods. In a similar way, the god-kings of ancient Egypt ordered the building of edifices to commemorate their existences and the European aristocracy of the Middle Ages commissioned portraits of themselves to ensure their posterity. They cultivated the popular conception that their world was not that of ordinary mortals; they were untouchable.

There are, of course, vestiges of this in today's celebrity temple. Behaviour designed to stake out unbridgeable distances between the celeb and Us is commonplace. Mariah Carey's well-publicized aversion to climbing – "I don't do stairs" – taxed tour arrangers trying to secure her appropriate accommodation (one hopes her chastening flop *Glitter* and subsequent expulsion by Sony helped improve her locomotive powers). John Travolta insisted on eight new £300 Armani tee shirts per day during filming. J.-Lo's catalogue of idiosyncratic demands for every appearance was legion. Beckham insists on a new pair of football boots for every game and saves every single pair. One suspects there are no functional reasons for the celebs' mandates, apart from affirming that They are not like Us and so need to be treated differently. For the most part, however, today's celebs, as I've suggested, have been sussed and fans are savvy enough to realize what the game is.

Fame before the age of television was hardly fame as we know it. It was carried largely by word of mouth: stories of great feats and the affectations of great people circulated widely through the various empires and, of course, in Alexander's case the coins and sculptures were reminders. Nor were those who tried to emulate military leaders or sages well known in the way that Hollywood stars were famous in the 1950s and 1960s or even radio stars in the decades before. In the absence of a mass media, there was no dependable, systematic way of sustaining fame. With the print medium came a way of distributing images and stories in a consistent, even routine way. Plus, printing and distribution were quick, making the press topical, current and responsive to change.

The media's saturation coverage of figures created an impression of intimacy, readers eventually gaining such an expertise in the personal lives of subjects that they experienced feelings of closeness that were at once real, yet artificially induced. Paper and magazine stories of people transformed them into public property: readers knew, at least in an abstract way, complete strangers they had never met, and were never likely to meet. This impression of intimacy was to become a crucial ingredient in the making of celebrities. However false the impression might be, the consumer had to believe that he or she knew the celebrity.

The celeb may have been a fully paid-up member of an elite, entry to which was restricted to only the blessed, but the consumers still had a conduit into their lives. Reports of their blemishes, flaws and frailties served as reminders that, gifted as they were, they were flesh-and-blood, not gods. The advent of the media in the late nineteenth century created a new class of celebrity, but exposed them as fragile mortals. It seemed almost incomprehensible that Beckham should injure his foot only seven weeks before the 2002 World Cup finals, but, as the news sunk in, the nation, perhaps the world, came to understand the fragility of even a chosen one.

Fame was available not only to those who performed great deeds, but also to those who were just newsworthy (like murder or kidnap victims). The film industry spawned the star system, a process carefully calibrated to ensure actors benefited from the publicity offered by the print media and, from the 1920s, radio. Names like Barrymore, Fairbanks and Valentino resounded through the airwaves and print media. Industrial processes were refined so that a warrantable assembly line of "stars" – a word contrived by Hollywood to insinuate celestial properties – was put into operation. This ensured that consumers became increasingly familiar with the stars, or at least familiar with whatever the system fabricated about them. A two-way relationship developed in which the film industry used the mass media for publicity purposes and the media used the film industry for good copy. It still works.

Allied to the film industry was the cinema newsreel, which permitted another level of intimacy: moving images of public personalities, not just stars, but also musicians, politicians, religious figures and, importantly, athletes. Some of these would have been dimly known or heard-of, but the sight of them in action provided primitive parasocial associations. Consumers could see and hear the images and sounds of the figures on the screen and relate to them in their own personal ways.

Television, as we've seen, was the medium that took parasocial relationships to a new level. Over a relatively short ten-year period, beginning in 1950, the appliance transformed people's lives. Rather than chart the number of ways television affected our lives, I'd rather ask: what parts of our lives have remained untouched by television? Imagine: prior to 1950, most people did not have a tv. What did they do? Life without television is almost incomprehensible to the 99.9 something per cent of us who have at least one tv, plus the obligatory videocassette recorder and, increasingly, the D V D player. Part of the estimable largesse brought to our lives by television was the opportunity to see not only stars, but also a new division of figures whose images were brought to our homes courtesy of video signals. These videated figures were not stars: they weren't necessarily known for great achievements. They were just *there* on our screens. Whether anchoring shows, linking programmes, forecasting the weather or hosting quizzes, the television personality, as this figure was known, became part of our lives. Celebrities were cast in this mould.

It's difficult to think of another invention that has made such an impact on our cultural lives as television. The internal combustion engine, which drives both cars and planes, and has had a comparably dramatic effect on our lives – maybe. The electric light? Nuclear power? The thing about television is that its influence on us is so pervasive that we hardly notice it. Think about your entire day, then imagine how it would be different without television. Every single aspect of it would be completely different.

Celebrities, in the way we understand them today, would simply not have been possible without television. Like Beckham, they're products of a culture habituated to a practice, once believed to be responsible for a catalogue of debilities, including inciting violence, inducing illiteracy, shortening attention spans and breaking up marriages. There are many more charges. We might add a few more: our wasteful absorption with people with undetermined talent (though a capability for becoming well known is perhaps a talent in itself); our unwholesome fascination with their private lives (if celebs can legitimately be said to have such things); and our occasional tendency to confuse our real lives with theirs (stalkers, threatening letter writers, marriage proposers and viewers who believe soap characters actually exist have this tendency).

Multiply-and-saturate, as opposed to divide-and-conquer, has been the most effective method of dominating popular culture. In recent decades, figures occupying our attention have reproduced like those furry creatures, tribbles, in the classic *Star Trek* episode. "The proliferation of media for publicising the individual has been reflected in a proliferation of celebrated individuals", writes Giles, attaching the important supplement "so individuals have had to *do* less in order to be celebrated, albeit for briefer periods than earlier" (p. 32). Unlike heroes, the progeny of television culture rely less on doing, more of being noticed. Representation, then, is one of the keys to being a celebrity: it is simply not enough to be or do; you need to be seen being and doing. Consumers need to be able to call up in their mind your portrayal and, in the case of celebs like Beckham, imagine what you are up to.

As Giles records, the status of a celebrity is conditional – on the continuing interest of the viewing and listening audiences – and ephemeral in the sense that the turnover of television personalities is crushing. Turnover, with its connotations of commerce, industry and regularity, fits the description well. "Although at one point in time the emergence of celebrity figures was a haphazard and arbitrary voyage of discovery," write David Andrews and Steven Jackson, "today the process is considerably more proactive in its focus on the cultivation of potential celebrities." Introducing their collection *Sport Stars*, Andrews and Jackson note how the "celebrity industry (the institutions and individuals responsible for the manufacturing of celebrity identities) has evolved into a multi-faceted, integrated, and highly rationalized phenomenon" (p. 4).

The media thrives on such changes, giving old celebs new images, or simply breaking fresh ground. Television networks respond with an endless flow of potential new celebs, some of whom they anticipate will fix viewers to the screen. In this sense, the creation we know as a celebrity is very much a product of television's never-ending quest for new faces that will captivate viewing audiences and thus attract advertising revenue.

Competition for advertisers among the commercial television companies makes it imperative that all stations try to maximize audience share. If they find a face that draws viewers, then they'll find all the riches of Croesus to keep them (which is why the British tv industry's average yearly salary for news-readers is about £1 million and why, in 2001, the USA's network NBC paid its anchor Katie Couric $42 million over five years). Ratings-driven television has been prolific in discovering or manufacturing talent: celebrities are, after all, *resources*; they bring viewers to screens, encourage them to read magazines and persuade them to buy goods, among other things.

Celebrities can be, indeed must be, created, though their staying power can never be guaranteed. Such is the fickleness of consumers that celebrity status is always fragile. As the small print in trust fund ads always states, the value can go up or down. Picture Britney Spears at the London première of her movie *Crossroads*, flouncing up to the red rope, refusing *en passant* to sign autographs for her gathered fans. In a bitchtacular transformation, the media turned her from beloved virgin-whore to abominated vicious-witch. A single event, a slipshod remark, over-exposure – the list of reasons why celebrities crash is limitless. Beckham, of course, had first-hand knowledge of how the process works, though he was able to engineer an astonishing comeback.

No amount of industrial damage maintenance can rescue some careers. Soap stars are especially vulnerable, as they are identified with only one character. A *cause célèbre* in 1986 was ruinous for Peter Adamson, formerly Len Fairclough of Grana-da's *Coronation Street*. *EastEnders*' Gillian Taylforth, by contrast, emerged from a well-documented indiscretion to feature in other television dramas after she left the show in 1999. Had Adamson been dismissed in the early twenty-first century, one wonders, would he have been able to marshal the might of the celebrity industry to restore his standing in the public eye? It's at least possible, if only because the new media complex of net-work, satellite and cable tv, internet, radio, cinema and print is so refined in its operation and so diverse in its ability to pro-duce, sustain and exploit interest.

Early evidence of this came when sports anchor Frank Bough was jettisoned by BBC television after his use of cocaine became known. He was snatched by a rival tv station, which sensed that his misdemeanour was not so heinous that it would turn the public against him; in the event, Bough enjoyed a new lease of celebrity life among the satellites. But, the exemplar here is surely Michael Barrymore, who seemed to lurch from scandal to scandal, resilient enough to bounce back from all except the final disgrace.

The upside of this, at least for aspiring celebs, is that scandals can and often do create celebrities, as if spontaneously. Nondescript Tory MP David Mellor might just have well have sprinkled himself with stardust when he donned his favoured Chelsea FC jersey and knelt to suck the toes of a female actor with whom he was having an affair. Once news of his peccadillo broke, he left his political office and walked into a number of high-profile media engagements, one of which positioned him waggishly as a football pundit.

One of the best defences against the vagaries of the not-unrelated media and public taste is talent. Ability, competence, proficiency or, even better, genius help. If none of these is present and the celebrity relies on just being liked, then one scandal can finish a career. Barrymore had little to offer once his "likeability" had gone. Vanessa-Mae, on the other hand, leapt to fame as a precocious coquette who could play the violin; after the initial enthralment went, her status as a seductress dropped, but she remained a celebrity virtuoso.

The lesson to be drawn is that even the best-laid plans can come to naught. The considerable allied forces of the communication, advertising, entertainment and fashion industries can maximize the chances of, but not absolutely guarantee, celebrity status. Longevity is even more elusive. There is as much art as science in the process of creating and sustaining a celebrity. Of course, the question that lurks behind this observation is: what are celebrities for?

———

We live in a time when every human need and want is replaceable. As soon as one set of needs has been satisfied, so another crops up. Our desires are shaped and inflated by an advertising industry dedicated to making us insatiably curious, ever inquisitive and desirous of the materials needed to enjoy the good life. Cars, houses, mobile phones, microwaves. Almost as soon as we've bought them, we start thinking about upgrading. Being a consumer is a never-ending Holy Grail-type pursuit. When that's seen for what it is – futile – the consumer turns to others who embody the narrow ideal and lives vicariously through them. In other words, we spend a good portion of our lives chasing commodities we think will make us happy and then discover that they rarely do. What can we do next? Attach parts of ourselves to others who are conspicuously happy. Celebrities are ecstatically happy. Who wouldn't be, with the glamorous lifestyle they have? So, we start to take a keener interest in them, not just to know about them, but to live through them.

People become things; things that are capable of being consumed just like any other item of trade. Beckham and other celebrities have been commodified: turned into objects that are desired by millions. They are acclaimed, adored and revered. The intoxicating prospect of sharing a relationship of whatever sort with Beckham confers a sense of unlimited power on the fan. Yet it may also signal a life bereft of authority, prestige, privilege or favour. Cheryl Harris and Alison Alexander's collection, *Theorizing Fandom: Fans, Subculture and Identity*, draws together various studies, many of which suggest that being a fan is in many ways an attempt – often a successful one – to negate the sense of powerlessness in every other aspect of a fan's life. The mere association of oneself with a celebrity is a private, yet wholly social, solution to the problem of being stuck at the margins of life, with no status and little hope of getting any. I wrote earlier that there's a Beckham that exists only in the imaginations of fans and here we should recognize again that Beckham the man does and says very little. This is why he's so perfect. Anybody can live through him without fear that he'll do or say anything to damage the fantasies they have about him.

Devotees of Beckham want not just to consume images of him, or even his body, in any rational way: in a genuine sense, they wish to *be* him. They wish they had his looks, his fame, his talent, his glamour, his wealth, his popularity, maybe his wife and perhaps even *him*. The types of attachment and identification that operate are more intense and perhaps more compulsive than those that tie consumers to inanimate objects of desire – cars, clothes, the tiniest mobile phones. The superabundance of celebrities makes it more and more difficult, if not impossible, for parents to shield children from the tantalizing world of glamour, money and status they grow into.

Beckham is a commercial for this world: he personifies endless novelty, change and excitement. He and his wife provide the stimulation to improve and upgrade through consumption, every bit as effectively as mass marketing itself. In this sense, the very existence of celebrities propagandizes the superiority of commodities over things, images over events and exchange values over worth. The way the media chronicle their lives encourages the contradictory ethics of hedonism and rude health, at the same time denying the significance of thrift and self-denial. Yet, there is more: celebrities advertise irrational freedom – to be trivial, whimsical, obsessed with others and, perhaps, to be others.

The impulse purchase that was once the archetype of irrationality has become an exemplar of reasonableness and common sense – everybody max's their credit cards, owes monthly payments and seeks immediate rather than deferred gratification. The very rationality of consumer culture is based on the irrationality of its individual actors.

It wasn't always like this. Not long ago, we followed the famous, but never actually consumed them. How did this change come about? Way back in the 1930s, the American writer Robert Merton wrote that our ultimate goal was material success, which we wanted to display and display conspicuously. Good clothes, cars, electrical appliances: these were all things that people wanted, perhaps craved. People valued their ability to consume and they were encouraged through various media, such as schools and particularly advertising, to maximize this ability – within certain boundaries. Merton's view was that the boundaries defined the legitimate means through which people could achieve their goals. There are right ways and wrong ways to achieve them. When people strove for material goods but lacked the means to get them, they often opted for the wrong ways. In other words, they stole the goods that the advertising hoarding and the radio commercials were telling them they should have. The "non-conforming" conduct, as Merton called it, was a response to this condition. This is a long-winded way of arriving at my point: today's celebrities provide for an alternative response. Instead of stealing the desired material that signifies success, people identify with celebrities who manifestly have an embarrassment of such material. They transfer their goals, not just fantasizing but living through the public experiences of others.

This might seem like an odd approach to understanding the appeal of Beckham, but stay with the argument: people still yearn for the prestigious cars and designer clothes, but many do something else too. They *wish* to be someone else. Wishing has become a crucial ingredient. We wish to be Them. This is not mere emulation, though every hairstyle, tattoo and body pierce of Beckham immediately excites countless imitations; it's vicarious fulfilment, imaginatively recreating personal accomplishment through the life of another. People have become commodities and we can buy them just like any other commodity. What's more, we use them in similar ways: not just to use them, but to consume, relish and delight in them. They satisfy our desires in a way inanimate objects can't. Let me expand.

Consumer culture was originally built on the avarice, envy and possessiveness that flourished in the post-war years. Merton's study had concluded that desire drives us towards appropriation: we want to possess the things we see dangled in front of us by advertising. The advertising industry had sensed that people didn't buy products just because they needed them: the needs had to be encouraged. Desire worked much better. If you desire something, the second you have it, the desire is gone. So the trick was to keep pumping up new desires: as soon as you upgrade the fridge, you start thinking about a new car. As soon as you get the car, you start thinking about a new house. "The accelerator of consumer demand", as Zygmunt Bauman calls it, is pressed hard down as new offers keep appearing on the road ahead.

In his article "Consuming Life", Bauman argues that one of the triumphs of the consumer culture is the liberation of the pleasure principle from the confines of the perimeter fence beyond which pleasure seekers once could venture only at their peril. "Consumer society has achieved a previously unimaginable feat: it reconciled the reality and pleasure principles by putting, so to speak, the thief in charge of the treasure box", Bauman concludes (p. 16). What we used to think of as irrational now strikes us as perfectly normal. Human desire has been transformed.

In other words: we still want to possess commodity goods, but we also allow ourselves the indulgence of whimsically wishing for things that we know are out of reach. We'd love that Porsche Boxster, of course, and maybe we can save enough to get it. But, that doesn't stop us wishing to be like Beckham or any number of other celebrities who have actually got one in their private stable of cars. We don't just want the attainable: we wish for the unattainable. It's totally irrational, yet it seems completely logical.

To work effectively, consumerism needs continually to invent new wishes and new discontents that can be assuaged only by devouring more commodities. There's a line in Bryan Singer's film *The Usual Suspects* in which one of the characters compares the mysteriously elusive arch-criminal Kaiser Soze, to the devil: "The devil's biggest trick is in persuading the world that he doesn't really exist." It may well be that the greatest deception of consumerism is not unlike the devil's. It executes this most effectively through its surreptitious use of celebrities. There's no need to advertise products when they can be seen or read about on celebrities. This isn't a control through direct manipulation or shaping of preferences: it's a dominion over the conception of what we earlier called the good life as depicted by the media. Images of luxury, romance and excitement radiate from every exposition of celebrities.

Because he actually does or says little of significance and confines his most provocative behaviour for the sports field, Beckham has few, if any, rivals to being the most perplexing yet mediagenic athlete ever: his public presence is apt to produce images that can be captured by the media and relayed in moments around the world. The images are typically filtered and refined in a way that makes them indistinguishable from fashion plates or movie posters. He is the embodiment of vicarious achievement, a figure through which aspirations may be lived. His followers aren't frustrated by their own comparative lack of material success or accomplishments. They displace their longing onto him. At the same time, they cringe, bowing to the unmistakable superiority of the celebrity's life in all aspects. The same paradox pervades the entire celebrity culture. Celebrities, like global brands and fictional figures, from Madonna to Lara Croft and Tiger Woods to Buzz Lightyear, dwarf and mock the very being of their fandom with their perfect digitalized existence. Fans cower, adoring but secretly enraged, in the shadows of these giant presences in their lives.

Some writers argue that celebrity culture has hijacked emotional life: the omniscient counterfeits have led to the loss of a stable, cohesive identity and the paroxysms of wrath that have become known as rages. The rages are, at one level, a vent of spleen against other consumers, locked in traffic, waiting at supermarket checkouts or standing impatiently in cashpoint queues, but at another, are part of the current condition of frantic over-stimulation. The shocks are delivered by celebrities, exciting us with visions of a good life in which goods and artifice are constituent parts of the self, enticing us with stories of their extravagance and excess, piquing us with shameful details of their intemperate self-indulgence and indifference to others. This is a world in which the celebrity defines aspirations: young people strive not to achieve but to become. Their ambitions are not to accomplish great deeds but to be like the rich and famous. They live in a constant condition of purgatory, trapped in mundane actualities, yet desperate for the kind of enchanted life they have dangled before them.

—————— twelve ——————

YOUR FIFTEEN MINUTES ARE ALMOST UP

Andy Warhol died in New York on 22 February 1987 after a gall bladder operation. David Beckham was then 11, a pupil at Chingford High School in Essex. Yet the two are connected. Follow the logic: Warhol prophesied, pursued and helped bring about a culture in which fame, celebrity and flamboyance came close to being absolute values. In his perfect world, the kind of fabulousness, once available to only a few select stars, would be dispersed among entire populations. Our lives would be structured not so much around people or things, but representations of them, recognizable images, such as those used in advertising. Warhol discerned the trends but didn't live long enough to see the tide turn. By the time Beckham emerged in the mid-1990s, a tsunami had arrived.

Warhol's masterpiece isn't in any gallery or private collection or even archived discretely away from the public gaze. It's in television shows, in tabloid newspapers, in advertisements everywhere. We've travelled a long way towards realizing his much-misquoted prediction: "In the future, everyone will be world-famous for fifteen minutes" (note: *world*-famous).

Beckham is part of this "future", in which fame is adored and sought for its own sake and representation has replaced substance. Or perhaps the future summoned by Warhol has not *quite* come to pass. "A world dominated by the avowed values of Andy Warhol would be one in which any form of critical commentary beyond 'gee' or 'fabulous' would be taboo," writes Kevin Jackson, in his article "Warhol's World Condensed", "and Posh and Becks would fill even more column inches, and sceptical jokes about them and their glitzy kind seem blasphemous or merely baffling" (p. 7).

Yes, there *are* jibes about the Beckhams; and incredulous analysts who question why the couple receive so much attention. There are also cynics who sneer at them, fans who barrack them. Jackson regards this as proof that Warhol's future has not completely materialized. There's still just enough critical distance between Us and Them to delay a verdict on what Jackson calls "the triumph of froth". In times of absolute triumph, we'd all be dotingly star-dazed, too transfixed to summon faculty enough to ask: why? In this book, I'm asking just that, of course.

There are people around who still find the inexhaustible public appetite for any titbit of information, gossip, half-truth or rumour about celebrities incomprehensible. The future, according to Warhol, would be completely overrun by people craving knowledge of the famous and fighting for their right to be famous, if only briefly. As we're discovering, the stampede may have just started.

There are several themes in Warhol that illustrate his influence as well as prescience. He's perhaps best known for his photographic silkscreens featuring multiple reproductions of famous subjects. Muhammad Ali, Elvis Presley and Marilyn Monroe were all iconic subjects of Warhol. Their representations were multiplied over and over again, as if reminding consumers that these weren't human beings but products, commodities to be bought and sold and consumed like any other piece of merchandise. The processes involved in their production were much like those involved in the manufacture of the other types of goods Warhol depicted, including Brillo pads and Coca-Cola.

Warhol, in many ways, called attention to the emerging milieu of vacuity and emptiness, where even people of great achievements are known for their appearances in ads as much as for what they actually do away from endorsing products. Warhol's cunning was in understanding desire. As I've written earlier in this book, consumerism encourages and sustains desire: it changes in response to brand innovation and the introduction of new commodities. Warhol introduced art-as-commodity, then changed it and kept changing it, switching mediums as he went (he diversified into music and film). He was also careful to leave his own market wanting more. Later, he took to wearing dark glasses and an assortment of wigs, which he would dye and hack about to make sure everyone knew they were artificial. His public appearances grew rarer and his interviews ever more perplexing. This was Warhol creating a commodity from himself. There was nothing more to him: no real character, no core personality, no inner identity. This made him more elusive, mysterious and, to use an over-used but, in this case, justified word, enigmatic. No respecter of the distinction between the creator and the created, Warhol inserted himself into his productions. He became a product.

Today, celebrities have little choice: their status is entirely dependent on their preparedness to become a commodity. Think of Beckham the creator: his actions on the field of play have moved many to compare his work with that of an artist. Think of him too as a creation: near-identical images of him adorn too many items to mention, each helping to shift products from shelves in the same way that logos and familiar labels shift soup and soft drinks. Yet, he remains studiously absent, only a public persona breaking through every so often. Everyone can desire, though no one can have the real Beckham, if indeed there is such a being. Still, as Warhol himself argued, the famous are there not to be admired or cherished and certainly not to be analysed, but to be bought and sold like anything else on the market.

Beckham exists in a world dominated by the avowed values of Warhol. Some time between the early 1990s and now, with the expansion of higher education, the supposed economic boom, the displacement of streetcorner gangs into undercover shopping centres, the disappearance of Laddishness and the appearance of bling bling, we've drifted into a world of representation. How things look seems more important than what they are. Imagery is everything and the mechanical reproduction of it is everywhere.

All of which sounds a curious way to begin a concluding chapter. But Beckham is a curious figure. Nobody has ever captured the public imagination in quite the same way he has.

Footballers will never quite be the same. And yet, as I've argued repeatedly in this book, he – that is, Beckham the person, the sportsman, the celeb – isn't special. The way he's consumed *is*.

A teenage Morrissey scrawled in his notebook: "I'm sick of being the undiscovered genius, I want fame NOW not when I'm dead" (quoted in Johnny Rogan's *Morrissey and Marr*, p. 92). "If I wasn't Robbie Williams right now, I'd probably be auditioning for the *Big Brother* household", the singer told writer Mark McCrum for his *Somebodysomeday*. Posh Spice declared that she wanted to be "as famous as Persil Automatic". These three became supreme celebrities. Just imagine the zillions of others who harbour similar ambitions. They clamour for appearances on reality shows, quiz programmes, confessional talk shows and open forums that usually disintegrate into full-scale slanging matches. Few of them are reluctant celebrities, if for no other reason than, as Chris Rojek puts it in his book *Celebrity*: "Most ordinary people suffer from achievement famine." This is a condition "that results from frustrated desires for material and romantic achievement of the sort the rich and famous enjoy" (p. 149).

Many, perhaps most, of us garner some degree of recognition, perhaps even some honour, among and sometimes beyond our circle of friends and close acquaintances. We still want more; achievement is prescribed. Nobody sees much virtue in being a loser; we are brought up to strive hard and accomplish as much as our ability will permit. Nowadays, people seem to want more: they don't just want to achieve something, they want to be famous for their achievement. In fact, they don't seem to mind if they get to be famous even without achieving anything. They want to be as famous as celebs. They're encouraged by the fact that, potentially, anybody can be famous: talent might once have been a prerequisite. Now, it's just a bonus.

The phrase "famous for being famous" is no longer sardonic: it's literally true of many celebrities, who have risen not because of any residual talent or achievement but because of how well they're known. There's even a certain respectability attached to it. This is resplendently distilled in Victoria Hervey aka the It Girl, a female with no known adequacy in anything, apart from being well known. There's any number of other bottom shelf celebs devoid of talent, lacking in accomplishments and destined to remain known for only as long as it takes a capricious media to tire and an equally capricious fandom to become bored. Our tv screens are populated by generic "presenters", many of whom become known for their lack of presentational skills – like inept athletes who leap to eminence thanks to cutely ironic nicknames ("Eddie the Eagle", "Eric the Eel") and the penchant of the media to laud abject failure, often more than success. An undistinguished and championship-lite career appeared to help Anna Kournikova to become the most celebrated and one of the highest earning tennis players in the world.

Beckham, or, at least, the commodified Beckham, has profited from the same kinds of process that create kings from fools, luminaries from dullards, It Girls from underachieving nymphets. All have been delivered to a vast audience courtesy of a media with a seemingly inexhaustible appetite for celebrities. Of course, Beckham differs from his vacuous contemporaries: he has the substance that comes from tangible athletic capabilities. Had he existed at an earlier time, he would still be widely regarded as a sportsman of considerable skill. That skill, while still recognized, is now just one facet of his remarkable make-up. It's actually not *his* make-up: rather a make-up constantly being created anew by his acolytes. Whatever he does or says is incidental to what fans believe, or want to believe, he does or says; as Garry Whannel concludes of this Beckham, "he's not 'real'" (p. 149). We might add: he's as much a construction as Harry Potter or Ali G – more a product of imagination and invention than of exploits.

None of this diminishes Beckham's stature or indeed his athletic proficiency: it underscores Whannel's point that "consumption is the new democracy". Anybody, no matter how lowly or humble, can devour whatever takes their fancy, digest whatever they like. As we've seen, Beckham is an advertisement, not only for the products he endorses, but also for the type of hollow democracy he inadvertently promotes. This is a system in which the lower orders can, indeed may, climb, but also one in which there are fallbacks in the likely event that they don't. The fallback is that they can wish: it costs nothing and has incalculable value, both for those who wish and for the consumer culture of which they're part.

We're part of a culture that has confidence in its own lack of rationality: thought and action need no reason, just stimulus. It's a culture in which ambitions are organized around quiz shows, like *Who Wants to be a Millionaire?* and *The Weakest Link,* in which twenty minutes of interrogation can end in life-altering riches. Reality tv compels viewers to peer at the conduct of "ordinary people" who are expected to perform like lab rats in a maze, learning and being rewarded for learning with the chance of celebrity status, albeit for the briefest of periods. Confessional shows, such as Jerry Springer's, bind us into a bargain, offering us a soul-baring glimpse into the intimate and usually embarrassing private relationships of volunteers but in exchange for our appreciation, not prurience. The bestseller lists are chock full of autobiographies of celebrity actors, singers and athletes, cook books by celebrity chefs, memoirs of celebrity politicians, even history books by celebrity academics. There are even celebrity journalists, like The *Mirror*'s 3am Girls, or the *Daily Mail*'s Baz Bamigboye, whose reputations are scored from writing about other celebs. Our enchantment with celebrities signifies a break with the reality principal and a flight into the realms of pleasure, of fantasy, of wishful thinking.

In Britain, this has become vividly and, often, painfully transparent through a tv series designed like an athletic contest in which only those possessed of "talent" win. In shows like *Pop Idol,* dozens of thousands of aspiring celebs clamoured for the chance to show their wares in front of fault-finding arbiters who cruelly reminded them of their ample limitations. Repeatedly, the hopefuls narrated to the camera that they had but one objective – *to become famous.* Even those with little capacity to perform confirmed their singular intentions: any other form of ambition was ruled out. They wanted to be pop stars; nothing else would suffice.

216

The central conceit of Paul Verhoven's movie *Total Recall* – based on Philip K. Dick's short story "We can remember it for you wholesale" – is that people don't need actually to visit places or do things when they can instead have embolisms planted in their memories, providing them with cheaper and safer ways of realizing all their ambitions. In the plot, Doug Quaid is a working-class nobody who aspires to go to Mars, but can't afford it. Instead, he opts for the experience of visiting Mars, which is delivered straight into his memory in less time than it takes to get a tooth filled. The story is predicated on the same reasoning that takes people to Tampa's Bush Gardens rather than the Serengeti, to Alton Towers where the rides are advertised as terrifying but no one comes to harm, and on packaged adventure holidays where the risks are minimal. In other words, we want to experience rather than do. It makes us privy to a province we secretly aspire to, but have no realistic chance of reaching.

The excitement, love, glamour and intrigue proposed not by Beckham but by the narratives drawn about his life say more about contemporary culture than about the player himself. They tell us that we now have a generation hooked on the irrational pleasures of celebrity watching, or, more accurately, celebrity fantasizing. People dream about becoming fabulously wealthy and globally famous but they have no effective means of achieving these ambitions. Their orientation, like all good consumers, is to carry on wishing. This includes watching tv shows that dangle tantalizing carrots, buying lottery tickets and following the pursuits of others who are already fabulously wealthy and globally famous. In short, consuming.

This is why we're guided to celebrities, why the media produces more of them and why the market commodifies them. Consumption is the new phoney egalitarianism in which anybody can be somebody. The danger is that the fickle and expendable hopes of consumers rest less on aspiration and ambition, more on the presence of others. These others embody the elusive, yet yearned-for properties that the consumer can never possess, but can still experience endlessly through the likes of Beckham.

This sounds a dispiriting way to conclude a book on one of the most seductively attractive and glamorous celebrities to have

217

emerged in recent times, particularly as he excites high emotions in consumers. He can make them feel good, perhaps even great. Of course, Beckham's ability to do this rests on the fact that they lack alternative ways of feeling good. This is a harsh, though not unfair assessment of Beckham's wide constituency of fans. And that includes Us. Are we sad? Maybe. Are we powerless? Probably. Do we use our imaginations? Definitely.

Beckham has no magical powers. He can't levitate or take flight. He can't win wars, save the planet or end famine. He can't change water to wine, heal the sick or communicate telepathically. He plays football. Yet he seems to glide so high that it sometimes seems he can do anything he turns his mind to. That we can have spun such an extraordinary aura around such an ordinary person is testimony to our inventiveness. It's also testimony to a culture that values a restricted idea of the good life, one that includes the kind of romance and glamour so often set before us, but rarely within our grasp. Yet, we go on chasing destinies that will forever elude us, slaloming between the real world and the parallel one where They live so exuberantly. This is the world where David Beckham looms large. There may be two worlds, but this is a single culture. It's a culture that nurtures, maintains and protects our right to be consumers.

This has been my focus: to understand how it's possible for an individual to provoke emotions and actions that might just about be comprehensible if he were a Nobel prize winner, or the discoverer of the cure for cancer. But a footballer? Of course, the deception is that Beckham is not just a footballer. Throughout the book, I've insisted that, while there's a physical Beckham, there's also a commodity Beckham and it's this product that engages us so much. On the surface, our almost worshipful devotion to, our exaggerated admiration of and our astounding pursuit of Beckham is a case of certifiable madness. On closer inspection, it's absolutely consistent with the kind of culture that now envelops and saturates us. It won't last, of course: the celebrities that fascinate us now all come with inbuilt time limits.

Over the next few years, we'll move on to newer celebs, each one a commodity that will capture the spirit of the times more faithfully than Beckham. They'll come from sport as well as other parts of the entertainment industry. And they'll march into our lives and demand our attention, perhaps as convincingly as Beckham. Then, most of them will disappear. Even Beckham will fade from view. He'll still play football, of course, and he may still have some heroic deeds ahead. As in all fairy tales, there will be unexpected twists. But the enchanted part of the story will end – and quite soon. Beckham's aura will start to vaporize long before he leaves football. But when? There are no guarantees in the age of the celeb. Well, just one: that when you get to be a celeb, you won't be one for very long. The exceptions are the ones that have mutated with the times, like species bent on survival. Madonna is the supreme case, of course. Or those, like Diana, John F. Kennedy or Martin Luther King, who died tragically young. Or those we actually respect – and I mean esteem, value and honour, rather than just like or even love. We mostly avoid degrading, insulting or interfering with the status of people we genuinely respect.

My account of the rise and rise of Beckham admittedly presumes an awful lot about the people who dote on celebrities – which is most of Us. Are we really so dumb as not to figure out what is happening here? Surely, we have already realized that we are not actually going to become another Beckham, another Posh, or a Morrissey, or a Robbie Williams, even though they all once ached for fame in their humbler moments. Our longing to enjoy the fruits of the good life is likely to remain just that – a longing. Versatile as we like to think we are, we're not going to be changed into a celebrity; not unless an ad agency's film crew drops in at our office and thinks we have the kind of face that would fit the new campaign. We're destined to go on yearning. And we know this. This doesn't take away the pleasure. The joy is in the yearning. As I've argued before, we don't just admire celebrities, we live through them, responding to every episode, crisis, accolade, even brickbat.

Beckham's power doesn't lie in his personal gifts, talents or capacities, though, of course, he may well possess out-of-the-ordinary aptitudes, perhaps even extravagant talents. This isn't the reason fans are drawn to him. It's because he provides

Figure 13 The globalization of Beckham was complete when he joined Real Madrid. Even at a club graced with world-renowned stars, Beckham commanded more attention than any of his colleagues. *Source*: Empics

something that excites and comforts, angers and consoles, violates and sanctions. Beckham can arouse these great emotions in us because he embodies so many of the ideas and values we share. The conspicuous talent, drama and sheer dazzle he parades might, in another era, offend. Today, they inspire.

Beckham is not just well suited to the requirements of a culture in which consumption is of paramount importance: he is perfect. Without knowing it, he conveys ideas that have become germane: that They, the celebs, are both different and yet the same as Us; that we could be like them, at least theoretically – if only we had a little more talent and a tad more industry; that this is a system that rewards and punishes according to just principles and that we all end up with what we deserve. Only one deserves to be Beckham, of course. But, by consuming him, we can all share in the experience.

220

BIBLIOGRAPHY

Abbas, Andrea (1996) "Masculinity", pp. 617–20 in D. Levinson and
K. Christensen (eds), *Encyclopedia of World Sport: From Ancient Times
to the Present* (Santa Barbara: ABC-Clio).

Andersen, Robin (1995) *Consumer Culture and TV Programming* (Boulder, Co: Westview Press).

Andrews, David L. and Jackson, Steven J. (2001) "Introduction: Sport
celebrities, public culture, and private experience", pp. 1–19 in D. L.
Andrews and S. J. Jackson (eds), *Sport Stars: The Cultural Politics of
Sporting Celebrity* (London: Routledge).

Bauman, Zygmunt (2001) "Consuming life", *Journal of Consumer Culture* 1 (1): 5–29.

Beckham, David (2000) *My World* (London: Hodder & Stoughton).

Beckham, David (2003) *davidbeckham: My Side* (London: Collins Willow).

Beckham, Victoria (2001) *Learning to Fly: The Autobiography* (London:
Michael Joseph).

Bent, Ian, McIlroy, Richard, Mousley, Kevin and Walsh, Peter (2000)
Football Confidential (London: BBC Worldwide).

Best, George (2001) *Blessed* (London: Ebury).

Boorstin, Daniel. J. (1992) *The Image: A Guide to Pseudo-Events in America* (New York: Random House).

Bolton, Andrew (2003) *Men in Skirts* (London: V&A Publications).

Bose, Mihir (2001) *Manchester Unlimited: The Rise and Rise of the World's
Premier Football Club* (London: Texere).

Boyle, Raymond and Haynes, Richard (2000) *Power Play: Sport, the
Media and Popular Culture* (Harlow, Essex: Longman).

Braudy, Leo (1977) *The Frenzy of Renown: Fame and its History*, 2nd edn
(New York: Vintage).

Burchill, Julie (2001) *Burchill on Beckham* (London: Yellow Jersey).

Bibliography

Chenoweth, Neil (2001) *Virtual Murdoch: Reality Wars on the Information Highway* (London: Secker & Warburg).

Conn, David (2001) *The Football Business* (Edinburgh: Mainstream).

Connell, Robert W. (1987) *Masculinities* (Cambridge: Cambridge University Press).

Crick, Michael and Smith, David (1989) *Manchester United: The Betrayal of a Legend* (London: Pelham).

Ferguson, Alex (2000) *Managing My Life* (London: Hodder & Stoughton).

Fowles, Jib (1996) *Advertising and Popular Culture* (London: Sage).

Frame, Pete (1993) *Compete Rock Family Trees* (London: Omnibus).

Gamson, Joshua (1994) *Claims to Fame: Celebrity in Contemporary America* (Berkeley: University of California Press).

Giles, David (2000) *Illusions of Immortality: A Psychology of Fame and Celebrity* (Basingstoke, Hampshire: Macmillan).

Giulianotti, Richard and Gerrard, Michael (2001) "Evil genie or pure genius? The (im)moral football and public career of Paul 'Gazza' Gascoigne", pp. 124–37 in D. L Andrews and S. J. Jackson (eds), *Sport Stars: The Cultural Politics of Sporting Celebrity* (London: Routledge).

Guttmann, Allen (1996) *The Erotic in Sports* (New York: Columbia University Press).

Harris, Cheryl and Alexander, A. (eds) (1998) *Theorizing Fandom: Fans, Subculture and Identity* (New York: Hampton Press).

Harris, Thomas (1991) "The building of popular images: Grace Kelly and Marilyn Monroe", pp. 40–4 in Christine Gledhill (ed.), *Stardom: Industry of Desire* (London: Routledge).

Hornby, Nick (1992) *Fever Pitch* (London: Indigo).

Hoskyns, Barney (2002) "The Brits: pop you can and should get out of your head", *Independent*, Friday Review, 22 February, p. 14.

Jackson, Kevin (2002) "Warhol's world condensed: The man who gave the 21st century its flavour", *Independent*, Weekend Review, 26 January, p. 7.

Katz, Daniel. (1994) *Just Do It: The Nike Spirit in the Corporate World* (Holbrook, MA Adams Media).

Kelly, Fergus (2001) *David Beckham: Portrait of a Superstar* (London: Scholastic).

Klein, Naomi (2001) *No Logo* (London: Flamingo).

Lasch, Christopher (1991) *The True and Only Heaven: Progress and its Critics* (New York: W. W. Norton).

Lazenby, Roland (2000) *Mind Games: Phil Jackson's Long Strange Journey* (New York: McGraw Hill).

Lewis, Lisa A. (ed.) (1992) *The Adoring Audience: Fan Culture and Popular Media* (London: Routledge).

Lovejoy, Joe (1999) *Bestie: A Portrait of a Legend* (London: Pan).

McCrum, Mark (2001) *Somebodysomeday* (London: Ebury).

McDowell, Colin (2002) "I'm (not) too sexy for Milan", *Independent Magazine*, 23 February, pp. 63–4.

McGill, Craig (2001) *Football Inc.: How Soccer Fans are Losing the Game* (London: Vision).

Madonna, Meisel, Steve (photographer) and O'Brien, Glenn (ed.) (1992) *Sex* (New York: Vintage/Ebury).

Marshall, P. D. (1997) *Celebrity and Power: Fame in Contemporary Culture* (Minneapolis: University of Minneapolis Press).

Merton, Robert K. (1969) "Social structure and anomie", pp. 254–84 in D. R. Cressey and D. A. Ward (eds), *Delinquency, Crime and Social Process* (New York: Harper & Row).

Messner, Michael (1992) *Power at Play: Sports and the Problem of Masculinity* (New York: Random House).

Monaco, James (1978) *Celebrity* (New York: Delta).

Morton, Andrew (2000) *Posh & Becks* (London: Michael O'Mara).

Pattenden, Mike (2000) "A cross to bear", *Inside Sport* 106 (October): 128–38.

Rogan, Johnny (1992) *Morrissey and Marr: The Severed Alliance* (London: Omnibus).

Rojek, Chris (2001) *Celebrity* (London: Reaktion).

Sherman, Len (1998) *Big League, Big Time: The Birth of the Arizona Diamondbacks, the Billion-dollar Business of Sports, and the Power of the Media in America* (New York: Pocket Books).

Simpson, Joe (1998) *Touching the Void* (London: Vintage).

Simpson, Paul (2001) *Paul Gascoigne* (London: Virgin).

Tench, Dan (2002) "Image-conscious? *Moi?* Celebrities turn legal eagles to gain self-control", *Independent on Sunday*, Business section, 17 February, p. 2.

Wahl, Grant (2003) "Big bend", *Sports Illustrated* 98 (25) (23 June): 60–70.

Wann, D. L., Melnick, M. J., Russell, G. W. and Pease, D. G. (2001) *Sports Fans: The Psychological and Social Impact of Spectators* (New York: Routledge).

Whannel, Gary (2001) "Punishment, redemption and celebration in the popular press: the case of David Beckham", pp. 138–50 in D. L Andrews and S. J. Jackson (eds) *Sport Stars: The Cultural Politics of Sporting Celebrity* (London: Routledge).

Walvin, James (1986) *Football and the Decline of Britain* (London: Macmillan).

INDEX

Note: page references in *italics* indicate illustrations. Abbreviations:
DB=David Beckham; VB=Victoria Beckham

A-list celebrities 4, 13, 20
ABBA 65, 108
Abbas, Andrea 149
AC Milan 63, 92
Adams, Tony 149
Adams, Victoria *see* Beckham,
  Victoria
Adamson, Peter 204
Adeyemi, Wale 196
adidas 7, 8, 32, 37, 54–5, 159,
  166, 167–9, 170, 191
advertising 20, 23, 95, 160, 163,
  191, 198, 203–4, 206, 208, 211;
  see also endorsements;
  sponsorship
Agassi, Andre 158
agents 2, 41, 64, 156–60
Alexander the Great 199, 200
Alexander, Alison 206
Ali, Muhammad 57, 179, 212
Ali G 150, 215
Alien (film) 194
American football 77, 91, 174;
  see also Dallas Cowboys
Americanization 98
Andersen, Robin 162

Andrews, David 185, 203
Arena Homme Plus 139, 153
Argentina, Red Card incident
  against 36–9, *38*
Arsenal 26, 49, 69, 73, 92
Ashby, Hal 1
Association of Tennis
  Professionals (ATP) 157
Aston Villa 73, 92, 157
Astoria, G.A.Y. club night 143

Babe Ruth *see* Ruth, George
  Herman
ballet 140–1
Bamigboye, Baz 216
Bananarama 102
Barcelona 109
Barcelona Football Club 26–7,
  28, 53
Barnes, Simon 185
Barrett, Slim 112
Barrymore, Michael 205
baseball 29, 76, 92, 93
basketball 29, 55, 98, 112, 158,
  166–7
Bates, Ken 73

Bauman, Zigmunt 208–9
Bayern Munich 63
BBC 85, 90, 135, 170, 205
Beatlemania 19
Beckham, Brooklyn (son) 43, 52, 109, 151, 181, 196
Beckham, David: birth of 25; clothes 11, 33–4, 47, 107, 108, 139, 179, 196; diversification 5; dual nature 12, 55, 206, 218; emotional appeal of 7–8, 61–2, 218, 220; epitome of ethos of sport 96; fashion model 3, 14, 23, 41, 47, 139–40, 165–6, 186; as father and family man 2, 12, 14, 48, 146–7, 151, 168, 179; globalization of 1, 5, 6, 11, 12, 13, 23, 30, 36, 39, 41, 54, 60–1, *171*, 220; image vs. the man 168–9, 178–81; lifestyle 107–8, 168–9, 174; marriage 32, 35, 62, 150, 186; OBE *171*; physical appearance 3, 10, 11, 14, 47, 117, *118*, 179, 180, 196; response to celebrity status 1–2, 5–6, 41; as role model 10, 47, 168–9, 176–7; and work ethic 108, 117, 168–9; *see also* brands; celebrity; commodities; consumerism; endorsements; family life; football career; gay icon; icons; image; masculinity; Posh and Becks
Beckham, Sandra (mother) 26, 27, 151

Beckham, Ted (father) 26, 50, 151
Beckham, Victoria 2, 18, 54, 65, 100–20, 160–2, 168, 173, 214; and attitude 104; contribution to DB's celebrity status 3, 7–8, 18–19, 114–20; legal actions over image rights (2001–2) 48; relations with Alex Ferguson 50, 63–4, 146–7; and work ethic 108, 116–17; *see also* celebrity; Posh and Becks; Spice Girls
"Becksdox" 11
Being John Malkovich (film) 195
Being There (film) 1–2
Being Victoria Beckham (tv documentary) 141–2
Bend it Like Beckham (film) 197–8
Bennett, Oliver 150–1
Bernabéu 25
Bent, Ian 94, 122
Berlusconi, Silvio 92
Best, George 17, 19, 22, 57, 60, 63, 66, 71, 86, 122, 123–4, 135, 136
Beverley, Joy 35
Big Brother (tv show) 177, 214
Billy Elliot (film) 140
Blair, Tony 128
Bogarde, Winston 129
Bolton, Andrew 139
Bono 14
Boorstin, Daniel 44
Booth, Mark 92
Bose, Mihir 37, 66, 73, 74, 77, 78, 79
Bough, Frank 205
Bowers, Dane 101

Bowie, David 4, 168
Boy George 187
Boyle, Danny 86
Boyle, Raymond 35, 97, 153
Boyzone 168
Bradford City ground fire
    (1985) 76
brands 63, 65–6, 191; DB as 12,
    13, 116, 196–210; ManU
    as 16–17, 31, 54, 66–82, 116,
    135, 137; Michael Jordan
    as 167; Spice Girls as 116,
    120, 161
Braudy, Leo 199
Brighton and Hove Albion 25
Brisco, Steve 79
Brit Awards (1996) 103
Brown, Howard 198, 199
Bryant, Kobe 158
Brylcreem 31–2, 159, 163–4, 165,
    170, 174
Brylcreem David Beckham
    Soccer Academy 163, 164
BSkyB 17, 30, 69, 76, 79, 85,
    87–90, 92, 95, 136, 159
Burchill, Julie 107, 151, 152, 154
Burton, Richard 35
Busby, Matt 70, 71, 72
Busby Babes 70

Campbell, Naomi 182, 183
Cantona, Eric 29–30, 31, 32, 33,
    66, 67, 68c, 77–8, 115
Carey, Mariah 200
Cassy, John 81
Cattaneo, Peter 153
celebrity and celebrities 2, 86;
    brevity of fame 6, 57, 198–9,
    205, 218–19; costs 196; DB

as 1–8, 11, 12, 15, 21–4, 30, 34,
    40, 42, 45, 59, 60–2, 98–9, 159,
    168 (contribution of VB 3, 7–8,
    18–19, 114–20); definitions 44,
    57; footballers as 19, 20, 22, 31,
    36, 63, 86–7, 108, 123–4, 160;
    function 205–10; Gascoigne
    as 19, 36, 123–4, 125, 132–3,
    136; journalists as 216; Posh
    and Becks as 34–5, 107,
    112–13; production of 183–95,
    203–5, 212; relations with
    fans *see* fans; Spice Girls
    as 104; in sport 5, 15, 57,
    94, 159–60; VB as 2, 43–4, 112–
    13, 115, 119–20, 162, 214
celebrity culture 14, 15, 22, 23,
    26, 56–62, 114, 160, 195,
    196–220; absence of
    rationality 207, 209, 216, 217;
    vicarious fulfilment
    through 208, 210, 219
Chadha, Gurinder 197
Challenor, Dave 199
Champions' League *see*
    European Champions'
    League
Channel 4: and NFL 77
Charles, Gary 126
Charlie's Angels (film) 113
Charlton, Bobby 17, 25, 71
Chelsea Football Club 73
Chenoweth, Neil 83
Chicago Bulls 29, 112, 166
Chisholm, Sam 89–90
Chrysalis Records 160
class conflict 137
Clear Channel
    Communications 158

Clooney, George 14
Close Encounters of the Third Kind
  (film) 194
Clough, Brian 145
Cobain, Kurt 96
Coca-Cola 95, 97, 106
Collymore, Stan 149
commodities,
  commodification 24, 95–9,
  206, 212, 213, 217; DB as 12,
  14, 24, 34, 54, 116, 164, 218;
  Posh and Becks as 15–16; *see
  also* consumerism
Compton, Denis 31, 163
Conn, David 69, 72, 89
Connell, Robert 148–9
Conroy, Paul 103
consumerism 24, 97, 162–3,
  190–2, 193, 201, 204, 212–13;
  DB and 6, 62, 154, 194,
  205–10, 213–20; Gascoigne
  and 124; *see also* commodities
Cooper, Henry 23
Coronation Street (tv
  programme) 183, 204
Cortéz, Joaquín 141
Cosmopolitan 5
Couric, Katie 204
Crane, Niles 155
Crick, Michael 70, 71
cricket 89
Croft, Lara 210
Crossroads (film) 204
Cruise, Tom 3, 141–2, 180
Cubic Expression 80
cultural awareness 98

Daily Mail 216
Daily Mirror 39, 129, 216

Daily Telegraph 11, 131
Dallas Cowboys 16, 68–9
Dash, Damon 120
Davids, Edgar 170
Davidson, Jaye 155
Davis, Marvin 91
Dein, David 73
Del Piero, Alessandro 32
Dell, Donald 157
democracy, consumption as
  new 215
Depp, Johnny 3, 120
desire 11–12; consumerism and
  celebrity culture 24, 207, 209,
  212, 213, 214, 219
Diana Memorial Fund 65
Diana, Princess of Wales 4, 13,
  44, 45, 65, 107, 112, 114, 219
diCaprio, Leonardo 173
Dick, Philip K. 217
digital technology 97
DiMaggio, Joe 35
Douglas, Michael 35, 65
Draper, Rob 65, 159
Dyke, Greg 69, 75, 88, 89

EastEnders (tv soap) 204
Edwards, Alan 103, 116, 168
Edwards, Douglas 70
Edwards, Louis 70–2, 73
Edwards, Martin 16–17, 28,
  67–70, *68*, 72–80, 89, 92, 110
Eisner, Michael 83
Elliott, Missy 7
Ellis, Doug 73
Emam, Hazem 171
EMI 103
emotions: celebrity culture
  and 210; *see also* fans

endorsements 95, 162–3, 185;
DB and 8, 14, 18, 20–1, 23,
31–2, 41, 54–5, 159, 163–75;
Gascoigne 135; Michael
Jordan and 158, 166–7; Spice
Girls and 105–6, 173
England East Asian tour
(1996) 128–9, 130
England Schoolboys team 27
England Under-21 team 31, 100,
115, 163
entertainment industry: DB
and 14, 42, 46, 47, 50, 67;
football becomes part
of 17–18, 20, 30–1, 35, 56–7,
83–99, 137, 160, 219; *see also*
fashion world; popular music
Essendouh, Roy 199
Eubank, Chris 66
European Champions'
League 29, 46, 52, 53, 80, 129
European Championships
(1996) 128, 129, 133, 137
European Cup (1968) 71, 74
European Cup Winners'
Cup 28
European football 76, 94; *see also*
individual competitions
Evans, Chris 133
Everton Football Club 16, 69,
129, 131

FA (Football Association) 46,
72, 76, 143
FA Cup 67, 78; (1991) 126;
(2003) 49
fairy tales 4, 9–24, 112, 219
fame 12, 34, 57, 113, 199–200,
201, 212, 214, 216, 219

family life: changes in 24; DB 2,
12, 14, 48, 146–7, 151, 168, 179
fans 2, 3, 6, 12, 14, 23, 38–42,
109–10, 200, 206, 215;
emotions 7–8, 61–2, 122, 218,
220; of football 20, 67, 77, 134,
135–6; homoeroticism 151–2;
and masculinity 20, 142–3,
150; reading DB as text 21–2,
34, 177–95; Red Card incident
(1998) 36, 38–42; respect
of 38–9, 219
fantasy 1, 10, 12, 22, 62, 216, 217
Fashanu, John 145
Fashanu, Justin 145–6, 149
fashion world 3, 14, 23, 41, 46,
47, 67, 133, 139–40, 153–6,
165–6, 186
feminization, football as process
of 154–5
Ferdinand, Rio 54
Ferguson, Alex 13, 28, 30, 42,
49–53, 54, 66, *68*, 108, 110, *111*,
112, 147–8, *148*; relations with
VB 50, 63–4, 146–7
FHM 153
Figo, Luis 54
films 97, 194, 201
Fimmel, Travis 155
football: authentication of
masculinity 47–8, 143–55;
Bosman ruling (1995) 26, 53,
73; decline and
reinvention 17–18, 76–8,
83–99, 122, 128, 135–7;
industrialization 105, 134 (*see
also* entertainment industry);
marketing 66–82, 92, 160
(*see also* endorsements);

maximum wage 25, 134; retain-and-transfer rule 25–6, 73; *see also* television

Football Association *see* FA

football career of DB 3, 14, 16, 25–42, 60–1, 100, 185, 188; early days 25–8, 27; loan to Preston North End 25, 28–9; at Manchester United 12, 16, 25, 27–30, 31, 38–42, 46, 52–3, 63–82, 84–5, 109, 110, *111*, 137, 147–8, *148*, 169; goal against Wimbledon (1996) 30, 107, 115, 163; Red Card incident (1998) 36–42, *38*, 108–9, 181; World Cup (1998) 36, *38*; World Cup (2002) 49, 96, 173, 201; Flying Boot incident (2003) 13, 49–52, 147; transfer to Real Madrid 8, 11, 13, 14, 53–5, 59, *61*, 82, 120, 156, 169, 172, *220*; faux pas 46–7, *61*

Football League 69–70, 71, 73, 74, 75–6, 78

footballers, as celebrities 19, 20, 22, 31, 36, 63, 86–7, 108, 123–4, 160

Footballers Wives (tv series) 86

Fortune 167

FourFourTwo 168

Fowler, Robbie 144, 179

Fowles, Jib 174

Fox network 85, 91

Frame, Pete 102

Francis, Trevor 73

Freedman, Edward 66, 77, 78, 79

Full Monty, The (film) 153

Fuller, Simon 21, 103, 108, 156, 160–2, 168, 189

Gallagher, Noel 128

Gamson, Joshua 177–8, 188, 192

Garbo, Greta 178

Gardner, Jim "Five Bellies" 130, 134

Gascoigne, Paul 16, 19–20, 31, 34, 36, 40, 59, 60, 107, 121–38, *123*, 149, 154

Gascoigne, Sheryl 129, 130, 132

Gates, Gareth 105, 161

gay footballers 145–6, 149

gay icon, DB as 6, 13, 20, 23, 47, 139–55, 179, 186

Gazzamania 126

Gerrard, Michael 135, 138

Gerrard, Steven 158

Giggs, Ryan 33, 67, 166

Giles, David 57, 197, 203

Ginola, David 141

Girl Power 18, 100, 104, 127

Girls Aloud 105

Giulianotti, Richard 135, 138

glamour 12, 86

Glasgow *see* Rangers

Glass, Jimmy 199

global communications 97–8

golf 157–8; *see also* Woods, Tiger

good life 22, 209, 210, 218, 219; Posh and Becks as symbols of 15–16, 56, 175

Goody, Jade 177

Gordy, Berry 102

gossip magazines 41, 44–5, 58–9, 117, 132

GQ 115, 153

Graf, Steffi 58

Greer, Germaine 19, 154

Guardian 10, 66, 81

Gucci 120

Gullit, Ruud 17
Guttmann, Allen 152

Halliwell, Geri 100
hand-holding, story on the
  significance of 10, 37
Hansen, Alan 158
Hardcastle, Paul 160–1
Hardman, Harold 71
Harris, Cheryl 206
Harris, Thomas 168
Haynes, Richard 35, 97, 153
Hear'Say 105, 189, 192
Heart Management 102
Heart of Midlothian 145
hedonism 207
hegemonic masculinity 148–9,
  155
Hello! 59, 65, 132
Henman, Tim 166
Herbert, Bob and Chris 103, 161
heroes 203
Hervey, Victoria 214
Heysel Stadium disaster
  (1985) 76, 88, 137
Hillsborough disaster (1989) 18,
  76, 88
Hingis, Martina 173
Hoddle, Glenn 130
Hodkinson, Mark 168
Holden, Amanda 182, 183
Holmes, Jon 156, 158, 162
Holyfield, Evander 50
homosexuality 180; in
  football 145–6, 149;
  homoeroticism of football
  fans 151–2; *see also* gay icon
hooliganism 18, 76, 186
Hornby, Nick 181, 191–2

Hoskyns, Barney 106
Hughes, Howard 178
Human Rights Act 64

icons 57; DB as 1–2, 6, 7, 12,
  41–2, 112 (*see also* gay icon);
  Michael Jordan as 167;
  Muhammad Ali as 179
identity 210, 213
illusion 62
image 207, 211, 213; DB 5–6, 7,
  13, 20–1, 41, 48, 62, 156–75,
  178, 188, 195; Spice Girls 109
image rights 48, 52, 63, 64–5,
  157, 159
In Bed with Madonna
  (film) 193–4
Independent 162
Independent on Sunday 150
indie music 190
Ingram, Charles 177
Inside Sport 107
International Management
  Group 157–8
Iraq War 13

J.-Lo 200
Jackson, Kevin 211–12
Jackson, Michael 50, 96, 170
Jackson, Phil 112
Jackson, Steven 185, 203
James, LeBron 55
Japan 8, 13, 59, 173
John, Elton 33, 120, 168
Johnson, Roy 167, 169
Jolie, Angelina 142
Jones, Catherine Zeta 35, 65
Jones, Vinnie 5, 125–6, 130
Jonsson, Ulrika 149

Jonze, Spike 195
Jordan (model) 149
Jordan, Michael 1, 5, 29, 66, 112,
 158, 166, 169, 179

Kamen, Nick 153
Katz, Donald 94
Keane, Robbie 158
Keane, Roy 159
Keegan, Kevin 22, 23, 46–7
Kelly, Fergus 46
Kelly, Grace 35, 168
Kennedy, John F. 219
Kenyon, Peter 52, 54, 66, 80, 81
Kewell, Harry 150
kidnap plots 11, 181
Killelea, Julie 67
King, Martin Luther 219
King of Comedy, The (film) 58
Klein, Naomi 94, 166
Klinsmann, Jürgen 17
Knighton, Michael 74
Kournikova, Anna 215
Kravitz, Lenny 120

Lad culture 127–9
Laporta, Joan 53
Lasch, Christopher 56
Law, Denis 17, 71
Lazenby, Roland 112
Lazio 127
Le Saux, Graham 144–5, 151
Leach, Robin 57
Learning To Fly (VB) 104, 146–7,
 168
Leeds United 46, 77
Leicester City 92
LeTissier, Matthew 16, 100
Levi's 153

Lineker, Gary 170, 174
Liverpool Football Club 69, 74,
 92
Lomu, Jonah 158
London Weekend
 Television 141; dinner to
 propose founding elite league
 (1990) 69–70, 76, 88, 89
Lopez, Jennifer 200
Lord, Bob 72
Los Angeles Dodgers 92, 93
Lovejoy, Joe 123
Lowe, Rob 96
Luttrellstown Castle,
 Ireland 43, 112
LWT *see* London Weekend
 Television

McAvennie, Frank 60
McCartney, Paul 151
McCormack, Mark 157
McCrum, Mark 149, 214
McDonald's Corporation 95
McDowell, Colin 140
McGill, Craig 94
McManaman, Steve 160
McManus, J. P. 80
Madonna 4, 20, 21, 44, 169, 173,
 192–4, 197, 210, 219
Magnier, John 80
Major League Baseball
 (MLB) 91
Malone, John 83
managers 2; business *see* Fuller,
 Simon; football *see* Ferguson,
 Alex
Manchester United 3, 12, 27–30,
 32–3, 42, 46, 49–53, 63–4, 109,
 110, *111*; DB's first

appearance 25; flotation on
stock exchange 74–5; Rupert
Murdoch's offer to buy 92,
93; transformation into a
brand 16–17, 31, 54, 66–82,
116, 135, 137; *see also*
Ferguson, Alex
manliness *see* masculinity
Maradona, Diego 37, 65, 179
Marketeer, The 165
marketing 7, 46, 66–82, 92, 94–5,
160, 168, 191, 195; *see also*
advertising; brands;
endorsements
Marks & Spencer 172
Marquee 157, 158
Marzell, Leoni 67
masculinity 19–20, 24, 28, 33–4,
47–8, 138, 139–55
Match of the Day (magazine) 134
Match of the Day (tv
programme) 90
Matrix, The 2
Matthews, Stanley 19, 135
media: and celebrity culture 19,
24, 58–62, 182–3, 184, 197,
198–210, 211, 215, 216;
creation of feeling of
intimacy 200–1; DB's
relations with 3, 5, 6, 10–11,
14, 16, 18, 20, 30, 36–42, 67,
137, 142, 194–5; and DB's
transfer to Real Madrid 8, 13,
54; and Flying Boot
incident 51, 147; and
Gascoigne 19, 122, 124–5,
126–8, 129, 131, 132–3, 134,
136, 137; and Madonna 21,
192–3, 197; and Posh and

Becks 13, 32–6, 43, 44–6, 48–9,
56, 107–9, 114, 117–20, 150–1;
and Spice Girls 104, 106, 109;
treatment of footballers 86–7,
149; *see also* multimedia;
television
media–sports cross-
ownership 92–4
Mellor, David 205
Merton, Robert 207–8
metaphor, DB as 55–6
Middlesbrough Football
Club 92, 131
Millichip, Bert 72
Minogue, Kylie 4, 113
Monkees 102
Monopolies and Mergers
Commission 79, 92
Monroe, Marilyn 35, 212
Montana, Joe 174
Morrissey, Steve 214
Morton, Andrew 36, 44, 45, 55,
101, 107
Mott, Sue 131
multimedia 98, 193
Munich air disaster (1958) 70
Murdoch, Rupert 17, 26, 30, 69,
74, 83–94, 95, 97–8, 132
Murphy, Chic 103
Murphy, Sheree 150
MUTV 75, 92
My World (DB) 151

Nanni, Silvia 172
National Football League
(NFL) 77, 85, 91
National Hockey League
(NHL) 91
nationalism 6, 46, 96

Neville, Phil 67
New Age 142, 147
New Kids on the Block 115
New Labour values 128
New Man 140, 142, 147, 151
New York Yankees 29
Newcastle United 92, 125, 137
News of the World 87, 88, 101
NFL 77, 85, 91
Nguyen Hong Son 171
Nike 8, 32, 55, 78, 95, 166–7, 169, 170, 191
Niklaus, Jack 158
19 Management 21, 103, 156, 160–2
Norton, Graham 155

Oasis 127, 128
OK! 44–5, 58–9, 65, 110, 184
O'Leary, David 131
Olive, Les 72
Olympic Games 95
Outside Organization 168
Owen, Michael 3, 39, 81, 94, 158, 159, 166

Packer, Kerry 89
Palmer, Arnold 157
paparazzi *see* media
parasocial relationships 197–8, 201–2, 206
Paris Saint-Germain 92
Parkinson, Michael 140
patriarchy 147
patriotism *see* nationalism
Pattenden, Mike 107, 108
Pearce, Stuart 130
Pelé 30, 162
Pellow, Marti 176

People 57
Pepsi 103, 105, 106, 170, 173
Peterborough United 48
"phallic anxiety" 154
Phillips, Nancy 101
Pippen, Scottie 112
Pitt, Brad 25
Platt, David 157
Player, Gary 158
Police 159, 172, 174
Pop Idol (tv show) 161, 180, 189, 216
Popstars (tv show) 189
popular culture 7–8, 12, 81, 203; changes 23–4; *see also* celebrity culture; entertainment industry
popular music 100–7, 110, 116, 127–9, 133, 189–90; *see also* Spice Girls
Portugal, England game against 46
Posh and Becks 13, 32–6, *37*, 40, 41, 51, 100, 101, 107, 110, 113–20, *119*, 141–2, 150, 164, 211–12; birth of Brooklyn 43; hand-holding 10, *37*; symbols of good life 15–16, 56; wedding 4, 43–6, 58–9, 110–12, 183–4
postfeminism 147
Prada, Miuccia 165
Premier League (later Premiership) 29, 64, 66, 67, 78, 80, 137; and tv 17, 33, 69–70, 76, 85, 88, 89–90, 91, 136
Presley, Elvis 212
Preston North End 16, 25, 28–9

ProServe 157–8
psychoanalytic theory 154
public, the 3, 14; *see also* fans
public/private life 5, 6, 15, 18, 23, 35, 39–40, 43, 64–5, 182–3, 213

quiz shows 216

racism 18, 76
Rage 165, 174
Rainier, Prince, of Monaco 35
Rangers 127, 129, 130
rap music 190
Raul, Gonzalez 54, 170
Ravanelli, Fabrizio 131
Real Madrid 52, 63, 69; DB's transfer to *see* football career
reality television 86, 216
Redgrave, Steve 173–4
Redknapp, Jamie 62
Reebok 166
Reeves, Keanu 3
representation 203, 211, 212, 213
Rice, Jerry 158
Ridgeway Rovers 26
Rivaldo 171
Roberto Carlos 3, 170, 171
Robson, Bobby 121
Robson, Bryan 31
Roc-A-Fella records 120
Rodman, Dennis 112
Rogan, Johnny 214
Rojek, Chris 214
Ronaldo 14, 54, 65
Rooney, Wayne 81
Ross, Diana 102
Rotherham United 73
Rowe, Matt 103

royal family 4, 107, 112, 114
rugby 90
Rugby Football Union 143
Rui Costa, Manuel 171
Rumbelow's Cup (1992) 25
Rusedski, Greg 158
Ruth, George Herman "Babe" 57

S Club 161
Sara Lee Corporation 163
Saturday Night Live (tv show) 106
Savage, Robbie 142
Scalpello, James 165
Scandals and celebrities 205
Scholar, Irving 77
Schwarzenegger, Arnold 50
Scorsese, Martin 58, 180
security concerns 181–2, *182*
Seles, Monica 58
sexual politics 153
sexuality *see* masculinity
SFX 21, 103, 156–9
Shallow Grave (film) 86
Shearer, Alan 31
Sheen, Charlie 96
Sheffield Wednesday *see* Hillsborough disaster
Sherman, Len 93, 96
showbusiness *see* entertainment industry
Simeone, Diego 36
Simpson, Joe 121
Simpson, Paul 124, 125, 128, 130
Singer, Bryan 209
Sky *see* BSkyB
Skyband 91
Slits, the 101–2

Smith, Alan 149
Smith, David 70, 71
Smith, Tommie 179
Smith, Walter 129, 131
soap stars 204
soccernet 65, 159
Sondico 166
Southampton Football Club 78
Spears, Britney 20, 170, 173, 204
spectacle: football turned into
    18, 83–99; Gascoigne as 124
Spice Girls 4, 7, 8, 18, 31, 32, 36,
    43, 65, 100–7, 108, 112–13, 116,
    143, 156, 161, 168, 170, 173
Spiceworld – The Movie 106, 115
sponsorship 17, 32, 77, 95, 160,
    172; *see also* advertising
Sponsorship Research
    Company 163
sport: commodification 24,
    94–7; *see also* celebrity; icons;
    and individual sports
Sports Illustrated 142
Springer, Jerry 216
Stage 102
Stallone, Sylvester 155
Stannard, Richard 103
Star 57
Stars In Their Eyes (tv show) 126
Stephens, Tony 110, 116, 156,
    157–9, 162
Stewart, Rod 125, 133
Sting 14
Sugar, Alan 88–9
Sullivan, Neil 30
Sun 26, 51, 87, 88, 93, 128, 132
Sunday People 172
Sunday Times 87, 115, 165
Supremes 102

Surprise, Surprise (tv show) 104
Sweeney, The (tv series) 26

Take That 115
talent 7, 116, 205, 214, 215, 216,
    220
Taxi Driver (film) 180
Taylforth, Gillian 204
Taylor, Elizabeth 20, 35
Taylor, Peter 47
television: celebrity culture 26,
    201–5, 211, 215, 216; DB
    and 11, 18, 20, 36, 39, 59,
    140, 141–2, 198; football
    and 17, 26, 69–70, 73, 76, 77,
    78, 84–94, 97, 98, 135–6;
    Gascoigne and 126;
    Manchester United and 28,
    30, 33; Spice Girls and 104,
    106; VB and 113
tennis 157, 215
text, DB as 21–2, 34, 177–95
Thatcher, Margaret:
    Thatcherism 26, 87, 125, 137,
    140
They Think it's All Over (tv
    show) 158
Thomas, David 162
3am Girls 216
Time Out 115
Times, The 87, 93, 115, 180, 185
timing: importance in
    development of DB's celebrity
    status 4, 23, 30, 40, 107
To Die For (film) 58
Tony Stephens Associates 157,
    160
Torquay United 73
Total Recall (film) 216–17

Tottenham Hotspur 16, 26, 69, 77, 89, 125, 126
Touch 103
Touching the Void (J. Simpson) 121
Travolta, John 200
Turner, Anthea 184
Turner, Ted 92
Tyson, Mike 130, 184

Uefa 94; *see also* European football *and individual competitions*
Umbro 166
USA 7, 8, 13, 65, 169, 173
Usual Suspects, The (film) 209

Vanessa-Mae 205
Van Sant, Gus 58
Venables, Terry 26–7, 89
Verhoven, Paul 217
Veron, Juan Sebastian 170, 171
Victoria's Secrets (tv show) 113
videos 197
Virgin Records 103
Vodaphone 172
vortextuality 45–6

Wachowski brothers 2
Waddle, Chris 66
Wahl, Grant 142, 148
Walkers Crisps: and Gary Lineker 170, 174
Walvin, James 76
Warhol, Andy 107, 211–13
Warne, Shane 174
Weakest Link, The (tv show) 216
Webber, Andrew Lloyd 112, 120
Wembley Stadium 157

Whannel, Garry 45–6, 151, 152–3, 215
White, Jim 11
White, Lesley 165
Who Wants to be a Millionaire? (tv show) 177, 216
Wilkins, Ray 73
Wilkinson, Jonny 61
Williams, Robbie 149, 214
Williams, Venus 166
Wimbledon: effect of DB's goal against (1996) 30, 107, 115, 163
Winfrey, Oprah 4
Wolverhampton Wanderers 132
women: admiration for sports stars 6, 12, 15, 186
Woodgate, Jonathan 149
Woods, Tiger 36, 61, 166, 210
work ethic 116–17, 220; DB 108, 117, 168–9; VB 108, 116–17
World Cup 95, 98; (1970) 30; (1990) 121–2, *123*, 133, 135, 138; (1998) 32, 33, 36–9, *38*, 42, 108, 130–1, 136; (2002) 49, 96, 173, 201
World in Action (tv documentary) 28
Wright, Billy 35
Wright, Ian 32

Yates, Simon 121
Yorke, Dwight 149, 171
Young, Will 161, 180, 192

Zamalek 171
Zidane, Zinedine 14, 32, 54, 166